KT-381-935

THE HISTORICAL ASSOCIATION
BOOK OF

# THE STUARTS

*In the same series*

The Historical Association
book of
THE TUDORS

# The Historical Association book of
# THE STUARTS

# Edited by K. H. D. Haley

*Professor of Modern History at the*
*University of Sheffield*

SIDGWICK & JACKSON

LONDON

This collection first published in Great Britain
by Sidgwick and Jackson Limited in 1973

Each essay originally published by
The Historical Association

Copyright © 1973 by The Historical Association

Introduction Copyright © 1973 by K. H. D. Haley

Stockton - Billingham
LIBRARY
Technical College

25077

942.04

I.S.B.N. 0.283.97891.0

Printed in Great Britain by
The Garden City Press Limited
Letchworth, Hertfordshire SG6 1JS
for Sidgwick and Jackson Limited
1 Tavistock Chambers, Bloomsbury Way
London WC1A 2SG

# CONTENTS

The dates given in brackets are those of the original
publication of the pamphlets

# INTRODUCTION

As one of its services to members the Historical Association provides each year three free pamphlets in its General Series. Some of the country's most distinguished historians have contributed, and, just as they commonly lecture to the Association's many branches up and down the country without charging a fee, so also they write the pamphlets without expecting royalties, in the common cause of fostering historical studies in Britain: the Association is glad to record its debt to them.

Non-members have always been able to buy copies of the pamphlets, and members have been able to buy past pamphlets, but it has been suggested that there would be a demand for a volume containing several of the pamphlets, on a common period, under the same cover. The present book, containing seven essays on seventeenth-century themes, is the result.

The pamphlets have never been planned by the Association's Publications Committee as a connected series: on the contrary, the aim has always been deliberately to provide variety to cater for many different tastes among members, and also much has naturally depended on the availability of authors. Sometimes the familiar game of watching for anniversaries has been played: it was impossible to allow the tercentenary of the execution of Charles I to pass without a commemorative pamphlet, and equally impossible to miss the chance to attempt a reassessment of his greatest opponent, Oliver Cromwell, on the three-hundredth anniversary of his death in 1658. Penruddock's rising in 1655 was similarly remembered. The collection which has resulted inevitably lacks the unity which would have been produced by the choice of one central theme to be followed through the whole of the Stuart period. Never-

theless the seven subjects to be found here should illumine
some of the central problems, political, social and economic, of
the age.

It is interesting that of the seven essays three are biographical in character, and this may perhaps be the unconscious
result of a presumption that the historical public is still largely
interested in the personalities of some of the most prominent
political figures of the time. If this is true, however, it does
not necessarily reflect a naive belief that historical development
is the result of the impact of a few 'great men', nor does it
imply that all the important issues can be personalized. It does
represent the fact that for many people much of the fascination
of history still lies in seeing individuals wrestling with great
problems and making choices of policy which were the result
of a combination of rationality and prejudice, idealism and
self-interest; in seeing the extent to which those choices were
really free or governed by circumstances; and in evaluating
the nature and extent of their influence.

What is surprising is less that Charles I, Cromwell, and
Charles II are perennial sources of interest than that two of
the three have still failed to attract satisfactory full-length
biographies. The life of Charles I, the 'Martyr-King', has a
certain tragic quality which, one might have thought, would
have invited biographical treatment; yet, for all the romantic
attachment which the Royalist cause attracted, both in
Charles I's lifetime and afterwards, and in spite of the
dramatic closing scene upon which 'he nothing common did or
mean', no one has come forward to make the attempt. When
Dame Veronica Wedgwood and her friends Mary Coate, Mark
Thomson and David Piper collaborated in 1949 to provide the
symposium which forms the first item in the present collection,
there was no biography of Charles I to which the student could
be referred; and this still remains true even though Miss
Wedgwood's own political narratives are described as *The
King's Peace* (1955), *The King's War* (1958) and *The Trial
of Charles I* (1964). Yet there is a sense in which, as Mr Brian
Manning has remarked, 'the decision men had to take in 1642
was not a decision about the best form of government for the
church or for the state, nor about changes in the social or

economic order, but simply whether or not to trust Charles I'.*
If the personal factor was such an important one, is it too much
to hope that Charles will some day find his biographer, at least
when the examination of England's social structure has been
completed and Puritanism has been fully described in all its
aspects? Or can it be that in spite of all the sentimental
devotion which the Royalist cause has aroused, Charles himself
remains profoundly antipathetic to would-be biographers?

Charles II, one might think, is an ideal subject for a
biography: his early life was unusually adventurous for that of
a king in modern times; after his Restoration his policies,
domestic and foreign, caused plenty of controversy both in his
own day and later; he was capable of a genuine (though sometimes coarse) wit which invites quotation; and if he was
immoral, he was never guilty of being dull. Many writers have
therefore been attracted to him. One, at least, Sir Arthur
Bryant, has found many readers. Since the essay in this
volume (V) was written, Mr Maurice Ashley has provided us
with another account, incorporating a good deal of recent
research. Yet somehow Charles has eluded portrayal; his secret
thoughts escape the penetration of modern scholars, just as
they perplexed contemporaries. Anything approaching a
definitive biography must still be awaited; it will need much
careful and detailed examination of the politics of thirty years;
and so far the most eminent scholars have not thought it worth
while to give Charles II the attention that they have given to
Cromwell.

There can be little doubt that Cromwell emerges the victor
from any 'battle of the books' with the Royalists. From the
time of Carlyle's edition of his letters and speeches, by way
of Sir Charles Firth's account and W. C. Abbott's monu-
mental four volumes of *The Writings and Speeches of Oliver
Cromwell* (Harvard U.P., 1937–47) down to modern times,
Cromwell's unique personality has clamoured for scholarly
attention, and the books on him are legion, and the interpretations of him correspondingly varied. S. R. Gardiner once
claimed him as 'the typical Englishman of the modern world'
– a rather startling idea, however appropriate it may have

* In an essay on 'The Outbreak of the English Civil War' in *The
English Civil War and After*, ed. R. H. Parry (1970), p. 3.

seemed in 1902. In the second essay in this volume Christopher Hill, the foremost present-day historian of the seventeenth century, picks out some of the paradoxes which make Cromwell's attitudes so difficult to define, in a sketch which will stimulate many readers to go on to look at his more recent book on *God's Englishman: Oliver Cromwell and the English Revolution* (1970). Yet the difficulty remains of grasping and describing such a great and complex personality, and that there will be further attempts, reflecting the changing preoccupations of our own lifetime, is certain: no historian could ever claim that his account of Cromwell was 'definitive'.

A constant diet of biographies would, however, be unsatisfying, and the remaining four studies here represent different approaches to the problems of the period. Professor Alan Everitt, the author of essay III on 'The Local Community and the Great Rebellion', has been the principal exponent in recent years of an approach which turns away from the more sensational events at Westminster and Whitehall and from the examinations of 'national' issues to look at Englishmen in their 'country' or county. Local antiquarians, of course, have for many years occupied themselves with the strictly military history of the clashes of Cavaliers and Roundheads in their areas. Recent work in local history, perhaps from the time of Mary Coate's study of Cornwall (1933), has been much more preoccupied with problems of social structure, with the nature of the alignments within counties, with the local loyalties which sometimes reinforced and sometimes cut across wider ones, with the parliamentary county committees (see *The Committee at Stafford, 1643–45*, ed. D. H. Pennington and I. A. Roots, 1957) and the possible emergence of new families – in short, with the 'local community'. Professor Everitt himself has made two important contributions to this kind of local study in *Suffolk and the Great Rebellion, 1640–1660*, Suffolk Records Society, iii (1960) and *The Community of Kent and the Great Rebellion, 1640–1660*. In his essay he turns his attention to the two Midland counties of Leicestershire and Northamptonshire.

Professor Woolrych's essay (IV) on Penruddock's Rising is an excellent example of the way in which the close study of an apparently minor episode illuminates more general issues. The rising itself occupied only a few days in 1655, and it is easy for us to look back on it now and to agree that its chances of success were always extremely slender, but it was intended to be on a much larger scale. Ill-co-ordinated Royalist conspiracies, weakened by the caution of the Sealed Knot and the lack of realism of others, produced a fiasco in which most of the Royalists failed to rise at all, and those few who did caused the Protector's troops little trouble before they surrendered in the little Devonshire village of South Molton. The Royalists failed to draw the obvious conclusion that they had small prospects as long as the army stood united and determined, and the over-optimistic plots of a few continued until in July 1659 another rising in Cheshire ended ignominiously with Sir George Booth, its leader, taken prisoner at Newport Pagnell, wearing a woman's clothes as an ineffective disguise. Oliver Cromwell and his Council, however, also failed to draw the right conclusions; fearing more plots, they overestimated the danger and instituted the famous regime of the major-generals, financed by the decimation tax. Their interference with local society not only created immediately a much greater hostility to the government than had previously existed, but became indelibly marked on the memory of the country gentry, who after 1660 were determined to allow no such 'sword government' to recur.

The last two pamphlets reprinted here (VI and VII) are both on economic themes. There was once a time when the economic history of the seventeenth century was neglected in comparison with the Tudor period which preceded it and the Agricultural and Industrial Revolutions which followed; but the picture has changed a good deal in the last twenty years, and Professor Charles Wilson's contributions have been second to none, from his *Profit and Power* (1957), analysing the economic and strategic considerations underlying the Anglo-Dutch rivalry, to his *England's Apprenticeship 1603–1763* surveying English development over a longer period. His pamphlet on *Mercantilism* is one of those most frequently requested from the Historical Association. This short treatment of the subject, which does much to dispel the confusion that has arisen round a much-abused word, is much in demand. It would obviously be wrong to think of mercantilism as either a purely seventeenth-century or a purely English phenomenon, and to that extent

Professor Wilson's account goes beyond the chronological and geographical limits suggested by the title which has been given to the book as a whole: there is a section on the mercantile system in Europe which extends as far as the time of Charles III of Spain, but no one is likely to cavil at this. In the same way Professor Ralph Davis's essay on 'A Commercial Revolution' refers to the changes which took place in the pattern of English overseas trade between the Restoration and the War of American Independence – virtually the period of 'mercantilism' – and the two articles make an interesting pair. Perhaps the word 'revolution' is another that historians tend to misuse; but if its meaning is extended to cover, not only sudden and violent change, but also change which is more gradual and peaceful but extremely far-reaching, then the term can surely apply to the development of English foreign trade in this century. Professor Davis describes not only an expansion of the volume of trade but changes in the commodities bought and sold, the replacement of trade with Europe by world-wide activities in which colonial produce played a large part, and changes in the general role of trade in the English economy: changes whose full significance is not always appreciated in the usual textbook political narratives.

Though contributors have made some minor changes from the text that was first published, the substance is unaltered. The date of first publication has been given in each case, and it should be particularly borne in mind that the articles on Charles I were *pièces d'occasion*, written for the three-hundredth anniversary of his execution: in any attempt to rewrite them much of their original point would have been lost. Bibliographical notes have been appended, but readers may like to know that the revised edition (by Mary F. Keeler) of the *Bibliography of British History: the Stuart Period, 1603–1714*, ed. Godfrey Davies, which appeared in 1970, appears to list works published down to about 1965, while the Bibliography of *Restoration England, 1660–1689*, ed. W. L. Sachse (1971) is less full but includes books and articles published more recently.

K. H. D. HALEY

# PART ONE

# Charles I:

# CHARLES I:
# THE CASE FOR THE EXECUTION

*by*

*C. V. WEDGWOOD*

The close of the third century since the execution of King Charles I presents an opportunity for taking stock of that momentous event – the first occasion in modern European history when a sovereign was formally brought to trial by his subjects. The various emotions which this 'horrid murder' or 'eminent act of justice' has aroused during twelve generations and the different interpretations which have been put on it are in themselves an object lesson in the manner in which all judgements of the past are affected by the experience and prejudice of the present. Try as we will to be dispassionate, the preoccupations of our own generation intrude upon our minds and shape our judgement.

In 1649 the execution of the King was regarded with dismay by the majority of his people and with real horror by a considerable number. The dismay evaporated quickly enough for the King's executioners to establish a relatively stable government almost immediately. The horror has worn off with the passing of time, the increasing tale of dethronements, revolutions, executions, murders and the general collapse of the hierarchical framework of society.

As our ideas on politics change and our factual knowledge increases, the seventeenth century in retrospect becomes infinitely more complicated. There is no simple choice today between the idea of 'horrid murder' and that of the 'eminent act of justice' which radical writers once gloried in defending.

In the first place the sum of our knowledge has greatly increased. New documentary sources have been found; local records have been more carefully examined; the quantity of auxiliary research increases every year. Private papers have thrown new light on the character and motives of the principals, have supplied small missing links of fact or tantalizingly suggested new clues to follow. But these effects are superficial compared with the extensive development of fields of research, besides the political and personal, during the last half century. The increasing attention paid to social, administrative and economic history has not only brought under review whole new classes of evidence, documentary and otherwise, but has altered the historian's attitude to the political evidence already known to him and gradually placed the whole central conflict of the seventeenth century in a different perspective.

For the first two and a half centuries after his death it is fair to say that the fate of King Charles was judged entirely within the narrow politico-religious framework. The different approach of the last half century has added so much to the picture as to throw quite out of proportion both the old-fashioned Whig attack on the King and the old-fashioned High Tory Anglican defence. (In parenthesis it must be emphasized here that to throw out of proportion is not necessarily to prove wrong; what is needed is not the scrapping of old theories which were sound enough on their premises, but a re-adjustment in relation to the additional facts.)

Thus for instance we have today the fashionable emphasis on the wealth of the Parliamentary party who organized the revolt against the King, an emphasis which is often so over-stated as to imply that all the property owners in the kingdom were on the one side. Charles has even been represented as putting up a solitary fight against something arbitrarily styled the 'money-power'. How, if he was fighting the 'money-power', he managed to finance his own war at all, and why the 'money-power' so often had difficulty in financing theirs, are questions that do not yet appear to have been fully examined. A dispassionate survey of the finances of both parties and of the distribution of private resources in England before, during, and after the war would be of the greatest value and is essential if any sound conclusion on this really important question is ever to be reached.

Extreme views apart, this economic interpretation of the Civil War contributed – and has yet to contribute – much of value to our understanding of the period. A war in which some property owners made a good thing out of mulcting other property owners, and in which the fanatics who suddenly and inconveniently set up a clamour for community ownership of land were instantly quelled, cannot precisely be represented as a war for popular rights.*

Our still far from adequate knowledge of social and administrative history has also modified the traditional view of King Charles's reign. In the earlier editions of his *Short History of the English People*, J. R. Green referred quite simply to the eleven years of the King's personal rule as 'the tyranny'. It was, of course, nothing of the kind; it was an indefinite intermission of Parliament during which the King governed by proclamation, usually – although not invariably – with benevolent intentions.

The addition of knowledge and of new aspects to our existing knowledge have thus broadened, modified and to some extent undermined the case against Charles I. But it is a change not in the extent of our knowledge but in our political outlook which has most effectively transformed our attitude to the Civil War. When manhood suffrage became the touchstone by which sound democratic government was judged, it became correspondingly more difficult to sustain the claims of the English Parliamentary party of the seventeenth century to have represented a movement towards the liberty of the people. Colonel Rainborough, who had apparently advocated manhood suffrage during the Putney meetings of October 1647, but was killed shortly after, became the first hero of the Civil War. Cromwell, with his emphasis on the property franchise, was immediately suspect.

It is easy to say that the English Civil War occurred a long time before Tom Paine proclaimed the Rights of Man, a long time before the French Revolution, and a very long time before manhood suffrage was introduced in any European country. It is easy to say it; it is not so easy to remember it. Our whole outlook is unconsciously moulded by these later conceptions and events. Thus the reputation of the opponents of King Charles has passed through a double misrepresentation. They received in the later eighteenth and the nineteenth centuries

---

* It was rarely so represented at the time. This is another confusion owing to the use of the term 'popular party' for Parliamentary party which came into fashion at a much later date.

credit for being more representative and more libertarian than in fact they were, and they have suffered in our own time from the reaction which will not allow them to have any claims to either of these pretensions because their claims are not strictly such as will pass in a modern Parliamentary democracy.

The historian who sets out today to defend the rebellion against King Charles and its most extreme consequence, his execution, can no longer do so on purely libertarian grounds. If he claims that the King's opponents stood for the liberties of the people, he is contradicted by the distressing fate of the Levellers at their hands. If he claims that they stood for the good of the people, he will have to face the inconvenient fact that there was more paternalistic benevolence of intention in the personal rule of Charles I than in that of any succeeding ruler for many generations.

There still seems to me to be, however, grounds on which the execution of King Charles I can, and should, be justified. It is to be justified on the long view not only of English but of European history; the Great Civil War belongs to the history of Western civilization quite as much as it belongs to the history of England.

The central problem of the sixteenth and seventeenth centuries is the same in all the western European countries: it is the struggle of the centralizing and essentially despotic tendency of the sovereign against the restraining power of elective or representative institutions. It is the struggle of a new and national or state efficiency imposed from above against the older and more diffused organs of government left over from a mediæval society. In the heyday of liberalism it was customary to regard the despotic monarchs as the reactionaries and the supporters of representative institutions as the progressives. Today the opposite view is often put forward: despotic monarchy (meaning the benevolent despotism of the central authority) is, it is argued, the more progressive movement; the reactionaries were those who preferred their local or class privileges to the new central authority.

The terms progressive or reactionary are alike out of place. In different countries the clash worked out in different ways. The success of either party depended to a great extent on its capacity to manipulate the forms in which it believed to suit the new demands made on government. Richelieu, for instance, was evidently a man of progressive ideas who developed the French monarchy into a highly efficient instrument of government; the *Etats Généraux* and the local French *Parlements* displayed little, if any, sense of that political perspicacity by which alone they might have opposed tthe encroachments of the Crown. Philip II in the Netherlands was highly progressive in a somewhat mistaken fashion; but here the local institutions, and such of the local nobility as co-operated in the revolt, showed the necessary capacity for creative development in opposition.

My own convictions are wholly on the side of representative institutions; I deplore their feebleness in France, while I admire and regret the triumph of Richelieu. It is because they were in fact feeble, incompetent and even reactionary in many European countries that the outcome of the English struggle seems to me all the more important. It is quite possible that without their rather startling victory in England it would have been impossible to arrest the decay of these institutions or to give them new life in other parts of the world.

The struggle links up very closely with that which had begun in the latter half of the sixteenth century in the Netherlands. The Dutch, clinging to their cumbrous local institutions, had rebelled against the attempts of the Spanish King not merely to impose uniformity of religion but to re-organize their methods of government. In the course of this struggle they found that they had to get rid of the King, which they did by an Act of Abjuration in the following terms: 'A prince is constituted by God to be ruler of a people, to defend them from oppression and violence . . . and whereas God did not create the people slaves to their prince . . . but rather the prince for the sake of the subjects . . . as a shepherd to his flock . . . when he does not behave thus but exacts from them a slavish compliance . . . then he is no longer a prince but a tyrant, and they may disallow his authority.' The words are the practical expression in politics of the doctrine of mutual obligations between subject and sovereign which had recently been put forward in the *Vindiciœ contra Tyrannos* ascribed to Duplessis Mornay. The theory was the outcome of the political atmosphere of the time; religious differences were fruitful of rebellion, and in one form or

another rebellion had to be justified in political theory. The op-
posing political theory on the King's side, which was of
slightly greater antiquity, was Divine Right.

In the Dutch revolt the issue is in part obscured by the
international element in the conflict. This was absent in the
second great move in the contest, the English Civil War. The
point at issue between King Charles and Parliament was a very
simple one. Ludlow asserts that when, during his trial, the
King heard himself described as being 'entrusted' by his
people, he interposed with the words 'No, they are mine by inheritance'. The term used by his accusers showed the very
centre of their argument against him. The King's answer was
his defence. The two attitudes are irreconcilable.

To turn from theory to practice: King Charles may not have
wanted to abolish Parliament. But he wanted to reduce it to
political impotence, to turn it into a body which offered useful
but not critical advice, which registered the laws he set before
it and voted the money for his policies. His first three Parliaments asserted with vigour their right to control the royal
policy. After getting rid of the third, Charles failed to call
another for eleven years. He was violating no law in keeping
Parliament in abeyance for so long, but he was certainly creat-
ing a precedent. The tendency of his policy cannot seriously be
questioned: it was towards a strong, centralized monarchy, independent of criticism or control.

The Commons, on the other hand, or that majority of the
Commons who supported the war when it came to war, were
determined to maintain the powers of criticism and control that
they had acquired, largely for economic reasons, during the
latter part of the sixteenth and the earlier part of the seventeenth century. King and Commons believed alike that their
point of view and no other was true to the laws of the land.
Neither saw themselves as innovators. *Stare super vias antiquas*
was indeed the favourite quotation of the King's most efficient
minister Strafford, as he showed his royal master how to play
the benevolent despot by establishing a highly efficient government in Ireland.

This then was the problem. A King working towards despotism and Parliament working towards a dominating control of
the Crown. The clash was inevitable, but, given the good in-

tentions of Charles's rule, why was it necessary that it should be stopped? The answer to this is best given by examining the probable results of Charles's victory.

Had Charles been a man of greater ability, had he above all been capable of choosing and supporting ministers of great ability, he might have had a comparatively easy success. There is a world of truth in Laud's comment on his master, when the war was in progress and he himself awaiting death in the Tower, that he was 'a mild and gracious prince who knew not how to be or be made great'. Had Charles been a prince who both knew how to be and to be made great, Parliament might have been reduced to impotence and an efficient despotism on the French model might have made its appearance in England. Almost everything that Richelieu did was cleverly calculated to divide the opposition to the Crown; he played one group off against the other. Almost everything that Charles did was ineptly timed to unite the opposition to the Crown. It needed, for instance, political ineptitude amounting almost to genius to force his English and his Scottish subjects to make common cause against him. But he produced even this result by 1640, and no one was more surprised than he.

The argument against despotism and the experience of almost all despotisms proves that the efficiency, in the interests of which they are usually created, is the characteristic which they soonest lose. Which is as much as to say that they rarely remain benevolent however they may begin. There is hardly one European country in which the authoritarian monarchies set up in the seventeenth century did not end sooner or later in the bitter convulsion of revolution, a convulsion producing after-effects far more lasting and serious to the body politic than any produced by the Civil War on English society.

The alternative to despotism, the persistence of Parliamentary control, may not have created an ideal government. It led to an upper-class oligarchy, with much corruption and vested interest; it may have retarded the introduction of social services (although this is by no means certain), and it certainly encouraged sectional as against national interests. But in the first place there is no guarantee that despotism will not also produce much the same effects – a bureaucratic oligarchy instead of a Parliamentary one, the vested interests and privileges of an even smaller Court clique, corruption of different kinds. Secondly, Parliamentary government has one advantage that despotisms conspicuously lack. It is capable of modification from the inside; that is, of growth. No total despotism can grow. All have in time become hopelessly decrepit or been violently shattered from without.

If this argument justifies the Parliamentary cause, as I think it does, it is still no direct argument in favour of the King's execution. But it is an indirect argument, for given the problem and given the protagonist – there was no other way out.

Charles I believed in his cause with a high religious fanaticism which was perfectly unamenable to any sort of argument. From the beginning of his English disasters in 1640 until the fatal autumn seven years later, he never had the slightest doubt that all his concessions to Parliament were so many manœuvres and subterfuges. He neither intended nor wished to come to any permanent constitutional understanding. When his personal rule ended in the revolt of the Scots and a financial *impasse* which forced him to call the Parliaments of 1640, he was not a changed and wiser man anxious to co-operate with the House of Commons. He regarded Parliament with the same suspicion and dislike that he had felt when he dissolved it eleven years earlier. He hoped, after he had solved his immediate difficulties, to pursue his original independent policy. Calling Parliament was a temporary expedient.

The immediate concessions which he made under pressure to Parliament were in several cases decisive. When he signed the death warrant of Strafford and when he agreed not to dissolve that particular Parliament, he made two strategic errors of the first magnitude. But they were errors; they were not the fruit of a changed policy. Because there was no change of policy and because there was a limit to the number of concessions that Charles I was prepared to make while manœuvring for position, the tension between King and Parliament came to war over the Militia Bill. Charles knew that if he lost control over the armed forces of the country he would never regain the full power that he believed to be his right in the state. And so war broke out in August 1642.

Totally defeated in the war, Charles found himself in 1647–8 in the hands of the Army. His point of view was still completely unaltered. So was his manner of procedure. He played for time, entertaining the overtures of Cromwell and the Army officers for a treaty of settlement on terms which he appeared to be considering seriously, while he was privately organizing a second English civil war coupled with an invasion from Scotland. So powerful was Charles's belief in his kingly office, that it is easy to see that this conduct seemed excusable to him, because it would serve the purpose of restoring him to his own. His attitude to all those who opposed him was always very close to the reputed dictum of the Jesuits – *fidem non servandam cum hœreticis*. He did not hold himself bound by any promises made to his opponents or by the normal decencies of treaty negotiations. But however sincerely the King believed himself to be justified, it is evident that his conduct was, from every point of view but his own peculiar one, as reprehensible as it was dangerous. A flat refusal to entertain the propositions of the Army leaders would have been more just and in the end safer. That would have brought about a deadlock from which Charles might or might not have been extricated through the exertions of his supporters.

What he did removed any basis of confidence on which further negotiations for a constitutional settlement could be conducted. It also touched off the explosive republican sentiments which lay only a little below the surface of Army politics. The decision to bring the King to justice, reached at the solemn meeting of the Army officers in May 1648, was inevitable in the circumstances.

Charles himself had half expected to perish obscurely as Richard II and Edward II had done. The extremists decided otherwise; they defied tradition and created a precedent by setting up a court to try the King. Of course the court organized for the purpose had no legal standing; of course the King was right to question its authority and refuse to plead. But if the King had to be removed from the scene, an open trial was by far the best way of doing it.

The men who carried the lugubrious drama through to its end were a comparatively small group, but the case they drew up against Charles was fundamentally the case of the nation against the King. They accused and condemned him for deliberately levying war on his subjects, and this was in cold fact precisely what he had done. Only it must be remembered that it was the *second* and not the *first* civil war which brought him to his end. The war which had broken out in 1642 over the Militia Bill might have ended in an accommodation with the King had the King been willing. The incontrovertible evidence that he was not willing and never would be willing was provided by the outbreak of the second civil war engineered by him from his confinement at Hampton Court in the autumn of 1647.

The final and dreadful crisis of public trial and death brought out not only all the King's qualities of courage and self-control. It brought out for almost the only time in his life a surprising measure of political acuity. By denying the justice of the court he managed to make the proceedings look even more shocking than they were. And on the scaffold he claimed, with calmness and sincerity, to stand for the just liberties of his people against the violence of extremists who had overthrown the laws.

In January 1649, he certainly had a case. The once representative Parliament which he had called into being eight years before had dwindled to a mere handful. There had been the secession of the Royalist members on the outbreak of war, the election to their vacant seats of men whose sympathies were with the victorious Parliamentary army, next the secession and expulsion of the Presbyterian members, finally the violent removal of all who objected to the King's trial. The rag of Parliament in 1649 was certainly not worthy of the name. Moreover the King's death was followed, as he had foretold, by the establishment of a military dictatorship.

Immediate appearances were however deceptive, for the war which had been begun in order to preserve the controlling power of Parliament over the Crown did in fact preserve it. The Restoration of King Charles II in 1660 marked a vehemently royalist reaction but it was not so royalist as that: nothing that Parliament had gained was thrown away. Moreover the signal death of a King on the scaffold, deeply as it was abhorred by the majority of Englishmen for several generations afterwards, undoubtedly acted as a restraining influence on the monarchy and thereby assisted the development of the Parliamentary system.

Speculation on what might have been the course of history had Charles not been tried and beheaded is necessarily vague. It did not seem probable in the winter of 1648–9 that he would ever again be in a position to make a monarchy such as he desired. But he had two very able soldiers among his followers, considerable support in Ireland and in Scotland, and he could perhaps have built on a revulsion of feeling in England. Given his abilities and his character it is improbable that he would have brought off after 1649 what he had failed to bring off in the early part of his reign. But given his political convictions he would never have ceased to try. Therein lay the danger, and therein the necessity, for destroying him. He died, as Isaac D'Israeli felicitously put it, the victim of 'his inevitable errors and his involuntary guilt'.

# CHARLES I:
# THE PERSONALITY AND THE
# KINGSHIP

*by*

*MARY COATE*

In the long line of English kings, only two have been styled
'martyr' – Edward the young king slain at Corfe in 979 after
but a few months of kingship, and Charles I, executed outside
his palace of Whitehall, on 30 January 1649, after twenty-four
years of his reign, and in the prime of his life. Did the words
of the Anglo-Saxon chronicle on the first occasion recur to
English minds at the second, with a singular appropriateness,
'There has never been among the English a worse deed done
than this . . . his murderers would blot out his memory, but
the Avenger on High has spread his fame in heaven and earth.
Those who would not bow to his living body, now bend on their
knees before his dead bones'?

The halo of reputed martyrdom is both a challenge and a
hindrance to any assessment of Charles I as king and man.
The issues bound up with his life and death are fundamental,
touching the very heart of the constitution and the very quick
of religion; therefore Charles I must always face his judges;
living or dead, his enemies will say of him, 'the evil that men
do lives after them' and many still agree with the verdict of
Macaulay in 1828, 'We detest the character of Charles I'.

But if we turn aside from political and religious bias, can
we then, with a more sympathetically detached approach, un-
lock the secret cabinet of Charles's curiously involved personality? It is not easy. Charles hid his personality behind a
chilling reserve, which only his wife and his friend, the Duke
of Buckingham, successfully penetrated. The causes may have
been both physical and psychological. A delicate child, slow
in being able to walk and with an impediment in his speech,
Charles only achieved a vigorous constitution with an effort.
But by the time he was sixteen, though not tall, he had plenty

of physical vitality; he could tilt at the ring and hold his own, could swim and dance and play tennis with ease and vigour. The Civil War was to show later that if the King's frame was slight it was wiry; he could endure long hours in the saddle, and did not lack physical courage. At Edgehill he took an active part in the battle, and would not quit the field at nightfall; while at Naseby he was on the point of charging the enemy at the head of the guards when the Earl of Carnwath turned his horse forcibly back, saying 'Will you go upon your death?' Defeat and imprisonment did not seriously impair his constitution; in 1647, as a prisoner at Hampton Court, he was happy enough to take a day's hunting and killed his stag in New Park. Those who saw him on the scaffold noted that his chestnut hair had whitened; but the post-mortem revealed that 'no man had ever all his vital parts so perfect and unhurt, and that he seemed to be of so admirable a composition and constitution that he would probably have lived as long as nature could subsist'. After all, he was only forty-eight.

The slowness of speech of his childhood persisted longer. James Welwood tells us that 'when he was warm in discourse, he was inclinable to stammer'. Whether it was this defect or something more psychological which affected him, Charles grew up to be a man of few words. It is possible that the loss of his elder brother at twelve years and of his mother at nineteen drove him in on himself, but whatever the cause, Charles presented, in his reticence and chilly gravity, a striking contrast to the cheerful garrulity of his father. His first speech to his first Parliament begins very characteristically: 'I thank God that the business of this time is of such a nature that it needs no eloquence to set it forth, for I am neither able to do it, nor doth it stand with my nature to spend much time in words.' He could express himself better on paper; he was a good letter writer, and his style was pointed and direct.

His reticence went further than verbal hesitation; it amounted to secretiveness. Clarendon says of him: 'He saw and observed men long before he received any about his person, and did not love strangers, nor very confident men.' In crisis he became the more taciturn. He was at divine service when a courtier whispered to him the news of the assassination of Buckingham. 'His Majesty,' says Clarendon, 'continued unmoved, and without the least change in his countenance, till prayers were ended; when he suddenly departed to his chamber and threw himself upon his bed, lamenting with much passion and with abundance of tears the loss he had of an excellent servant and the horrid manner in which he had been deprived of him.'

Beneath the cold exterior and dignified manner, Charles concealed an active intelligence and a capacity for affection.

Clarendon, writing in his second exile of the 'martyr king', might be thought partial when he says that Charles had 'an excellent understanding', though he adds shrewdly, 'but was not confident enough of it'. Long before, Charles's abilities were recognized by that shrewd judge of men and books, the Conde de Gondomar. Writing in 1620 to Philip III, when the negotiations for the Spanish marriage of the prince were in full swing. Gondomar said: 'The Prince is of good disposition and ability. He knows several languages well and particularly Latin. He is a good horseman and daily, after hearing Divine service, occupies himself in the exercises suitable for a Prince.'

Charles's mind differed from his father's; he was less interested in the technicalities of scholarship, more in a broader culture. Well trained in theology by the Oxford divine, Dr Hakewill, Charles read widely in the subject, and the papal agent George Con was surprised to find him so well read in the Fathers and so able to argue on the history of the Church and the Papacy. As a young man, Charles had told the Spanish theologians, perhaps a little tactlessly, that he had no scruples or doubts as to his religion; it was for them to open the debate. He went to Spain a Protestant and returned a confirmed one. His studies strengthened his beliefs and gave an intellectual basis to his faith. Neither the affection of a Catholic wife, nor the prospect of the scaffold shook the King's firm conviction that the Church of England was truly the Church Catholic; with this he would live and with it he would die.

Charles's other intellectual interests were literary and artistic. In the last days of imprisonment he was reading Tasso's *Gierusalemme,* Hooker's *Ecclesiastical Polity,* and the historical plays of Shakespeare. He enjoyed music and acting, and supported Massinger and 'rare Ben Jonson', who lived on to 1637. But more distinctive was the King's taste in art; here he was a real connoisseur. 'He had a singular skill in limning and pictures,' we are told, 'nor unskilful in music.' He had knowledge and discrimination. He could distinguish the special quality of a painter and knew merit when he saw it. History confirms his artistic judgements. He early showed his interest in art. From his journey to Madrid he brought back the full-length portrait of Charles V by Titian, but according to Hume's account, he was unable to persuade Don Juan de Espina to sell to him his two volumes of original drawings by Leonardo da Vinci.

Charles used his diplomats as agents to seek out and pro-cure paintings for him, and he also employed the painter Daniel Nys similarly. About 1628 Nys secured for the King the greater part of the famous collection of the Duke of Mantua, including 'The Triumph of Cæsar' by Mantegna. About the same time Charles bought the famous cartoons of Raphael for the tapestries for the Sistine Chapel.

Charles's taste was wide; he bought Flemish and Spanish as well as Italian paintings, and was also interested in sculpture. Unfortunately the magnificent bust which Bernini made of him from the painting of three heads of the King by Van Dyck perished or disappeared in the great fire at Whitehall in 1698, but the fine equestrian statue in bronze by Le Sueur remains at Charing Cross to this day.

> 'Comely and calm, he rides
> Hard by his own Whitehall:
> Only the night wind glides:
> No crowds, nor rebels, brawl.' . . .

> 'Armoured he rides, his head
> Bare to the stars of doom:
> He triumphs now, the dead,
> Beholding London's gloom.'[1]

Charles gathered round him the artists and men of taste of the day. Rubens painted for him the ceiling of the Banqueting House at Whitehall; Van Dyck was his court painter; Inigo Jones designed the masques in which he and his queen delighted to perform. To these men Charles showed his best side, sensi-tive, appreciative, discriminating. He was one of the greatest among the great collectors of works of art. When, after his death, the regicide state took possession of his collection, it comprised 400 pieces of sculpture and 1,400 paintings. Princes and statesmen of Europe competed in purchasing the great masterpieces which Charles had so lovingly assembled, and the English visitor to the Prado and other famous galleries views with mixed feelings works which might still be in his own country. Many less valuable works were sold to Englishmen. Others, including the Mantegna Triumph and Raphael's Cartoons, were retained by the State. Many of the pictures were retrieved by Charles II at the Restoration, and others have since returned to this country; but deprived of its masterpieces, the collection has lost for ever its outstanding character.

Charles I was not only a cultivated and widely read man: he was an affectionate and faithful husband and father. His marriage to Henrietta Maria was not politically wise, for it rested on a falsehood. The concessions which Charles had promised in his marriage contract to English Catholics were, he knew, impossible of fulfilment. The penal laws were on the statute book; the most he could do – and even this was disputable to Puritan opinion – was to grant dispensations from them; to revoke them could only be done by Parliament.

The marriage nearly came to shipwreck in the first two years. Charles was nearly ten years older than his girl bride; not until he expelled her French attendants ('the Devil go with them', he wrote irritably to Buckingham), did he win her affection or obedience. But after that, the marriage was a success in spite of the difference in religion. Up to 1642 it seems it was Charles who made the concessions, conniving at his subjects going to Mass at the Queen's chapel and receiving Papal agents at his court. But when it came to the difficult days of 1646, when Henrietta Maria was in Paris and Charles a prisoner, then the King showed himself unyielding. He would purchase neither life nor throne by yielding up episcopacy permanently. To the Queen, Anglicans, Presbyterians and Independents were all one, heretics every man of them, and the episcopacy of the English Church to which Charles clung so fiercely not truly Catholic in her eyes. She was in despair at seeing the King so resolute in what touched episcopacy and so little concerned with his own future and that of his children. Charles protested his grief in differing from her, but he was stung to reply: 'Make the case thy own, with what patience would thou give ear to him who should persuade thee for worldly respects to leave the communion of the Roman Church for any other?'

Long before, in 1624, Laud had heard Charles say that he could not be a lawyer, for 'I cannot defend a bad nor yield in a good cause'. In 1645 he had written to Ormonde in Ireland: 'I will rather choose to suffer all extremities than ever to abandon my religion.' The furthest he would go in negotiating with the Parliament was to concede the form of Presbyterian government in England for three years, reserving to himself in the interim Anglican worship for his household, and referring the ultimate religious settlement to an assembly of divines, including among them his own nominees. He neither dissolved the episcopal government of the Church nor alienated its property. But there was no heart or reality in his concessions and his enemies rightly gauged that, with that curious mixture of optimism and obstinacy which was part of the King's make-up, he was possibly still hoping that the wheel might turn and King and bishops enjoy their own again.

Both as a man and as a father, Charles was loyal to his faith. All his children were baptized according to the Anglican rite, and only the youngest, the Princess Henrietta, was brought up in France as a Roman Catholic by her mother.

Charles was a devoted husband. His last message to his wife, given to his daughter the Princess Elizabeth in a farewell interview on 29 January, and recorded by her, was this: 'He bid me tell my mother that his thoughts had never strayed from her, and that his love should be the same to the last.' It was the truth but the message was never given in person, for the young Princess, worn by grief and imprisonment, died in Carisbrooke Castle in 1650 at the age of fourteen. Charles's affection for his children was fully returned and when in July 1647, in his captivity at Caversham, his three younger children were allowed to see him, the stern Cromwell with tears in his eyes found it 'the tenderest sight that ever his eyes beheld'.

So far we have thrown the high light on the more attractive aspects of Charles I, the promising youth, the cultivated monarch, and the affectionate husband and father. But with all these gifts, Charles also combined a rigidity of mind and a lack of warmth and generosity to all but his family and his few friends. He had said he could not be a lawyer, but he had much of the narrowness of the law in his composition. He lacked entirely the flexibility and political wisdom of Queen Elizabeth and the shrewdness and accessibility of his father. He stood on technical rights when the question at issue could only be solved by the broadest political wisdom. In 1628, deep in the quarrel with his third Parliament over the impeachment of Buckingham, he put to the judges the question of the extent of his right to punish those who 'defamed his government within the walls of Parliament'. The shrewd comment of the Venetian agent at his court that 'with the key of the laws he seeks to open the entrance to absolute power' is true of the whole reign; whether it were ship money or the enforcement of obsolete forest law, what mattered first to Charles was the technical merit of his case. That secured, he went ahead, inflexibly trampling over the susceptibilities, religious or economic, of his people. To those who opposed him, he could be unmerciful, witness his refusal to free the dying Eliot from the Tower and even to give back the poor body for burial in his native county. It was characteristic of this side of his mind that when at his execution the executioner asked for the customary pardon, the King replied: 'I forgive no subject of mine who comes deliberately to shed my blood.' 'He was not in his nature bountiful', says Clarendon of Charles I, and it was true. His refusal of the earldom to Wentworth grates on us; it was so well earned, and when at length he conferred it, the grant had lost its savour. His dismissal of Prince Rupert after the surrender of Bristol might have been militarily unavoidable, but it was harshly put.

There was a certain mental obtuseness in Charles I with all his intelligence. He often had technical right on his side, but he allowed too little for the lively political capacity of his people or for the strength of their Puritanism.

In 1642 he felt that he had gone to the limit of concessions; he had sacrificed Strafford against his conscience and judgement as the *Eikon Basilike* shows; he had abolished the Star Chamber and the High Commission and given Parliament the power to control its own existence; no more would he grant, and to the demand for the control of the militia he presented a firm negative. The result was civil war.

Undoubtedly the King had technical right on his side; the control of the armed forces was a royal prerogative; whatever a parliamentary ordinance might be, it was not law without his assent. What he failed to appreciate was the real issue. Could a reformed and limited monarchy be achieved by a balanced compromise between royal prerogative and parliamentary government? If not, and it took all the years of war between 1642 and 1648 to prove the impossibility, then the deposition of the King was inevitable. There were moments in the war when compromise seemed near; it was almost but not quite so in 1647 when the Heads of the Proposals were offered by the Army. But two things made a limited monarchy impossible – Charles's stubborn adherence to episcopacy, and his failure to prove himself a man of his word. No doubt some of his vacillation between Parliament and Army, Scots and Irish, was a real seeking for a possible solution of the dilemma; a prisoner, he grasped at straws and any chance seemed possible. But this was not all. He had an almost arrogant and unjustified belief in his powers as a negotiator. His weak if pacific foreign policy after 1630 might have taught him differently, but almost to the last he was playing a part with successive opponents, with the fatal result that at last they rose in their wrath and resolved to destroy him. Oliver Cromwell, who had clung to monarchy as late as 1647, now repudiated it, and with indecent haste drove through the farce of a trial and the speedy execution.

'If I cannot live as a King, I will die as a gentleman,' Charles had written to Digby in March 1646. But now, when it came to the last, he did not die just as a gentleman; he died as a King. In that illegal court he would not plead. 'Let me know by what authority I am called hither. I do stand more for the liberty of my people than any here that come to be my pretended judges, and therefore let me know by what lawful authority I am seated here and I will answer it; otherwise I will not answer it.' The only answer was the sword. There was no legality behind that court, and the people of England knew it. But it could not unking the King, for he was neither tried nor convicted; they might sentence him to death, but it was as 'Charles Stuart, King of England'. By his death Charles I saved the monarchy. It was only a question of time before it was restored, for though the English had created a first-class

• •

army, they were too legally minded a people to be ruled by force.

In the brief hours left to him Charles I recovered all his native dignity. The inner citadel of his faith was intact. With the consolations of his religion, administered to him by Juxon, he went unflinchingly to his death. In the city which had turned against him in the war, the vast crowds that came to see him die were quiet, as if partly stunned by the unusual spectacle. Few could have heard his final speech; there were too many guards round the scaffold for that, but in his last hour all hesitation dropped away from Charles I. He spoke nobly and without rancour, and his words rang true. 'For the people truly I desire their Liberty and Freedom as much as any body whatsoever, but I must tell you that their Liberty and Freedom consist in having of Government those laws by which their lives and their goods may be most their own.'

So died Charles I by violence, not by law. His critics then and now say that had he succeeded in his absolute policy, England would have lost her Parliament and gone the way of continental despotism. This is true, but it is equally true that had the naked rule of the sword persisted in England and the English not recovered a stable monarchy, social anarchy might have followed and the framework of local government, which held intact in 1640, would have collapsed also. The death of Charles I and the manner of it prevented this. The cause of monarchy was reborn. The rule of the sword stood self-condemned to be necessarily transient.

'Vanquished in life, his death
  By beauty made amends:
The passing of his breath
  Won his defeated ends.

'Brief life and hapless? Nay:
  Through death, life grew sublime.
Speak after sentence? Yea:
  And to the end of time.'[2]

# THE EXECUTION OF CHARLES I AND THE DEVELOPMENT OF THE CONSTITUTION

*by*

*MARK A. THOMSON*

The Civil War did not begin as a struggle between those who wished to abolish, and those who wished to preserve, the monarchy. The monarchy, indeed, appeared alike to Parliamentarians and Royalists to be an element of the constitution so essential that its absence could scarcely be conceived. The aim of Charles's opponents was to compel him to accept certain constitutional changes alike in Church and State. His supporters were originally mainly those who opposed ecclesiastical changes; but for his championship of the Church, Charles would have found few to fight for him. The great statutes of 1641, however much they might be disliked by the King, were not a grievance to most of the Royalists. Thus it may be said that, until shortly before Charles's execution, the great majority of Englishmen were constitutionalists, firmly attached to the monarchy, to Parliament, and to an established Church. About the precise functions of King and Parliament* and about matters ecclesiastical there was disagreement, a disagreement sharpened as the struggle continued by increasing fears and mistrusts, but the area of disagreement was restricted by this constitutionalism. It was Charles who so widened it that a settlement became impossible during his life.

But the King who did not know how to rule or how to agree with his adversary knew how to die. In his speech on the scaffold, moreover, Charles claimed, doubtless in good faith, to have been the opponent of arbitrary power and the rule of the sword. In point of fact, his execution was followed by something very like the rule of the sword. Until the Restoration the

---

* The King was, and is, part of Parliament, which consists of King, Lords, and Commons. This fact should never be forgotten in studying the seventeenth century.

army was the strongest organized force in England; without its support no regime could survive. But the support of the army alone could not make any regime stable, however efficient it might be – and the Protectorate was efficient. The mass of Englishmen remained constitutionalists. Charles's execution, therefore, so far from being a blow to the cause of monarchy, actually strengthened it. It is true that the execution was followed by a series of constitutional experiments. Those who were responsible for the killing of the King had to try to find a substitute for the old constitution, which they thought had been shattered on 30 January 1649. But all the new systems were damned by their illegitimacy, which carried with it the taint of arbitrary power. Before Charles's execution there had been many disputable constitutional points, but much had been certain. Afterwards the whole constitutional terrain became an area of possible conflict. What was the power of the body that was called Parliament? No man could give a satisfactory answer. Who could exactly define Cromwell's powers after he had become Protector? The fact that Cromwell was strongly urged to take to himself the title of King is evidence of the desire to secure a greater measure of certainty in constitutional matters.

The Restoration, indeed, when it came, was far more than the acceptance of Charles II as King, and more than the recall of a dynasty; it was professedly, as said in the service for 30 January, and to a great extent really, a return to the 'ancient government in Church and State'. Charles I had been executed because of his personal defects; but Charles II was not called to the throne because of his personal virtues. The Restoration was a triumph for constitutionalism. That triumph was in part due to the execution of Charles I. While alive Charles I had been a liability to the royalist cause; after his death he became an asset. But he became an asset because he became a symbol. More and more he was thought of as the champion of the good old constitution, which in retrospect contrasted so favourably with the experiments of 1649–59. Again, those Englishmen – and they were many – who favoured episcopacy and loved the Book of Common Prayer venerated the memory of the royal martyr, who had, they believed, died for the established Church. Hence that extravagant laudation by Anglican divines of

Charles I, and hence their frequent references to non-resistance as a doctrine of the Church of England. Resistance to the monarch appeared to be inseparably connected with enmity to the Church. During the reign of Charles II the alliance between Church and King remained firm, in spite of various stresses and strains, and some Anglicans, both clerical and lay, wrote and talked of the King as though he were absolute. Very few of them meant what they said. The real temper of the country can be gauged by the conduct of the members of the Cavalier Parliament, which never hesitated to stand up for what it conceived to be the rights of the Church or of Parliament itself. About the precise extent of those rights there was plenty of room for debate. The Restoration, though it purported to be a return to the old constitution, did not, and could not, put an end to constitutional disputes, which are an inseparable concomitant of a vigorous political life, but the area of possible disputes remained limited for many years, since the substantial continuance of the old constitution was a generally accepted belief.

The prevalence of this belief did not mean that the events of 1642–59 had been forgotten. That would have been impossible. On the contrary, it was because they had left so many unhappy memories that reference was often made to them to point a moral. Persecution of Dissenters could be defended on the ground that Dissenters were likely to be rebels. The principles that led to Dissent could be represented as logically leading to regicide. Such arguments came naturally to those zealous Anglicans who believed, or professed to believe, that republicanism was still potent as well as pernicious. Fear of republicanism was natural enough in the Restoration period, but the grounds for it were not strong. Neither before nor after 1660 did those who disliked certain features of the established Church necessarily incline to republicanism. The Restoration, indeed, had been largely due to the Presbyterians. Republicanism after 1660 was the political creed of a small minority, which included no great man of action. It could never have been a major political force. But the very real and widespread fear of republicanism was often exploited by propagandists. Those who held that the monarchy was limited and that a king who endeavoured to go beyond the limits of his lawful authority could be deposed were often denounced as republicans.

The Exclusion controversy showed the interaction of the then political forces. The strength of the agitation for Exclusion was a commentary at once on contemporary English feeling, on the past policy of Charles II, and on the reputation of his brother. The case for Exclusion was that the old constitution and the Church would not be safe if the Papist James were allowed to succeed to the throne. Charles showed his appreciation of the situation by offering to assent to a bill imposing such limitations upon a Roman Catholic successor as would have robbed him of almost all prerogative power. This offer was well calculated, for it took much of the force out of the Exclusionists' main argument. But it also amounted to a profession of willingness to accept a revolutionary constitutional change. It is small wonder that some republicans are reported to have favoured the limitations scheme; it is small wonder that many conservatives disliked it. For the opposition to Exclusion was essentially conservative in character. It could be argued that the existing laws were an adequate safeguard against any designs that James might form after his accession; loyalty to the dynasty, to the Church, and to Parliament were still compatible with one another; on the other hand, Exclusion would lead to civil war. Considerations such as these were weighty. Ultimately, fear of change and its consequences proved the deciding factor in the struggle over Exclusion.

The reign of James II showed that a choice must be made between conflicting loyalties. If the constitution were not to be subverted and the Church endangered, resistance to the King was inevitable. In 1688 the great majority of all classes hoped for the success of William of Orange's expedition, the professed aim of which was to secure the calling of a free Parliament, to whose decision all debatable matters were to be committed. What actually happened was what nobody expected. James, largely because he was terrified by the memory of his father's fate, fled the country, and thereby created a constitutional vacuum, which the Convention Parliament filled by the tender of the Crown to William and Mary. Unless they had been willing to recall James on his own terms, there was nothing else to be done. But, though necessity compelled the decision, it made many rather uncomfortable. Not that James was much regretted. Mary Woodforde, wife of an Anglican divine of conservative opinions, expressed a pretty general feeling, when in February 1689 she wrote in her diary: 'The Prince and Princess of Orange were proclaimed . . . King and Queen . . . God grant they may reign in righteousness and . . . make them a blessing to this unhappy land . . . And good Lord bless our late King James (wheresoever he is) . . . Open his eyes to the ways of truth . . . that tho' he has lost his earthly crown, he may obtain a Heavenly.'[3] None the less, many found the substitution of William and Mary for James hard to reconcile with views previously professed. It could be argued that James had been deposed because he had broken the original contract between King and people. Those who believed this had no qualms of conscience. But this argument could not be invoked by that large section of the community which had long defended the doctrines of non-resistance and indefeasible hereditary right. Other grounds had to be found to justify their conduct and found they were. The supreme authority, it was contended, was not the King, but the legislature; this authority had not been resisted at the Revolution; the person of the King, indeed, was inviolable, but no violence had been offered to James's person; of his own volition he had withdrawn from the country, and thereby created a vacancy of the throne. Thus the Revolution could be justified on very different grounds; but its real justification was that it preserved what Englishmen rightly valued – the monarchy, Parliament, and the Church. Preservation, however, involved change. After 1688 the functions of the monarchy and of Parliament were not what they had been before. Again, the passing of the Toleration Act was an admission that there could be more than one Church in the same State, that the Church of England was not to be, even in theory, the Church of all Englishmen.

In fact a great deal more happened at the Revolution than many of its supporters perceived. The widespread disposition to minimize the extent of the change, the retaining wherever possible of old forms, were evidence of fear – fear of a renewal of the civil strife and confusion of the years 1642–59. The great argument of the Jacobite minority was that the Revolution meant a breaking down of all the old bounds and the subversion of all lawful authority in Church and State; only a second

Restoration could save England from the alternative perils of arbitrary power or anarchy. This argument was conclusively refuted by experience. William III was not a Cromwell nor did England fall into anarchy. The memories of 'old unhappy far-off things' invoked by the Jacobites actually helped to preserve the Revolution settlement, because they acted as a moderating influence, when political passions were stirred.

In 1702–4 Clarendon's *History of the Rebellion* was first published with a preface and dedication to Queen Anne, written by his younger son, Rochester, himself a prominent Tory. Rochester was careful to point the moral that might be drawn from his father's tale: 'Where any King by ill judgement, or ill fortune, of his own, or those who intrusted by him in the chief administration of his government, happens to fall into an interest contrary to that of his people, and will pursue that mistake, that prince must have terrible conflicts in the course of his reign, which way soever the controversy ends; on the other hand, that people, who, though invaded and oppressed in their just rights and liberties, shall not rest satisfied with reasonable reparations and securities, but, having got power into their hands, will make unjustifiable use of it, to the utter subversion of that government they are bound in duty and allegiance to support, do but at last make rods for their own backs, and very often bring upon themselves from other hands a more severe bondage than they had shook off.' Armed resistance to the monarch is not justifiable; grievances can be remedied 'in a Parliamentary way'. Queen Anne, who 'succeeds to a Revolution as well as a Restoration, has the advantage of a retrospect on all these accidents, and the benefit of reviewing all the failings in those times; and whatsoever was wanting, at those opportunities of amending past errors, in the management of affairs, for the better establishment of the Crown, and the security of the true old English government, it will be your Majesty's happiness to supply in your time.' In this 'true old English government' the Church was included: 'The religion by law established is such a vital part of the government... that men generally look upon it as a good part of their property too; since that, and the government of the Church, is secured to them by the same provision.' Rochester was a High Churchman, but not a Jacobite. He and his like accepted the Revolution settlement, even if unenthusiastically. But they were ready to revive the old cry that all Dissenters were potential rebels in order to make propaganda for the Occasional Conformity and Schism Bills which were designed to strengthen the Tories at the expense of the Whigs.

The Whigs, on their part, were equally adroit in their appeals to history. At Sacheverell's impeachment, when the Commons propounded, and the Lords accepted, what was to become the classic Whig doctrine, Sir Joseph Jekyll, one of the managers of the impeachment, could say: 'Nothing is plainer than that the people have a right to the laws and the constitution. This right the nation hath asserted and recovered out of the hands of those who had dispossessed them of it at several times. There are of this two famous instances in the knowledge of the present age. I mean that of the Restoration and that of the Revolution; in both these great events were the regal power and the rights of the people recovered. And it is hard to say in which the people have the greatest interest, for the Commons are sensible that there is not one legal power belonging to the Crown, but they have an interest in it.' Eighty-one years later these words were quoted with approval by Burke in his *Appeal from the New to the Old Whigs*.

Thus to bracket the Restoration and the Revolution was something more than propaganda. It was an affirmation that certain essential elements of the old constitution had been preserved. Preservation, indeed, involved modification. Burke could proudly declare: 'In what we improve, we are never wholly new; in what we retain, we are never wholly obsolete' (*Reflections on the Revolution in France*). Many reasons, some of them highly controversial, could be given for this. But it is certain that a great lesson had been learnt in the seventeenth century. James Boswell's father is said to have observed that the execution of Charles I taught Kings they had a joint in their necks. This was true enough, but it was not the whole truth. Bitter experience taught the English and their rulers that constitutional disputes must be settled without recourse to arms. Englishmen, though they long refused to acknowledge the fact, learned to treat their constitution as flexible; once this had come to pass, almost any kind of peaceful change in response to new needs and pressures was possible.

# THE PORTRAITS OF CHARLES I

*by*

*DAVID PIPER*

The development of Charles I's appearance from an early age can be followed through a relatively large number of portraits. He was the greatest English royal patron of the arts, and it was owing to him that Van Dyck came to England; what is not so well known, however, is that his patronage extended far beyond Van Dyck, and that the latter's interpretation of Charles is but one of several.

There are a number of pictures of Charles as a boy and a young man in his 'teens, in varying costumes, and by various artists, but all working in the archaic, slightly wooden manner of the late Elizabethan painters. They show a smooth, rather long and thin face, with an unusually large forehead, the hair tending to stand up from the brow in front. It is somewhat surprising to find a long-standing confusion between these early portraits of Charles and those of his elder brother, Henry, Prince of Wales, and a number of them have only recently been re-converted from the name of Henry. On close inspection the faces of the brothers prove clearly distinct, particularly in their proportions: if Charles's face be considered as an oval, then Henry's is near to an equilateral triangle – compare the miniatures of the two by Isaac Oliver, or the paintings formerly at Ditchley (that of Charles is now no. 2562 of the National Portrait Gallery).

Between 1620 and the death of James I the portraits become more numerous, and the patterns are often repeated; the number of versions still broadcast in continental collections makes it probable that portraits of Charles were already being sent abroad as instruments of diplomacy. At this period portrait-making was a business which comprised that of both the photographer and the modern portrait-painter. The painter, then, from one or more sittings of his subjects, would take a likeness – probably a drawing of the head only, with perhaps a sketch of the pose of the body demanded. Then, often with the help of assistants, he would complete a painting from this; if it was a success, and the sitter a person of importance, there would no doubt follow orders for copies of this same *pattern*. In the case of royal portraits, this might amount almost to mass production: they had been used for prestige at home, and for embassies abroad (particularly by missions seeking marriage-alliances) since the fifteenth century at least. Mytens was now the principal painter employed, a Fleming, showing already the influence of Rubens in a freedom of manner that must have been remarkable in England about 1620. From his hands from 1623, and perhaps earlier, comes a series of studies of Charles, which built up an image entirely credible, not spectacular yet not inelegant. Typical of the early portraits is the whole length of 1623 by Mytens (in the Royal Collection: reproduced by Millar, pl. 47). Charles wears his hair dressed neatly, rounded just below the ears, a slight moustache, but the rather heavy chin clean-shaven. Then in 1624, just before his accession, he shows for the first time a beard, a small fluffy tuft on the point of his chin (examples of this portrait are in the Royal Gallery, Copenhagen, and in the National Gallery of Canada, Ottawa, no. 768). So he appears for the first five years of his reign, with a slight thickening and darkening in time, and a gradual elaboration of costume: but his accession is not marked by any re-casting of his portrait – only by the crown and sceptre placed on a table by his side. There are two or three stock patterns in use: for example, 'his Majesty's picture at large with a prospect, and the Crown and Sceptre, in a scarlet em-broidered suit' – perhaps the pattern, with variations in back-ground and dress, which is represented in the National Portrait Gallery (no. 1246), the Maritime Museum, and at Chatsworth, and which seems to have been used by both Cornelius Jonson and by Mytens.

But in 1632, Van Dyck arrived; apotheosis begins, of which he is the painter. The Charles of Mytens is a dignified figure, yet of considerable charm, human and accessible. (Charles's dignity, it should be noted, was not inevitable: the very com-petent Dutch painter, H. G. Pot, makes an absurd mannikin

of him in the strange group in Buckingham Palace[4] – Pot, however, does not seem to have flourished long in Charles's
favour.) In Van Dyck's first portraits of Charles allegory is at
once apparent, and the visual material of the legend of Charles
the King, Charles the Martyr to be, is to hand.

A description of how this transformation is achieved may be
found in any work on Van Dyck; the most important points
may be recapitulated here. Van Dyck was, of course, among
other things a genius as a technician: he knew a great deal
more about paint than Mytens could ever learn, and the
seduction of this technical mastery must not be forgotten when
accounting for the domination that Van Dyck won in the eyes
of his contemporaries. Moreover, he could compose a picture,
where Mytens could only arrange it. To the influence of a close
contact with Rubens, he added the experience and knowledge of
his own Italian journey; from Rubens (who himself painted
Charles as St George) and from Titian he had learnt not only
the formulae of the heroic, but had caught the spirit of it; and
this sense of the heroic was the element that appealed perhaps
most deeply to Charles. Once Van Dyck had shown Charles
his own ideal reflection, it did not remain confined to the painted
portrait: it appears in the equestrian statue by Le Sueur, at
Charing Cross, while behind the medals later issued by Charles
for award to soldiers valiant in some 'forlorn hope' (such as the
medal struck from Rawlins in 1643) lies the idea of the hero
king distributing his image to his satellite heroes. From Van
Dyck himself we have the great equestrian portrait in the
National Gallery, of about 1637 (obviously strongly influenced
by Titian's *Charles V*, which Charles I must surely have seen
in Madrid, in 1623), the other colossal equestrian portraits and
various studies in armour. But there are other conceptions
besides the military: Charles as the Royal Father and Husband
in the family group of 1632 at Windsor; as what we can now
recognize as the Royal English Gentleman in the famous group
at the Louvre, where he stands in a landscape, his equerry
holding his horse; and again in the almost funereal Dresden
portrait in which the pose of the head is nearly identical.

Yet the technical accomplishment, the heroic apparatus, are
not alone responsible for the extraordinary magic of Van Dyck's
portraits, which still bewitches today the Cavalier partisans.

There is some flattery beyond doubt, but, although the Princess Sophia of Bohemia was so distressed by the discrepancy between Van Dyck's presentation of Henrietta Maria and the toothiness of the reality, the blandishment was not gross in Charles's case. Its nature can be best understood now by comparison of Mytens's portraits with those of Van Dyck, though allowance must be made also for Mytens's own brand of flattery: there is, in particular, a double portrait of Charles with Henrietta Maria, a laurel wreath in their hands. E. K. Waterhouse has suggested,[5] with probability, that the earliest painting of this type, at Welbeck Abbey, is by Mytens: this pattern is of about 1630, and it was developed a year or so later by Van Dyck. He does remarkably little to it – he ties it together as a composition largely by a simple adjustment of the hands and of the background – yet at the same time he generally loosens it, releases it, so to speak, completely into three dimensions, so that the atmosphere is changed utterly, and the portrait lifted out of the quiet, familiar world (which by comparison seems bourgeois) into a rarefied air.

Little, if any, development of Van Dyck's idea of the King is visible during the nine years he worked for him; having stated his theme, he performed variations, to every one's immense satisfaction; he was copied, or aped, almost at once (even by Mytens), until his contemporaries had all learnt to see with his eyes. This is evident already in the Hoskins miniature of 1632, which may or may not be a copy from him; it may be seen perhaps most clearly in Briot's two *Dominion-of-the-Sea* medals. The first of these, of 1630, shows the King in profile to the right, and is perhaps Briot's own view, noted from the life; but in the second medal, of 1639, the head, in exactly the same pose, is obviously, if not actually based on Van Dyck, then certainly conceived in his mode. For what it is worth, I remark that the actual physical proportions of the images on these two medals are not the same: in the later medal there is a pronounced drawing-out, a lengthening in brow and nose, as though to balance the increased length of beard: this lengthening is perhaps the characteristic of Van Dyckian flattery for his male sitters, the foundation of that melancholy, the remote and elegant, if a little equine, incarnation of aristocracy, which succeeding generations have agreed almost unanimously to perceive in them. To realize how arbitrary this impression is, turn to the bust of Bernini, which was made up in Italy exclusively from Van Dyck's three-in-one portrait of Charles's head. (The original marble was destroyed by fire, but a copy is now in the Royal Collection; rep. Millar, text vol., fig. 27.) Van Dyck is swamped by the stronger vitality of the Italian, under whose hands Charles turns into a restless, domineering, almost swashbuckling type. But Bernini's version was never widely known.

In December 1641 Van Dyck died, just before the disruption of the Civil War began. Charles continued to patronize the arts; Dobson, for example, is said to have painted much for him until his own death in 1646, although no portrait of Charles by Dobson is known. Indeed only two major images were made during the last eight years of Charles's life. First (about 1645?) Lely's portrait: a double portrait of this type shows Charles with James, Duke of York (a version is in the Scottish National Portrait Gallery, no. 858), and similar pictures of the King alone are known. This pattern was also used by Sir Edward Walker when he had the double portrait, of Charles and himself on the battlefield, made up (no. 1961 in the National Portrait Gallery), and a good engraving by Faithorne is founded on it. Yet this image is little known. In it Charles's face appears broader and coarser, the Vandyckian beard is trimmed down almost to a lip-tuft. Secondly, there is a pattern known as *Charles I at his trial*, originated by a painter called Edward Bower of Temple Bar, and manufactured, with variations, in some profusion (Millar, pl. 91). Here Charles is seated in a high-backed chair, three-quarter length, wearing a dark cloak and a tall, broad-brimmed hat; his beard is more roughly grown than in any other image, fully covering the jawbone. Though doubtless based on sketches from the life made about the time of the trial, there is here a reminiscence of the Vandyckian atmosphere. In the engravings of this picture, made about the beginning of the next century by Simon and by Faber, the groomed Vandyckian mask with the familiar pointed beard is substituted for the rather gaunt and uncouth face which actually appears in Bower's paintings.

Indeed the Vandyckian image had established its monopoly some years before Charles's head fell; the failure of other

painters after Van Dyck's death to supplant or even to supplement it may be due not only to historical events, but to
Charles's own refusal to promote the publication of portraits,
which, he may have felt, fell short of the ideal figure presented
by his favourite painter. It is this figure that is used in
the cult of Charles the Martyr. It is at least as much an attri-
bute – so to speak – of the royal saint as are the crown of
thorns, or the earthly and the heavenly crown in the ray of
light, which appear in the engravings prefaced to the various
editions of the *Eikon Basilike*; it is the Van Dyck profile which
is stamped on the memorial badges and medals, the Van Dyck
head which appears on the frequent posthumous miniatures.
Apart from the fact that Van Dyck's shop produced a considerable number of versions of the image, later copies and engravings (the British Museum *Catalogue of Engraved Portraits*
lists almost a hundred different engravings after Van Dyck) are
innumerable, while reproductions of portraits by other artists
are comparatively rare. When men think of Charles I in visual
terms, they think of him in terms of Van Dyck – and probably
Charles himself would have no objection to history seeing him
exclusively through Van Dyck. That, however, is not the whole
picture, and a selective illustrated iconography is long overdue.

## NOTE ON REPRODUCTIONS

The argument above is expanded, and illustrated by reproductions, by
this writer in his *English Face* (1957) ch. 4, and a summary selective
account of the portrait-types is included in the entry for Charles I in his
*Catalogue of the 17th Century Portraits in the National Portrait Gallery*
(1963). The most comprehensive body of reproductions of painted portraits of Charles is to be found in Oliver Millar's *The Tudor, Stuart
and Early Georgian Pictures in the Collection of Her Majesty the Queen*
(2 vols, 1963), both in the volume of plates and in the comparative
material illustrated in the text volume (referred to above as *Millar*). For
reproductions of Van Dycks, see also G. Glück, *Van Dyck* (Stuttgart,
1931; in the *Klassiker der Kunst* series): M. Whinney and O. Millar,
*English Art 1625–1714* (the Oxford History of English Art, vol. VIII,
1957.
    The Coins and Medals are well illustrated in Helen Farquhars' articles
(*British Numismatic Journal*, 1906, vol. II; 1909, vol. V); or see the
plates to *Medallic Illustrations* (British Museum, 1904-05, pls. XIX-
XXXIV).

NOTES

1. Lionel Johnson, *By the Statue of King Charles at Charing Cross.*
2. Ibid.
3. *Woodforde Papers and Diaries*, ed. D. H. Woodforde, London, 1932, p. 21.
4. J. Skelton, *Charles I*, p. 114 (wrongly attributed to Mytens); a version, with Charles alone, is in the Louvre.
5. *The Studio*, 1948, vol. 135, p. 136. See Millar, text volume, figs. 12 and 14, reproducing both Mytens's and Van Dyck's versions of this design.

PART TWO

# Oliver Cromwell

# OLIVER CROMWELL

*by*

### CHRISTOPHER HILL

> The historian's quarrel with the biographer ... is that he wrests a complex figure from a complex setting, seeking to epitomize history in the far too simple terms of the individual. (W. K. Jordan, *The Development of Religious Toleration in England,* III, p. 476)

## I

Ever since the death of Oliver Cromwell 300 years ago his reputation has been the subject of controversy. The royalist view of him was expressed by Clarendon: 'a brave bad man, an ambitious hypocrite'. This interpretation was supported by many former Parliamentarians: Edmund Ludlow regarded Cromwell as the lost leader who jettisoned his early radical ideas on rising to power himself. The only aspect of Cromwell's policy that the next generation praised unreservedly was his aggressive foreign policy and support for trade. Pepys's famous phrase – 'What brave things he did and made all the neighbour princes fear him' – is only one of many rueful assessments made while the last two Stuarts were squandering the heritage of the Interregnum. But after William III resumed the policy of trade wars and colonial expansion there was less reason for remembering Oliver.

When radicalism revived in the later eighteenth century, the Yorkshire Association and Major Cartwright, the Corresponding Society and Cobbett, recalled Hampden, Pym, Prynne; but Cromwell was viewed critically by radicals like Mrs Macaulay no less than by Tories like Hume. The Vicar of Wakefield looked back with admiration to the Levellers, Blake and Wordsworth to Milton, but literary eulogies of Cromwell are far to seek. In Crabbe's *Frank Courtship* a dour and old-fashioned country trader who admired Oliver kept his portrait face to the wall, to be turned round only in the safe company of chosen friends. Crabbe may have drawn on a sub-literary tradition among the middling groups; the phrase 'in Oliver's days' to describe a time of exceptional prosperity was still in use in the West Riding in the early nineteenth century (Mrs Gaskell, *Life of Charlotte Brontë*). But men of letters were agreed, down to Sir Walter Scott in *Woodstock*, that Cromwell was both ambitious and a hypocrite.

A more balanced estimate emerged with Macaulay's Essay on Hallam's *Constitutional History*. It was clinched by Carlyle's *Letters and Speeches of Oliver Cromwell*, published in 1845. This was an epoch-making book, though today it is easier to see its defects than its virtues. By printing Cromwell's own words and relating them to his actions, Carlyle established that Cromwell was not, in the normal sense of the words, either personally ambitious or a hypocrite. What was he then? For Carlyle he was a Hero with a capital H, a God-sent leader such as, in Carlyle's view, was needed in nineteenth-century England, trembling on the brink of democracy, Chartism and other evils. But that was in 1845. In 1848 and 1867 middle-class England shot its Niagara, without needing to be saved by a military dictator; its God-sent Hero was Mr Gladstone; and it came to see Cromwell not in the light of the French Revolution or Chartism but through the spectacles of liberal non-conformity. That very great historian, Samuel Rawson Gardiner, himself a nonconformist and a descendant of Cromwell's, invented the conception of 'the Puritan Revolution' to describe what Clarendon had called 'the Great Rebellion'. Gardiner's Cromwell was in part Puritan Hero; but he had lost the naive simplicity of Carlyle's. Gardiner saw a man who, coming to power by military means, nevertheless wished for 'bit-by-bit' reform, opposed 'the exaggerations of Puritanism' and was frustrated in his attempt to found a constitutional monarchy only by the circumstances of his day. He was a liberal in advance of his time; a russet-coated Gladstone even less successful with the Irish problem and even more apt to confuse theology with foreign policy.

This is an ungenerous caricature of Gardiner, whose work must be the starting-point for all study of the period. Like all of us, Gardiner was aware of the present whilst looking at the past, and his liberal prepossessions may well cause less distortion than the late W. C. Abbott's laboured comparisons between Cromwell and Hitler. Nevertheless, recent experience has given us new insights into Cromwell the revolutionary and dictator, whose world was so different from that of Victorian England. Moreover, research during the last fifty years has posed problems about the relation of economics to politics, and about the nature of 'the Puritan Revolution', of which Gardiner was hardly aware. Professor Nef and others have shown that economic developments in the century before 1640 helped to prepare Parliament to challenge political power. Professor Tawney's *Religion and the Rise of Capitalism*, and Professor Haller's *Rise of Puritanism* have shown the economic and political links of 'Puritanism'. We can no longer speak of 'the Puritan Revolution' without asking further questions. Recent contributions to the *Economic History Review* from Professors Tawney and Trevor-Roper and Mr Stone agree only in assuming that the causes of the Civil War are to be sought in economics rather than in religion.

Since Carlyle the English Revolution has too often been seen as Cromwell's revolution, almost as his creation. Cromwell himself needs to be placed against his background. Yet so long as no agreed interpretation has replaced Gardiner's, it is difficult to agree on the exact role of Oliver Cromwell. Mr Ashley saw him as 'the conservative dictator', Professor Abbott as a proto-fascist. Professor Trevor-Roper sees him as a declining gentleman, a 'country-house radical' and a 'natural back-bencher', who could lead a revolution of destruction but had no positive political ideals or abilities. Dr Paul sees him as the Christian trying to make God's will prevail in this world, torn between religious ideals and the necessities of political action. But the theological interpretation of Cromwell is really tautological. If we assume that God did not in fact speak to him, as is perhaps safest in the present state of the evidence, we then have to consider *why* Oliver thought that

God willed this, that or the other course of action. And so we are brought back again to the world in which Cromwell lived.

## II

There can be such varying interpretations of Oliver's character, motives and place in history because his character and actions bristle with paradoxes. I shall list and illustrate some of these paradoxes, and then comment on them.

(1) First is the paradox already noted, that the revolutionary of the forties became the conservative dictator of the fifties. At a time when Parliament claimed to be fighting *for* the King *against* his evil counsellors, Cromwell was reported as saying that 'if the King were before me I would shoot him as another'; and that he hoped to live to see never a nobleman in England. He was 'that darling of the sectaries,'[1] and he played the leading part in bringing Charles I to the scaffold. Yet Cromwell was no theoretical republican. He was described as 'king-ridden'; in 1652 he asked 'What if a man should take upon him to be King?' (II, 589); in 1657 monarchy was virtually restored, with the Lord Protector as monarch. By that date his former radical allies had broken with him – Lilburne in 1649, Harrison in 1653, Lambert in 1657. George Fox thought Oliver deserved the ignominious treatment he received at the Restoration because he failed to keep his promise to abolish tithes.

(2) Closely allied is Cromwell's attitude to constitutional government. He organized an army to fight for Parliament against the King. He sponsored the Self-Denying Ordinance which ordered all members of the two houses to lay down their military commands: yet Oliver retained his. In 1647, though he tried to mediate between Parliament and Army, in the last resort he sided with the Army in every crisis. In December 1648 he acquiesced in the Army's purge of Parliament; in 1653 he himself used the Army to dissolve Parliament. Except as Lord General he would never have become Protector. Yet from 1654 onwards he aimed, apparently genuinely, at a 'settlement' by which the military basis of his rule would be ended, and a parliamentary constitution estab-

lished: and was defeated in this aim by his Army. 'What's for
their good, not what pleases them', had been his object in
1647 (C.P. I, 277). In the fifties he could claim to be imposing liberty by the means of tyranny. Through the Major-
Generals he enforced a greater degree of religious toleration
than any Parliament elected on a propertied franchise could
approve of. ' 'Tis against the will of the nation,' Calamy said of
the Protectorate, 'there will be nine in ten against you.' 'But
what,' Oliver replied, 'if I should disarm the nine, and put a
sword in the tenth man's hand? Would not that do the business?'[2]

(3) Another paradox is to be found in his attitude towards
those unrepresented in Parliament. Promotion in his Army
went by merit, regardless of social or political considerations.
'I had rather have a plain russet-coated captain that knows
what he fights for, and loves what he knows, than that which
you call a gentleman and is nothing else.' 'It had been well
that men of honour and birth had entered into these employ-
ments, but why do they not appear? ... But seeing it was
necessary the work must go on, better plain men than none.'
'The state, in choosing men to serve them, takes no notice of
their opinions; if they be willing faithfully to serve them, that
satisfies' (I, 256, 262, 278). Cromwell was appealing, consciously if reluctantly, to the lower classes for the fighting
support his own class had failed to give. Yet he opposed
demands for manhood suffrage. In his speeches to his first
Parliament he equated poor men with bad men, and said that
if a Commonwealth must suffer, it was better that it should
suffer from the rich than from the poor (III, 435, 584). The
Levellers, with whom he worked in 1647 and in the winter of
1648-9, and whose leaders he imprisoned and shot in the
spring of 1649, had some reason to regard Cromwell as a
doublecrosser.

(4) Even in those political convictions which he most
strongly and genuinely held there are obvious contradictions.
Cromwell wrote to the General Assembly of the Kirk of
Scotland: 'I beseech you in the bowels of Christ, think it
possible you may be mistaken,' and said to the Governor of
Edinburgh Castle, in words that shocked many nineteenth
century nonconformists, 'Your pretended fear lest error should

step in, is like the man that would keep all the wine out of the country lest men should be drunk' (II, 303, 339). Yet he justified the massacre of Irish Catholics at Drogheda as 'a righteous judgement of God upon these barbarous wretches', and said: 'if by liberty of conscience you mean a liberty to exercise the mass, . . . where the Parliament of England have power, that will not be allowed' (II, 127, 144).

(5) Cromwell was not a hypocrite. And yet he sometimes comes very near hypocrisy in the absoluteness of his self-deception. 'He will weep, howl and repent, even while he doth smite you under the first rib', wrote men who had some experience of Oliver's methods.[3] The Irish have always found it difficult to take at its face value his declaration that 'We come (by the assistance of God) to hold forth and maintain the lustre and glory of English liberty in a nation where we have an undoubted right to it; wherein the people of Ireland . . . may equally participate in all benefits, to use liberty and fortune equally with Englishmen, if they keep out of arms' (II, 205). Cromwell was never quite sure whether his main duty was to the people of England or to the people of God. He assumed that 'the interest of Christians' was identical with 'the interest of the nation' (IV, 445), but not all the 'ungodly' majority would have agreed. Thurloe, Oliver's secretary, on one occasion differentiated sharply between the 'vile levelling party' and 'the good and godly' (C.P. II, 245). In Cromwell's foreign policy Firth saw a mixture of commercial traveller and Puritan Don Quixote.[4] Cromwell always talked of the Protestant interest; but it is difficult to think of a single instance in which he supported Protestantism to the detriment of England's political and commercial interests. His famous intervention on behalf of the Vaudois seems to have done the persecuted heretics little good in the long run; but it was excellent for England's prestige, and helped to force France to conclude the treaty of October 1655. In the Baltic Oliver advocated a Protestant alliance; but it was when Charles X threatened to establish Swedish power on both sides of the Sound, to the detriment of English trade, that the Protector most persistently sought to divert his energies into attacking Papist Austrians and Poles. We all know of the famous scene at Whitelocke's departure for Sweden, when Oliver adjured him:

'Bring us back a Protestant alliance!' But we shall search in vain in the official instructions given to Whitelocke for any such ideological purpose. It is all sordid, commercial and diplomatic.

(6) Finally, Oliver curiously combines hesitation, waiting on the Lord, with sudden violent action. At many of the crises of the period he was either missing, or played a highly ambiguous role. In the first four months of 1647, when the quarrel between Parliament and Army was coming to a head, he took no part in the negotiations. To this day historians do not know how far, if at all, Cromwell authorized Joyce's seizure of the King at Holmby House in June 1647. We know only that after the seizure had occurred he threw in his lot with the revolutionary Army. At the time of Pride's Purge he was far away, apparently prolonging quite unnecessarily his stay at the siege of Pontefract. When he returned he said 'he had not been acquainted with the design, but since it was done he was glad of it'.[5] Again in the winter of 1652–3 there were long delays and hesitations, and much criticism from his fellow-officers, before Cromwell finally lost his temper and dissolved the Long Parliament. 'It hath been the way God hath dealt with us all along,' he commented, 'to keep things from our eyes, that in what we have acted we have seen nothing before us — which is also a witness, in some measure, to our integrity' (III, 64). Cromwell's share in the dissolution of the Barebones Parliament is shrouded in mystery. He denied solemnly that he knew beforehand what was going to happen; but he accepted the *fait accompli*. In 1657 there were interminable delays before the final rejection of kingship; and then in 1658 the final explosion, brushing Fleetwood's protest aside with 'You are a milksop; by the living God I will dissolve the House!' (IV, 728). The conversations recorded by political opponents like George Fox, Edmund Ludlow and John Rogers make attractive reading because of Oliver's obvious sincerity; but those to whom he listened so attentively were often disappointed by his failure to adopt the point of view they had put before him. There is something mysterious about the way in which Oliver took his political decisions, about his mental processes. Did he control events, or did they control him?

Some of these contradictions can be explained by the accidents of Cromwell's personal history. He was far more tolerant than most men of his time and class. One has only to read the debates in the second Protectorate Parliament on the Nayler case to be reminded of the frightened savagery with which the average gentleman reacted to doctrines which he thought socially subversive. Only in his intolerance towards Irish Papists did Cromwell fail to rise above the standards of his age. But others of the paradoxes stem from specific features of the English Revolution and from the Puritan ideas which guided its leaders. To them we now turn.

## III

The Calvinist doctrine of the church contains a fundamental ambiguity. In one sense the church is all the people in a given community; in another sense it is the elect only. For the elect, Calvinism was a doctrine of spiritual equality: any good man was better than a peer or a king who was not in a state of grace. Puritan preachers sometimes presented this as though it was a doctrine of human equality: the qualifications were not always insisted on as carefully as they should have been.[6] It was easy for many laymen to proceed direct from Calvinism to Lilburnian democracy. But for the true Calvinist some men were undoubtedly more equal than others: the elect had privileges, rights and duties, because they were elect, which raised them head and shoulders above the sinful mass of mankind. In opposition the emphasis was on spiritual equality, with appropriate vagueness about the precise individuals who were equal: in power Presbyterians naturally wished to subordinate and discipline the sinful masses. Any seventeenth-century Calvinist would have agreed with the Rev. Jabez Bunting two centuries later, who opposed democracy because he opposed sin. Yet a linguistic ambiguity remained, just as it remained in the vocabulary of Locke, who talked of 'the people' in a dual sense: sometimes he meant all the inhabitants, at other times he meant the propertied class, and assumed that 'the people' had servants.[7] Those who loosely used Calvinist or Lockean language were liable to deceive those whose interpretation was stricter. The latter, in Wildman's expressive phrase at Putney, were 'cozened, as we are like to be' (*C.P.* I, 404).

Cromwell can be identified with no sect. But he was a Calvinist, and thought democracy manifestly absurd. For those with 'the root of the matter' in them, yes: for them no privileges were too great, no barriers should prevent them serving the state. But 'the root of the matter', 'the godly'—they are woefully imprecise phrases. In the moment of battle those who fight bravely on your side clearly have this root. But in peace visible saints are difficult to identify. It is easy to slip into interpreting 'the root of the matter' to mean 'agreeing with me'; then 'disagreeing with me' comes to mean 'ensnared by fleshly reasonings' (I, 696). Oh, Sir Harry Vane! This identification of yourself with God's cause was all the easier if, like Cromwell, you really did earnestly seek the Lord in prayer before any action; and if the Lord consistently blessed you with success, and thus gave *prima facie* proof of the rightness of your actions. So Oliver, contemptuous of the Divine Right of Kings, came close to believing in the Divine Right of Oliver. Major-General Harrison, George Fox and Lodowick Muggleton, among others, similarly identified their wishes with the will of the Almighty.

The Calvinist discipline, in France, the Netherlands, Scotland, had ensured unity during and after revolution, whilst preserving the dominance of the propertied classes through lay elders in presbyteries. But in the English Revolution the erastianism of the classes represented in Parliament made them suspicious of a full Scottish presbytery: religious toleration precluded any discipline imposed from above. So Calvinism in England disintegrated into fragments in the moment of its victory.

Puritanism therefore united the opposition by concealing divergences. The doctrine of the spiritual equality of believers could sound like a doctrine of the equality of men. Add to this the comradeship in arms of a victorious Army, and we can see how those who looked to Cromwell for leadership against lordly bishops and aristocratic Presbyterians might think him more of a democrat than he was. Nay, Oliver himself, in moments of emotion, may have been deceived too: 'would that we were all saints!' (I, 646). Yet after the fighting was over, after Cromwell had broken, one after another, with Lilburne, Vane, Harrison, all of whom had seemed godly at one time: where then shall we find consent? This tendency within Puritanism towards an ultimate anarchy of individual consciences seemed to Cromwell to justify military dictatorship as the only means of preserving the essential gains of the Cause. He came to see himself as the unwilling constable set not only over the people of England, but even over the good people in England.

## IV

Calvinism was one formative influence. Cromwell's own political experience was another. At Huntingdon in the 1630s he opposed the transformation of the town council into a close oligarchy, and helped to protect the rights of poorer burgesses. An early letter shows him pleading with a London merchant for continuance of money to maintain a lectureship 'in these times wherein we see they are suppressed with too much haste and violence by the enemies of God his truth' (I, 80). On behalf of fenmen whose common rights were endangered he opposed the drainage of the Fens by the Earl of Bedford and his associates. This was no mere philanthropic gesture. Cromwell arranged, in a business-like manner, contributions from all the commoners affected, with which he promised to hold the drainers in suit for five years. His attitude appears to have been inherited with his estates: his uncle had also opposed fen drainage. So we have here something more than an accident of personal biography – kindness of heart, or factious opposition. Common material interests linked a section of the gentry with humbler countrymen against privileged great landlords exploiting court influence. As 'Lord of the Fens' Oliver was already occupying in his county a political position similar to that which he held nationally a decade later: the country gentleman leading freeholders and people against courtiers and peers. In both cases his stand was liable to be misunderstood. Leader and led seemed to have identical aims when they only had common enemies. In the 1650s it was the Levellers who supported commoners against exploitation by fen drainage.[8]

When the Lord of the Fens had become Lord General he sent troops to protect drainers against commoners; as Lord Protector he consented to an ordinance in favour of Bedford and against the fenmen.

In 1640–2 diverse groups were united against the government. Commoners, yeomen and some gentlemen opposed enclosing landlords and court patentees. Congregations, led by their richer members, looked to London merchants to help them to get the preaching of which the hierarchy deprived them. Townsmen opposed royal attempts to remodel their government. Most men of property opposed arbitrary taxation; men and women of all classes opposed monopolies.

The House of Commons elected in the autumn of 1640 was not a revolutionary assembly. Elected on the traditional propertied franchise, the M.P.s were a cross-section of the ruling class. Nevertheless, they had been elected under pressure of popular opposition occasioned by the final fiasco of the Scottish war. The wider the franchise in a constituency, the more likely were opponents of the Court to be returned. But from 1641 the atmosphere began to change. In many counties there were enclosure riots, one of which Cromwell defended in the Commons; tenants began to refuse to pay rents; in London unruly crowds got into the habit of visiting Westminster to put pressure on M.P.s. Sectarian congregations emerged from their underground existence and began openly preaching seditious doctrines. In December 1641–January 1642, amid scenes suggestive of the French Revolution, the Royalist clique of aldermen which controlled the City government was overthrown and replaced by radical Parliamentarians.[9] Men of property began to have second thoughts. The King took heart, withdrew from London, and started to collect an army.

Gentlemen all over England tried hard to be neutral. But neutrality was increasingly difficult. As the King formed his army, all but the staunchest Parliamentarians in the north and west came to heel. Nearly 100 M.P.s with estates in counties occupied by the royal forces changed to the King's side. They included a stalwart like John Dutton, M.P. for Gloucestershire, who had once endured imprisonment for the parliamentary cause; but now it was a matter of 'the preservation of his house and estate'.[10] We can imagine how men of lesser conviction behaved. Many gentlemen, especially in the north and west, abandoned Parliament when opposition was pushed to the point of rebellion. These were the 'constitutional royalists', of whom Hyde made himself the spokesman. A second consequence of the social anxiety of 1641–3 was the determination of most of the solid and respectable families supporting Parliament to end the war as quickly as possible. The initiative in *fighting* the King came from socially lower groups – from the clothing districts of the West Riding, which practically forced Fairfax to lead them into battle, and from towns like Manchester; from the "Moorlanders" in Staffordshire, who banded together with little help from the gentry, and were led by 'a person of low quality'.[11] Within the familiar distinction between economically backward and Royalist north and west, and economically advanced and Parliamentarian south and east, we must also see a division between 'compromise-peace' rich and 'win-the-war' plebeians. The former are those whose representatives at Westminster we call 'Presbyterians'.

## V

Their 'Presbyterianism' had two essential features: (i) It was the price of the Scottish alliance; (ii) it envisaged the preservation of a national church, subordinated to the central control of Parliament and to the local control of the men of property (elders were nominated in the acts setting up presbyteries). As against the 'Presbyterian' desire for a limited war, fought by county militias officered by the local gentry (or by a professional Scottish army hired for the purpose), the 'Independents' were prepared for a war without limits. 'It must not be soldiers nor Scots that must do this work,' said Oliver Cromwell, 'but it must be the godly' (I, 216). Religious toleration was the means of ensuring the widest possible unity among the Parliamentarians; for 'religious toleration' in seventeenth-century terms meant freedom of assembly, discussion and organization.

So divisions at Westminster reflected divisions in the country. The counties which supported Parliament were run by committees composed of their leading gentry. As the war progressed, splits appeared in all those county committees which

TO 20422

have so far been studied. The majority wished for a limited war, and concerned themselves mainly with safeguarding their own estates. A minority, drawn from those most active in the field, called for an all-out war. For organization and leadership they looked to London; for support they relied on lower social groups in their counties, outside the charmed circle of the ruling class. Sir William Brereton found that he had to replace the military governor of Stafford, who came from one of the best county families, by a rich Walsall merchant. Soon Brereton was heading a party in Staffordshire, composed of religious and political radicals, which aimed at taking control of the county away from the old families. In Kent and Nottinghamshire too, county government passed into the hands of social inferiors.[12]

The Lord of the Fens had perhaps less to learn than Sir William Brereton about political alliances. Cromwell allowed his men complete freedom of political and religious discussion; appointments went by efficiency only, regardless of social rank. Contemporaries even alleged that Cromwell went out of his way to choose officers 'such as were common men, poor or of mean parentage'. The logic of war brought Cromwell's principles, and Cromwell himself, to the top. What, after all, was the use of a general like Manchester, who said: 'If we beat the King ninety-nine times, yet he is King still, but if the King beat us but once we shall all be hanged'? Cromwell's retort was unanswerable: 'If this be so, why did we take up arms at first? This is against fighting ever hereafter' (I, 299). Since Charles had now got enough support to make him obstinate on points to which even conservative Parliamentarians attached importance, the war had to go on. It could be won only with the help of a Scottish army or by replacing the county militias with an efficient English army, nationally financed and nationally controlled. The Self-Denying Ordinance marks the triumph of Cromwell's principle of the career open to the talents: it forced the surrender of their commissions by all who owed them only to rank. In the New Model Army the vastly superior resources of the Parliamentary areas were first fully utilized. A national system of taxation — the assessment, the excise, plus the system of compounding with delinquents — allowed the Army to be paid as regularly as Cromwell's own troops had always been. Once that stage of organization was reached, the war was won. 'Combination carries strength with it; it's dreadful to adversaries' (I, 128).

By the end of the war Cromwell had won a unique position. He was the idol of the Army, not only because he was a consistently successful general, but also because he had shown himself determined and courageous in sinking political differences for the sake of unity. Half of the men in the New Model were volunteers. They believed that Cromwell stood for the political principles which united them and gave them the self-imposed discipline which at Marston Moor and Naseby had proved irresistible. His resolute advocacy of toleration, his defence of Anabaptist officers against witch-hunting generals, his campaign against officers who did not really want to win the war, his readiness to serve under a general like Waller who would fight, his lead in the struggle for the Self-Denying Ordinance, even though it looked like ending his own military career — all this made Cromwell the darling not only of the sectaries but also of the Army. Outside the Army such prestige as he had was with the radicals. In Parliament he was viewed less sympathetically. Many a gentleman who in 1644–5 had supported toleration and the New Model Army as lesser evils had reason to be alarmed at the Frankenstein monster that had been created. In 1641–3 there had been agrarian disturbances and riots at Westminster; in 1647 a cross-section of the people of England, combined into the most powerful military machine in Europe, proclaimed their right to a say in settling the destinies of their country.

The Royalists had been beaten: the battle now began between the old ruling families, whose representatives sat in Parliament, and the civilians in uniform living on free quarter in the Home Counties. Cromwell, unique among Englishmen, had not only a foot in both camps, but a share in the strongest feelings of both sides. With the radicals and the Army he demanded toleration; with the conservatives he wanted to preserve existing social relations. 'A nobleman, a gentleman, a yeoman: that is a good interest of the nation, and a great one' (III, 435). In March 1647 Parliament took its foolish and fateful decision to disband the Army and send some of its regiments to Ireland, with their arrears unpaid. The Army revolted, and Oliver

Cromwell was sent down as Parliamentary Commissioner to investigate.

## VI

In May 1647 Cromwell and the officers threw in their lot with the rank and file. The result, Cromwell explained to the House of Commons, was to bring off 'the soldiers from their late ways of correspondency and actings between themselves', and reduce them 'towards a right order and regard to their officers' (*C.P.* I, 98). Six months of uneasy co-operation followed. On 4 June Cornet Joyce seized the King, after the Agitators had told Cromwell that 'if he would not forthwith come and head them they would go their own way without him'. Cromwell came. An Army Council, representing rank and file as well as officers, was set up, and issued its Declaration of 14 June, that it was no mere mercenary and hireling Army, but a body of citizens who at the call of Parliament had rallied 'to the defence of our own and the people's just rights', and so had a duty to see these rights fully established before disbanding.[13] The Army, again at the instance of the Agitators, moved on London, and the first purge of Parliament took place, the withdrawal of eleven M.P.s. named by the Army. Cromwell and Ireton then started tortuous behind-the-scenes negotiations with Charles I. Rumours of what was afoot leaked out, and the Army was in an uproar. Five cavalry regiments displaced their Agitators and elected new ones; pamphlets were circulated telling the rank and file 'Ye can create new officers!'[14] In debates in the Army Council at Putney which started at the end of October two conceptions of the future constitution of England confronted one another: the Heads of Proposals put forward by the Independent officers, and the Leveller Agreement of the People.

'Agreement of the People' is English for Social Contract. The Leveller theory was that in the civil war the old constitution had broken down; the Agreement was to refound the state on a new basis. Acceptance of the Agreement was to be necessary to citizenship, but all who accepted it should be free and equal citizens. The property franchise would be replaced by a much wider suffrage. The Levellers had no intention of submitting the Agreement to Parliament; for Parliament was part of the defunct constitution whose breakdown had left England in the state of nature. So radical and revolutionary a solution appalled the generals, who came from the propertied class themselves. Many of them had received substantial grants of land from Parliament. Unlike the doctrinaire Ireton, Cromwell was prepared to consider concessions to Leveller views. Some copyholders by inheritance, perhaps, might be allowed to vote; though not wage labourers or recipients of alms. But to scrap the existing constitution, he thought, would be to throw too much into the melting-pot – law, order, property, social subordination and social stability.

The profound divergences revealed at Putney explain the policy adopted by Cromwell and the Independent Grandees towards the Levellers during the next two years. In November they broke decisively with them. Aided by the timely flight of the King to Carisbrooke (so timely that unkind contemporaries suspected Cromwell of engineering it) they disbanded the Army Council, suppressed an incipient Leveller mutiny and restored traditional military discipline. Faced by a new Royalist threat, soon realized in the second civil war, the Army *had* to reunite; and Cromwell's prestige was too great for it to reunite without him. When the House of Lords released Lilburne from prison in the hope that he would add to Cromwell's difficulties by attacking him, Lilburne on the contrary offered his provisional support against the common enemy.

But nothing had been solved, as was shown after the Army had won the second civil war. Levellers and 'Silken Independents' again entered into conversations, since Cromwell knew that 'if we cannot bring the Army to our sense, we must go to theirs, a schism being evidently destructive' (I, 569). A revised Agreement of the People was hammered out, in which the Levellers made many concessions. But when this was not forthwith submitted to the people, but only to the Rump of the Long Parliament – i.e. to one of the parties to the compromise – the Levellers not without reason felt that they had been double-crossed. They had hoped that the Rump would dissolve itself, giving way to a Parliament elected on the new franchise. A series of mutinies early in 1649 registered the protest of the rank and file. All were suppressed. In November 1648 Cromwell had told Hammond there was no need to fear the Levellers; four months later he said that unless they were broken the Levellers would break the Independent government. By then he probably knew that the Levellers had begun to extend propaganda activities outside London and the Army. Their programme – opposition to social and economic privileges, to enclosure, tithes, excise, conscription – might prove very attractive to the unenfranchised 80 per cent of the population if the Levellers were given a few years' freedom to propound their views. Henceforth Oliver was consistently unfair to the Levellers, deliberately using them as a bogy to scare men of property by attributing to them communist and anarchist views which most of them certainly did not hold (III, 435–8, 581–6; IV, 267–8).

## VII

The break with the Levellers was a decisive moment in Oliver's career. Till then the Revolution had moved steadily to the left. Henceforth, unevenly at first, a reverse trend set in which ended only with the Restoration. So it is important to realize the dilemma which Cromwell had to face in 1649. The Leveller programme seems very sensible now that it has been achieved by nineteenth-century liberal democracy. But the Levellers were democrats without an electorate. Manhood suffrage, with a largely illiterate population voting by show of hands in the presence of the parson and the squire, might well have destroyed all that had been fought for in the civil war. The Leveller attempt to circumvent this by restricting the vote to those who accepted the Agreement of the People, and by establishing certain fundamentals which were not to be changed, could have worked only if there had been a long period of dictatorship during which the Army was used, in Hugh Peter's words, 'to teach peasants to understand liberty'.[15] But apart from the obvious dangers of thus 'forcing men to be free', the Army itself was divided. Its generals and officers did not accept the social revolution which the Agreement assumed, and were not prepared to allow the years of peaceful political education which the Levellers would have needed to achieve an electorate capable of working the new constitution.

Yet the generals had no electorate either. 'A free Parliament', whether elected on the pre-1640 franchise or on any new propertied franchise that could be devised, would inevitably contain a majority of men similar in outlook to the Presbyterian majority in the Long Parliament. Yet the officers had decisively broken with the Presbyterians at Pride's Purge. So to the right there was a solid mass of opponents – Cavaliers, Presbyterians. After 1649 enemies were added on the left – Levellers, Republicans, Fifth Monarchists. Cromwell was left sitting on a thin line of bayonets. The huge Army seemed more and more to remain in existence only to collect taxes to pay for the Army to collect taxes to pay for the Army . . . After 1653 Oliver was desperately trying to arrive at a 'settlement', some agreement with a Parliament by which the Army could be reduced and the burden of taxation lessened. Yet the dilemma was inescapable. Any Parliament would demand the subordination of the Army to itself. Oliver and the generals could never fully accept this, for it would jeopardize not only their lives and liberties but the whole cause for which they had fought, including toleration, to which all Parliaments were fanatically opposed. Professor Trevor-Roper's view that only a little 'parliamentary management by the executive' was lacking appears to be an unwarranted over-simplification.[16]

In April 1653 Cromwell dissolved the Rump because its efforts to perpetuate itself seemed an obstacle to any settlement acceptable to those who counted in the country. The Barebones Parliament revived some of the radical policies which had been jettisoned in 1649. Its dissolution left the dictatorship of the generals naked but ashamed. The Instrument of Government spread a fig leaf over this nakedness by providing a parliamentary constitution, which disfranchised smaller freeholders and gave votes to copyholders and leaseholders more generously than did the 1832 Reform Bill. In those days of open voting, when landlords marched 'their' freeholders to the polls, such a franchise might in time have produced an independent electorate. But the first Parliament returned under the Instrument, like the first Parliaments after 1832, showed no significant change in social composition or outlook. The

Instrument also endeavoured to perpetuate the veiled dictator-ship of the generals by writing into the constitution, as a first charge on the revenue, an Army of 30,000 men; and by nomin-ating to the Council the generals, their friends and relations, and making it virtually impossible to remove them. Even a purged Parliament rejected this constitution.

But the rule of the Major-Generals which followed finally demonstrated the unviability of military dictatorship without radical support. The Major-Generals were efficient. But they encountered solid opposition from precisely those groups which Parliament represented – town oligarchies, country gentry. For the Major-Generals took over command of the militia from local authorities; they purged corrupt ruling groups in corporate towns; they supervised, bullied and put pressure on J.P.s. For the last time in English history before the nineteenth century local government was run from Whitehall. It was worse than the days of Laud and Strafford, for now the representatives of the central authority were low-born intruders, with troops of horse to add persuasion to their unpopular commands. The opponents of Star Chamber had not fought a civil war to *strengthen* the power of central government. The Major-Generals ran the elections of 1656, and decided to exclude nearly 100 M.P.s., against the Protector's advice; even so they could not secure a friendly Parliament. Their rule probably did more than anything else to make the 'natural rulers' of the country determined to have a constitutional monarchy – whether under Cromwell or Stuart was a secondary consider-ation. The long omnipotence of the J.P.s began in 1660; hatred of standing armies became a decisive political prejudice for the British ruling class.

A first attempt was made in 1657 to restore the parliamentary constitution as it would have existed after 1642 if Charles I had been prepared honestly to accept it. The Humble Petition and Advice subordinated Council and armed forces to Parlia-ment; taxation was to be reduced to a stated *maximum*, which precluded a large Army: 'no part thereof to be raised by a land tax' (as the bulk of the revenue had hitherto been). Some-thing as like the old House of Lords as possible was to be revived; Oliver was offered the crown. This was too much for the generals. They blackmailed Oliver by threatening military revolt if he accepted the crown. There was even talk of reviving an Army Council representing the rank and file (IV, 531). Feverish negotiations went on, in public and behind the scenes, at the end of which the constitution was accepted, without the title of King, with an enhanced revenue, with a Council subordinate to Parliament – but with the generals and their friends firmly entrenched in the second chamber, able to veto any legislation they disliked. The apparent solution had only transferred the problem to a different plane. When Parliament met, with the excluded M.P.s admitted, the Commons refused to recognize the Other House, and started a furious attack on it.

Cromwell was perhaps fortunate in the time of his death. It is difficult to see what way forward there could have been. His unique prestige with the Army made him the indispensable head of state so long as the Army was a power in the land; his genuine desire for a parliamentary settlement continually raised hopes that he might yet square the circle. But, just because Oliver owed his position to the Army, he could never in the last resort break from it. He had created it, yet without it he was plain Mr Cromwell. For this reason no one could succeed him. Richard Cromwell had no status with the Army, and therefore no power to bargain with Parliament. None of the professional generals was acceptable to Parliament, not even the ex-Royalist Monck. Oliver could ride the two horses, like a trick rider at the circus, though he could never transfer his weight from one to the other, transform military rule into parliamentary government. But his delicate balance resulted from his unique personal position: after him – Tumbledown Dick. The Grandees were left plaintively murmuring that any constitution must include a 'select senate' composed of themselves, with a right to veto legislation; until the Restoration swept them away.

## VIII

If we return now to the paradoxes of Oliver Cromwell, we may be able to see in them something more than the peculiarities of his personality. They were, I suggest, paradoxes of the English Revolution. All great revolutions are necessarily contradictory, ambiguous. They can begin only by a breach within the ruling class itself, a 'revolt of the nobles'. But in order to overthrow an old-established government and make profound changes in society, wider support is needed, especially from the unprivileged classes. To rouse them to effective political action, ideas have to be let loose which may prove inconvenient to those who later establish themselves in power. A halt at some stage has to be called: the more conservative revolutionaries break with their radical supporters, the Directory succeeds the Jacobins. The uniqueness of Cromwell is that he was Napoleon to his own Robespierre, Stalin to his own Lenin and Trotsky. Hence the accusations of self-seeking and treachery showered on him by the radicals who felt he had deceived them.

He had not deceived them. He may have deceived himself, but there was a dualism in his personality which made him the ideal leader of the revolt and the ideal leader of the Independents, those who first co-operated with the radicals and then led the move towards restabilization. Cromwell's passion for toleration aligned him with sectaries and Levellers against most of his own class; yet, despite his real interest in humanitarian law reform and his alleged hostility to tithes, he retained too many conservative prejudices to go far with the radicals. 'We would keep up the nobility and gentry' he told Parliament in 1656 (IV, 273). He could not have law reform as well. His cousin Edmund Waller rightly saw in the Lord Protector

> One whose extraction from an ancient line
> Gives hope again that well-born men may shine.[17]

He was the ideal mediator, too, between Army and Parliament because he shared so much of the outlook of the average M.P. He always wanted 'a settlement of somewhat with monarchical power in it'. But he could not be 'wedded and glued to forms of government' (C.P. I, 277), since he owed his power to the Army. God had called him there, by a series of inscrutable providences. Some of the principles which the average M.P. most deplored in Oliver, like toleration, he and his Army colleagues regarded as God's will. So considerations both of interest and of principle made it impossible for Oliver to sacri-

fice the Army. The most he could do was to straddle his two
horses.

The paradox that Oliver's real tolerance did not extend to
Papists is no paradox at all if we recall that they had been
'accounted, ever since I was born, Spaniolized' (IV, 264). The
Armada and Gunpowder Plot were vivid memories in Oliver's
youth, when the House of Hapsburg seemed to be undoing
the Reformation, with the connivance of the English King and
bishops. In the civil war Papists were solidly Royalist. Ireland
was a back door to foreign invasion; exaggerations about the
'Irish massacres' of 1641 were accepted by almost all English
Protestants as gospel. There were sound political reasons for
refusing facilities for worship and organization to men believed
to be a foreign fifth column, quite apart from Oliver's genuine
conviction that the mass was idolatrous and therefore forbidden
by God's word. Nevertheless, the historian of toleration in
England considers that 'the Catholics gained from Cromwell
a more reasoned and consistent toleration than from the House
of Stuart'.[18]

Cromwell's critics lay heavy emphasis on two aspects of his
Irish policy: the massacres of Drogheda and Wexford, and
the 'Cromwellian settlement'. Cromwell is by no means free
from blame for these atrocious proceedings, but there are
points to be made in his defence. Of Drogheda and Wexford
it can be said (i) in accordance with contemporary laws of war
a garrison which had prolonged resistance unreasonably and
so caused unnecessary loss of life might, after due warning,
be put to the sword; (ii) civilians were not intended to be
involved; (iii) the severity helped to bring to an end the
ghastly Irish war, which had dragged on for eight years. Dr
Paul pertinently compares the use of the atom-bomb in 1945
(although this massacred mainly non-combatants).[19] It is
reasonable to condemn both Cromwell's behaviour and the use
of atom-bombs; but it seems hypocritical to condemn the one
whilst defending the other. The 'Cromwellian Settlement'
(evicting the Irish and sending them 'to Hell or Connaught')
was not Cromwellian at all in the sense that the West Indian
campaign was. It was the putting into more drastic effect of
what had been English policy since the reign of Elizabeth. The
transplantation was initiated before Cromwell controlled policy;

it was mitigated after he became Protector. There is no reason
to suppose Oliver abhorred it, as he should have done; but only
Levellers like Walwyn and Prince conceived in the seventeenth
century that the common people of England and Ireland might
live in peace together.[20]

Refusal of liberty of worship to 'prelatists' has given rise to
misunderstandings. England was not yet divided between
Anglicans and Noncomformists. Oliver's state church was the
Church of England. The great majority of the population,
ministers included, continued to accept it – as men had accepted the Church of England in its various manifestations
from Henry VIII to Elizabeth. The only consistent opposition
to Oliver's state church came from the Laudians, 'prelatists' on
principle. They formed the nucleus of the party working for
the restoration of Charles II.[21] Here too there were substantial
political reasons for refusing freedom of public worship and
organization; though again there was much more toleration
under Oliver *de facto* than *de jure*.

His foreign policy also loses some of its paradoxicality if
regarded in historical perspective. The 1650s saw the beginning of that purposeful application of the resources of the
state to commercial war and the struggle for colonies that
characterized English foreign policy for the next 150 years.
This was not Cromwell's personal policy. It goes back to
Hakluyt, Ralegh, the Earl of Warwick – whose grandson mar-
ried the Lord Protector's daughter in 1657 – and to the Provi-
dence Island Company which had supplied so many of the
leaders of 1640. But it had never before been adopted as consistent government policy. Slingsby Bethel suggested that
Oliver's alliance with France against Spain made possible the
subsequent preponderance of Louis XIV.[22] But in so far as
English mistakes contributed to this preponderance, it was
Charles II's disbandment of Oliver's Army, neglect of his
Navy, and sale of his conquest of Dunkirk that are to blame.
One might argue that Cromwell's foreign policy exceeded the
available resources of the country, so that a generation of con-
solidation and economic advance was needed before it could be
resumed; or that grandiose imperial designs were not in the
best interests of England. But for good or ill the 1650s mark a
turning-point in English foreign policy.

The paradox underlying Oliver's attitude to foreign affairs –
the Protestant interest or the interest of the nation – is not
peculiar to him. We find it in Gustavus Adolphus. It had
existed in the minds of Englishmen ever since Hakluyt advocated colonization of America for the good of the souls of
Indians and the pockets of Englishmen. But God did seem
to have put aces up the Protector's sleeve. If he had allied
with Spain against France, this would have been in order to
help the French Huguenots; when England in fact allied with
France against Spain, it was because the Spaniard was 'a
natural enemy . . . led on by superstition and the implicitness of
his faith in submitting to the See of Rome' (IV, 261), and
because France treated Protestants relatively well. This may
have convinced the godly; it certainly appealed to traders like
Martin Noell who looked for an expansion of exports once the
Spanish monopoly of American trade was broken open. If
the Protestant interest had been primary for Oliver he need
have allied with neither France nor Spain. He could have
established closer relations with the Protestant Netherlands, at
the price of sacrificing the Navigation Act which protected
English trade and shipping. But 'there were no greater considerations in England', Secretary Thurloe wrote of the Protectorate, 'than how to obviate the growing greatness of the
Dutch'.[23] This is no place to discuss the psychological connections between Calvinism and the capitalist spirit. But the
connections are deep and long-lived: they are paradoxes of
the English Revolution itself.

Finally, the clue to Cromwell's delays and sudden violent
actings is to be found in the famous maxim 'Trust in God and
keep your powder dry'. Because one is fighting God's battles,
one must be more, not less, careful to run no risk of failure.
On the battlefields Cromwell rarely attacked until he had local
military superiority. In politics, too, since the cause was the
Lord's, every avenue must be explored, every contingency
foreseen, before Cromwell committed himself to any course of
action. In his periods of delay and hesitation Cromwell not only
sought the Lord, he also consulted Ireton, Vane, Harrison,
Lambert, Thurloe, Broghill – anyone whose opinion might be
of significance. When he had completed his reconnaissance, and
was sure of his dispositions, then he struck hard and with

confidence that he was acting righteously. But to contemporaries 'waiting on the Lord' might seem like waiting to see which way the cat would jump.

Again this is a paradox of Puritanism. 'Trust in God and keep your powder dry' perfectly expresses that tension between predestination and free will which lay at the heart of Calvinism. God has his purposes for this world which are preordained; but God may act through human agents. If we are privileged to be so used, we must be absolutely sure at every stage that we are genuinely striving to realize God's will. 'We are very apt, all of us,' said Oliver himself, 'to call that faith, that perhaps may be but carnal imagination.' Just because our cause is God's we dare not fail or mistake. 'The greater the trust, the greater the account' Cromwell reminded Hammond (II, 418). For Oliver's famous schoolmaster, Dr Beard, the world was 'the theatre of God's judgements'. God intervened directly in history. Those who acted for God would be supported by Him and tended to succeed, however weak and powerless they would otherwise have been. Their success justified them. 'I can say this of Naseby,' Cromwell wrote, 'that when I saw the enemy draw up and march in gallant order towards us, and we a company of poor ignorant men ... I could not (riding alone about my business) but smile out to God in praises, in assurance of victory, because God would, by things that are not, bring to naught things that are. Of which I had great assurance; and God did it' (I, 365). What Marvell aptly called Oliver's 'industrious valour' helped God to achieve his ends.

But 'the providences of God are like a two-edged sword, which may be used both ways'.[24] After 1660 Puritans had to grapple with the terrible problem posed by defeat. Had God spat in their faces, as Fleetwood thought? Or had His cause been misconceived? Perhaps His kingdom was not of this world, as Bunyan and the Quakers came to believe? At all events, in that dark hour of the crash of Puritan hopes, the ways of God needed justifying to man. It is significant that Milton started to wrestle with this cosmic problem from the mid-fifties, as he began to lose confidence in Cromwell. The Restoration was for him only the outward confirmation that the cause was spiritually lost. But in the 1640s not only Crom-

well and Milton but thousands of lesser men had drawn tre-
mendous moral energy from the conviction that God had chosen
them to serve Him. Here again the explanation is ultimately
social: problems exist, and certain men feel themselves quali-
fied to solve them. It therefore becomes their duty to make their
contribution to setting society right. A revolutionary situation
breeds men with this sense of mission. Without them, revolutionary change could never take place; yet they would not act
unless they were stimulated by the confidence that God, or
Reason, or History, was on their side. Demanding reinforce-
ments in 1643, Oliver wrote: 'As if God should say, "Up and
be doing, and I will help you and stand by you". There is
nothing to be feared but our own sin and sloth' (I, 245). Here
Oliver personifies not only the English Revolution but all great
revolutions. Perhaps the most characteristic act of his life
occurred when a dispatch to the Speaker came up for sig-
nature in September 1645. Reading it through Cromwell paused
at words attributing the fall of Bristol to the prayers of 'the
people of God with you and all England over who have waited
on God for a blessing'. Was that what he had dictated? It
certainly was not what he had meant. He took up his pen,
crossed out 'waited on' and substituted 'wrestled with'. God
would help his world to be changed only by those who helped
themselves (I, 377).


## IX


Cromwell is the most quotable great man in English history.
His sayings have a racy, earthy character. 'What shall we do
with this bauble? Here, take it away' (II, 643). Many of them
have become proverbial. This is appropriate for the man who
led a popular revolution, whom Gardiner described as 'the
typical Englishman of the modern world'.[25] We may perhaps
differentiate two types of revolutionary – the man committed
to change society in accordance with preconceived ideas, like
Tom Paine, Robespierre or Lenin – and the pragmatic, em-
pirical revolutionary, like William the Silent, Cromwell or
Washington. The distinction is not merely a matter of date,
for Lilburne in the seventeenth century, and Calvin in the

sixteenth, were clearly men with a mission. If Oliver had a political mission, it is hard to define it precisely. 'I can tell you, sirs, what I would not have, though I cannot what I would';[26] 'no one rises so high as he who knows not whither he is going' (I, 472). Whether Oliver used those words or not, they are certainly plausible. His theory of government always tended towards that ultimately established in 1688 by the most pragmatic and untheoretical of all revolutions.

The achievement of 1688 is summarized in two couplets:

'For forms of government let fools contest;
Whate'er is best administer'd is best.'

'There can be no pretence of government,
Till they that have the property consent.'[27]

Oliver would have accepted both. But the constitution was not his main interest. He rightly declared that religion was not the cause of the civil war, 'not the thing at the first contested for, but God brought it to that issue at last' (III, 586). Religion became the great bond of union between those who opposed Charles I and Laud, and Cromwell's passionately-felt undenominational Puritanism made him the ideal leader to unite those social groups who had never hitherto been allowed to worship and discuss and organize as they pleased. If Cromwell had not been a profoundly religious man he could never have been the revolutionary leader of the 1640s. If he had not accepted unquestioningly the assumptions of the propertied class he could never have co-operated as he did in the fifties with hard-headed businessmen like Thurloe, unscrupulous politicians like Ashley-Cooper, and renegade Royalists like Broghill and Monck. The very fact that he was not 'wedded and glued to forms of government', that he thought them 'but a moral thing', 'dross and dung in comparison of Christ' (C.P. I, 370), made it easy for him to reflect the views of those with whom he associated – the rising revolutionary feeling of the forties and the growing conservatism of the fifties: for him political, constitutional and economic issues were secondary.

When the historian looks back at God's 'working of things from one period to another' in the great turning-point of the seventeenth century, he will agree with Oliver that 'such things ... have not been known in the world these thousand years' (III, 591–3). But he has to add that it was the political, constitutional and economic revolutions that succeeded: the Puritan Revolution failed. And the Protectorate, as Milton foreboded, was the period in which this outcome became inevitable. Herein lies the final paradox, the historic irony and the personal tragedy of the career of Oliver Cromwell.

## NOTES

Quotations indicated in the text by a volume and page number, with no further reference, are from W. C. Abbott, *The Writings and Speeches of Oliver Cromwell* (Harvard University Press, 1937–47). In quotations from *The Clarke Papers* (ed. C. H. Firth, Camden Soc., 1891–1901) the reference is preceded by the letters *C.P.*

1. F. Guizot, *History of the English Revolution* (1884), p. 183; *Camden Miscellany*, VIII (1883), fifth item, p. 2; R. Baillie, *Letters and Journals* (1775), II, p. 76.
2. C. H. Firth, *Oliver Cromwell* (World's Classics), p. 411.
3. D. M. Wolfe, *Leveller Manifestoes* (1944), p. 370.
4. Firth, op. cit., p. 382.
5. Ibid., p. 211.
6. See W. Haller, *The Rise of Puritanism* (1938), *passim*.
7. Cf. C. B. Macpherson, 'The Social Bearing of Locke's Political Theory', *The Western Political Quarterly*, March 1954.
8. Cf. J. D. Hughes, 'The Drainage disputes in the Isle of Axholme', *The Lincolnshire Historian*, Spring 1954.
9. V. L. Pearl, *London and the Outbreak of the Puritan Revolution* (1961), Chap. IV, *passim*.
10. D. Brunton and D. H. Pennington, *Members of the Long Parliament* (1954), p. 150; M. F. Keeler, *The Long Parliament* (1954), *passim*.
11. D. H. Pennington and I. A. Roots, *The Committee at Stafford, 1643–45* (1957), p. lxii. For the West Riding see Mr B. S. Manning's contribution to a discussion reported in *Past and Present*, No. 13, p. 70.
12. Pennington and Roots, op. cit., *passim*; A. M. Everitt, *The Community of Kent and the Great Rebellion* (1966), chap. V, *passim*; A. C. Wood, *Nottinghamshire in the Civil War* (1937), chap. XI.
13. Firth, op. cit., p. 160; W. Haller and G. Davies, *The Leveller Tracts* (1944), p. 55.
14. *A Call to all the Soldiers* (1647), p. 7.
15. *Mr. Peters Last Report of the English Wars* (1646), p. 6.
16. H. R. Trevor-Roper, 'Oliver Cromwell and his Parliaments', in *Essays Presented to Sir Lewis Namier* (1956), p. 45.
17. Waller, 'A Panegyric to my Lord Protector', in *Poems* (Muses Library), II, p. 15.
18. Jordan, op. cit., pp. 193–4.
19. R. S. Paul, *The Lord Protector* (1955), p. 218.

20. T. Edwards, *Gangraena* (Part II, 1646), p. 27; *Walwins Wiles* (1649), in Haller and Davies, op. cit., p. 310; T. Prince, *The Silken Independents Snare Broken* (1649), pp. 6–7.

21. R. S. Bosher, *The Making of the Restoration Settlement* (1951), *passim*.

22. In *The World's Mistake in Oliver Cromwell, Harleian Miscellany* (1744), I, pp. 280–8.

23. S. von Bischoffshausen, *Die Politik des Protectors Oliver Cromwell* (1899), p. 221.

24. *Parliamentary Diary of Thomas Burton*, ed. J. T. Rutt (1828), I, p. xxx.

25. Gardiner, *Cromwell's Place in History* (1902), p. 113.

26. Sir Philip Warwick, *Memoirs* (1813), pp. 193–4.

27. Pope, 'Essay on Man', Epistle III, in *Collected Poems* (Everyman), p. 204; Defoe, *Jure Divino* (1706), Book II, p. 12.

## BIBLIOGRAPHICAL NOTE

Mr Ivan Roots's book *The Great Rebellion 1642–60* (Batsford 1966) appeared since this pamphlet was published in 1958. It should certainly be read by anyone interested in Oliver Cromwell; it is especially good on the 1650s. A fuller bibliography will be found at the end of my *God's Englishman: Oliver Cromwell and the English Revolution* (1970).

C.H.

PART THREE

The Local Community
and the Great Rebellion

# THE LOCAL COMMUNITY AND
# THE GREAT REBELLION

*by*

*ALAN EVERITT*

The local history of the Great Rebellion cannot be described
as a neglected branch of English historiography. Many towns
and most counties have produced some kind of account of
their part in the Civil War: Staffordshire, Nottinghamshire,
Hampshire, Lancashire, Dorset, Suffolk, Cornwall, and Kent,
to name but a few.[1] Almost before the war was over, indeed, it
began to throw up a crop of local histories, principally of the
more startling kind and about the more dramatic events, such
as the relief of Gloucester or the siege of Colchester. Quite a
number of the twenty thousand or so tracts in the famous
Thomason Collection in the British Museum are in fact local
history of a kind. The great bulk of them are purely ephemeral,
of course; but some, like Matthew Carter's *Most True and
Exact Relation of that as Honourable as Unfortunate Expedition of Kent, Essex, and Colchester* (1650), are serious works
of history in their own right, based on manuscript sources and
eye-witness accounts. A few, like *L'Estrange his Vindication to
Kent. And the Justification of Kent to the World* (1649) are
still immensely good reading, sharp, vivid, observant, and not a
little scandalous.

After 1660 the Great Rebellion became a sensitive and embarrassing subject in most local communities. If you were a
country squire and had not actively supported the King, or at
least been sequestrated, it was usually best to keep as quiet
about it as possible, and leave it to your descendants to invent
a loyalist grandfather. Everywhere Cavalier legends were
spawning themselves, like mushrooms in the dark, even in such
unlikely counties as Suffolk and Northamptonshire. For this
reason the Restoration era was no more conducive to scholarship in the field of local history than to common sense in the

field of politics. And despite a mass of local information in the great county historians of the next century, such as Edward Hasted and John Nichols, there was little serious re-examination of the local history of the Civil War period until the reign of Queen Victoria.

During the nineteenth century, however, the Great Rebellion once again became a popular subject of study. Local histories abounded, and edited texts were published with increasing frequency. The first four volumes of *Archaeologia Cantiana*, for example, printed the complete journal of Sir Roger Twysden of Roydon Hall, in the Kentish Weald; one of the most graphic of all Civil War diaries, a perfect mine of information on what it really felt like to live through that traumatic period. Later volumes of *Archaeologia Cantiana* printed a valuable series of letters of Thomas Stanley of West Peckham, also in the Weald; a very detailed account book of his neighbour James Master of Yotes Court, and several other important manuscript sources for the history of Kent in the seventeenth century. About the same time, one of the early volumes of the Camden Society was devoted to an edition of Sir Roger Twysden's *Government of England*, another to a manuscript collection entitled *Proceedings, principally in the County of Kent ... in 1640*, and part of a third to the Civil War papers of Thomas Weller of Tonbridge Castle.[2] The county of Kent, it is true, was probably better served than most by nineteenth-century editors interested in the Great Rebellion; but its fortunes in this respect were certainly not altogether untypical.

Generally speaking, the Victorians performed a more valuable service to the local historian in printing original sources than in writing full scale accounts of this period. Twysden's journal gives a far more revealing picture of life in Kent at this time than H. F. Abell's rather superficial and unscholarly sketch of *Kent and the Great Civil War* (1901). The weaknesses of the straight Victorian histories of the time are not far to seek. In the first place they paid far too much attention to local sieges and skirmishes. The cynic's remark that the only battle that matters in any war is the last is no doubt an over-simplification: the sack of Leicester, after all, was a decisive and disastrous event for Leicester itself, even if its consequences for the nation at large were reversed a few days later at Naseby. But it must be confessed that the average tale of local skirmishes usually makes rather dreary reading for all but the specialist military historian or the dedicated antiquary.

The second defect of most of the older local histories is that they make very little attempt to relate political events to the development of local society. They often tell us about the fortunes of a few particular families; but they rarely envisage the local community as a whole. They do not see the people of the town or county they purport to describe as a self-conscious and coherent society with a distinct life of its own, developing at a different pace and in different ways from the economy of the country at large. The tensions set up between the local and national community, if perceived at all, are explained simply in personal terms or in terms of one or two well-known local leaders, instead of as a conflict between two distinct organisms, each with its own independent existence. Perhaps the first local history to avoid these pitfalls with complete success was Mary Coate's *Cornwall in the Great Civil War and Interregnum,* which was published in 1933 and is still one of the best local studies of the period.

## The Conflict of Allegiance

It would be absurd to blame the Victorians too severely for their limited conceptions of Civil War historiography. Our own are no doubt more limited than we realize, and in any case we all stand upon our predecessors' shoulders. Nevertheless, their historical ideas were limited, and if we are to improve upon them it is important to start from a new standpoint. The point I wish to set out from is the recurring problem that faced so many provincial people in this period, the conflict between loyalty to the local community and loyalty to the state. The conflict is evident in urban communities as well as rural, as important recent studies of Newcastle upon Tyne and the parliamentary boroughs of Kent have shown.[3] But for reasons of space and simplicity I shall confine myself principally to county society and to its leaders, the local gentry. Although, after a good deal of time spent in studying the county community, I now find urban society a fresher and more rewarding field of research, there is no getting away from the fact that the country gentry played the decisive part in both the Revolution and the Restoration.

The allegiance of the provincial gentry to the community of their native shire is one of the basic facts of English history in the seventeenth and eighteenth centuries. Though the sense of national identity had been increasing since the early Tudors, so too had the sense of county identity, and the latter was normally, I believe, the more powerful sentiment in 1640–60. There were many factors in the development of regional loyalty: the growth of county administration, the development of county institutions, the expanding wealth of the local gentry, their increasing tendency to intermarriage, their growing interest in local history and legal custom, the rise of the county towns as social, cultural, and administrative centres: these and many other elements entered into the rise of what Namier once called the 'county commonwealths' of England.

In some respects the Civil War period, by greatly adding to the complexity and volume of local government, increased this sense of county awareness. Certainly the inevitable collision between local and national loyalties implicit in the social development of the sixteenth and seventeenth centuries was precipitated by the political events of 1640–60. Quite apart from the politics of the Civil War, however, there was much in the development of English society that fostered the sense of county cohesion. Despite the well-known fact that many gentry attended the universities and some of the wealthier families spent part of the year in London, the vast majority of country gentry passed most of their lives within a few miles of their native manor-house, in a circle often as limited as that of their tenants and labourers. The brief years at the university and the Inns of Court were no more than an interlude, principally designed to fit them out for their functions as justices, squires, and landlords in their own county. After the time spent at Oxford or in London, most of them quickly settled back into the old routine of country life. Henry Oxinden of Maydeacon in East Kent, for example, apparently visited London only once in his life: and when he was there he told his wife that, if he could only get clear of it, he desired never to come thither again.[4] The mother of Edward Hyde, the great minister of

Charles I and Charles II, is said to have spent the whole of her
life in the county of Wiltshire, and never once to have stepped
over its borders into the neighbouring shires. Not surprisingly
when people like Mary Hyde and Henry Oxinden spoke of
their 'country', they did not mean England, but Wiltshire or
Kent, Leicestershire or Northamptonshire, Cumberland or
Durham.

The basis of this intense attachment of most provincial
gentry to their native soil, despite the social changes of the
previous century, is not difficult to understand in the context
of the time. In speaking of the gentry of the mid-seventeenth
century one has to think oneself back into a world which was
very different, not only from that of Victorian England, but in
many ways from that of George III as well. In 1640 armigerous
families were far thicker on the ground than in, say, 1800,
perhaps twice as numerous in counties like Devonshire,
Suffolk, and Kent. In Suffolk there were 700–750 gentry in
1640, and in Kent about 850. While I am not aware of any
late eighteenth-century figures, the decline is clear both from
county histories like Hasted, from genealogical sources, and
also from the number of manor-houses which, by 1800, had
declined to the status of farms.[5] As a consequence the average
landed estate was probably far smaller in 1640, too small to
enable these families to maintain a second household in
London, and too small to let them pay a mere casual attention
to its prosperity. The average Caroline estate in Suffolk, Kent,
and Leicestershire cannot have been more than about 1,000
acres, and in most counties there were probably hundreds of
parochial squires like Henry Oxinden of Maydeacon whose
property extended to no more than 600 or 700. Such people
had of necessity to be much 'taken up with the business of
farming', as one of them later described it.[6] Every manor-house,
except a few of the very largest, was quite as much a farmhouse
as a hall, and the centre of a local agrarian commonwealth. On
the rare occasions when Henry Oxinden was away from home,
his letters were full of inquiries about his harvests and his
labourers. His countryman Sir Edward Dering evidently spent
a great deal of time and thought upon his famous orchards at
Surrenden Dering, where he cultivated more than 150 varieties

of fruit-tree, and kept a very detailed orchard-book recording their prosperity from year to year.[7]

The simple fact was that in 1640 farming in England was not yet always looked down upon as the dismal occupation of yeomen and boors. The change of attitude towards it seems to have come with the latter-day Cavaliers, who spoke of the older generation of men like Oxinden and Dering as 'the female gentry of the smock'.[8] In some counties at least the change of attitude was furthered, from 1660 onwards, by the gradual amalgamation of smaller properties, partly due to inter-marriage, and partly because many Cavalier gentry who had failed to pay detailed attention to husbandry were forced to sell out.[9] Only local research would show whether this kind of development was universal; but the very large number of Caroline manor-houses in counties like Norfolk, Suffolk, Kent, and Devon which, during the eighteenth and nineteenth centuries, declined to the status of mere farmhouses suggests that it was a widespread phenomenon. As a result of amalgamation, and the general increase in the national wealth, the margin of prosperity for the landed family increased: there was not the same urge to pay scrupulous attention to every detail of one's property, and it often became possible to maintain a second household in the county town or in London. The deep local roots of the gentry, though certainly not yet severed, were in some cases beginning to be sapped.

In 1640, however, local attachments were, if anything, becoming deeper rather than more superficial. For this reason the Civil War was not simply a struggle between gallant Cavaliers and psalm-singing Roundheads. If one studies the history of any particular county community in this period, particularly if one is fortunate enough to find an extensive *corpus* of family correspondence, one finds that only a small minority of provincial gentry can be classified exactly in either of these conventional categories. This does not mean that most English people were indifferent to the political problems of the time, but that their loyalties were polarized around different ideals. For them, bounded as they so often were by local horizons, a more urgent problem was the conflict between loyalty to the nation and loyalty to the county community. This division cut across the conventional divisions, like a geological fault. The unwillingness of most people to forgo the independence of their shire and to admit that allegiance to the kingdom as a whole must override it was certainly one of the reasons why the Civil War was so long drawn out. In some respects the England of 1640 resembled a union of partially independent county-states, rather as Canada today is a union of self-governing provinces, or America of federated states: and that union, as we all know, is not always a very simple or easy relationship.

During the Civil War, there were three periods of peculiarly intense crisis, and on each occasion the conflict between loyalty to county and to state was one of the basic issues. In the winter of 1643–4 a crisis occurred over the attempt to form various groups of counties into regional associations. As is well known, these associations were set on foot specifically in order to counteract the tendency of each shire to confine its activities to raising and paying troops for its own defence alone, to the neglect of the safety of neighbouring shires. The effort to associate the counties often provoked intense opposition, and the only thoroughly successful amalgamation – though even there not without difficulties – was the famous Eastern Association under the Earl of Manchester.[10] The South-Eastern Association, which comprised Hampshire, Sussex, Surrey, and Kent, never really held together and was little more than a name. The Midland Association, which included such counties as Northamptonshire, Buckinghamshire, and Leicestershire, was also rent asunder by disturbing feuds.

The second time of crisis came a year later in 1644–5, when the abler and more forceful leaders on the Parliamentarian side, such as Fairfax and Cromwell, realised that these county associations themselves were inadequate to solve the problem of local allegiance. The only solution was the formation of a newly-modelled, nationally-organized army. Hitherto the Parliamentary regiments had been raised, paid and officered by each county independently, so that they were regarded as existing primarily for local defence, and as being responsible to the counties who raised them rather than to Parliament. Even in the loyal Eastern Association, local leaders were of the opinion that the 'safety of the kingdom ... was not our work.'[11] In the New Model Army of 1645, however, though the regiments were still raised locally, they were commissioned by

Parliament, paid for by the Treasurers at War in London, and controlled far more completely by the Committee of Both Kingdoms than by the counties. At the same time, and for similar reasons, the King's armies themselves underwent a good deal of reorganization.[12] The consequence was to provoke the final, decisive battle for which the more militant leaders on both sides had been pressing for years, and the moderate majority, by and large, had been endeavouring to avoid. Naseby was the triumph of the state over the county community as much as of Parliament over the King.

The third crisis came with the Second Civil War in 1648. Naseby had been a great military victory; but it had been the triumph of organization rather than the effect of a widespread change of feeling in provincial society. In 1648, therefore, in Kent and elsewhere the county community rose once again in an effort to curb the authority of the central government. The Cavaliers made a desperate bid to convert what was essentially regional loyalty into thoroughgoing support for the King. But they were unable to form any sort of union between the rebellious shires. The Kentish leaders refused to enter into negotiations with Surrey, Sussex, Essex, or Suffolk, and, with the storming of Maidstone and the siege of Colchester, the movement was overwhelmed by the victorious New Model Army. Paradoxically the cause of county independence was a victim once again of the obstinacy of local allegiance.[13] Not until 1660, after years of frustration, interference, and insecurity, were the counties willing for a time to forgo a measure of independence and join with the real loyalists, the Cavaliers, in an effort to restore the monarchy. Even then it was only a few months before Charles II began to find himself up against the same problem of provincial intransigence as his father and his usurper before him.

### The War in the East Midlands: Two Case-Studies

I have endeavoured elsewhere to delineate this conflict of loyalties in the two counties of Suffolk and Kent. In Cornwall the same phenomenon has been described with a wealth of detail by Miss Mary Coate. In Staffordshire, Nottinghamshire,

Wales, and other districts similar developments have been noted by other scholars.[14] There is no point in repeating here what has already been better said elsewhere. Instead, in the limited space available, I should like to trace the story of two Midland shires in this period – Leicestershire and Northamptonshire – where somewhat similar problems were at issue. In some ways these two counties form an especially interesting and perhaps rather surprising illustration of my theme. Since they are both small inland counties, surrounded on all sides by other shires, one would expect local allegiance within them to be less pronounced than in counties like Cornwall or Kent, which are larger in area and geographically more isolated from other regions. But though Leicestershire and Northamptonshire undoubtedly were less isolated, they were nevertheless remarkably independent in their reactions. Moreover, despite the fact that they adjoined one another, and the fact that both were subject to the ebb and flow of warfare, their fortunes in this period were remarkably dissimilar. First I shall outline some of these differences, and then explore some of the reasons for them and some of their consequences.

The salient fact in both Leicestershire and Northamptonshire in this period, when compared with the counties of the east, the south-east, or the far north, is that they were always in the front line of fighting. Both counties were equally unfortunate in this respect. The tide of warfare was continually flowing to and fro across them, whereas counties like Suffolk, Kent, and Cumberland experienced little of the horrors of civil strife. In fact the final issues of the war were decided in these two counties, with the sack of Leicester by Prince Rupert in May 1645, and the defeat of the King at Naseby, fifteen miles away in Northamptonshire, a few days later. Throughout the war, the people of Leicestershire and Northamptonshire were subject to raiding and plundering, and in both counties there were several well-known garrisons. The two county-towns were held for Parliament, and a number of the great country houses of the region, such as Belvoir and Ashby de la Zouch, for the King. Apart from Northampton, none of these garrisons was very powerful, but from the point of view of the local population they had almost unlimited nuisance value. Yet despite the superficial resemblance between them, the two counties of

Leicestershire and Northamptonshire responded to their common situation in very different ways.

The reactions of Leicestershire were remarkable for their hesitancy and indecision. At the risk of some rather tedious detail, we must outline the principal military events in the county during this period.[15] Like other English shires, when war broke out in 1642, Leicestershire endeavoured to maintain its neutrality and join neither side in the dispute. But the attitude of indecision lasted much longer there than elsewhere, in fact right up to the eve of the battle of Naseby in 1645: a period of more than three years since the first tentative efforts to secure the county magazine and the militia in the spring of 1642.

In March of the latter year the House of Commons had nominated the Earl of Stamford Lord Lieutenant, and when he arrived in Leicester he was, to all appearance, enthusiastically received by the townsmen. The King, who alone had legal power to appoint to this office, retaliated by forbidding the raising of troops in the county under Stamford, and the local Royalist leader, Henry Hastings, successfully prevented many people from obeying Stamford's summons to appear for Parliament. Stamford, however, was successful in removing a large part of the county magazine from Leicester to his own mansion at Bradgate Park, a few miles from the town, and in holding recruiting meetings at Melton Mowbray, Copt Oak, Kibworth, Broughton Astley, and Queniborough. Henry Hastings replied by making a series of raids against Bradgate Park itself and these forays achieved a fair measure of success. When the King visited Leicester on 22 July 1642, he is said to have been warmly received by a crowd of 10,000 people. Though the reports of this welcome were probably exaggerated, there was no doubt some truth in them. According to Edward Hyde, however, 'if the king were loved [in Leicester] as he ought to be, the Parliament was more feared than he'.[16] As a consequence, despite the apparent welcome, Charles I was asked by the county to leave the magazine in the hands of Stamford, whom he had already declared a traitor. In fact the Leicestershire magazine was never secured for the King; but, despite this rebuff, Charles I did not give up his attempts to win over the county. When Prince Rupert, after Charles I had left

Leicestershire to set up his standard at Nottingham, demanded a levy of £2,000 from the townsmen of Leicester, the King indignantly repudiated his high-handed action. Unfortunately for the town, it seems that Rupert never forgot this incident, and it may have influenced his decision to sack it in 1645, when once again the violence of his supporters was deplored by the King.[17]

During the following winter of 1642-3, Leicester was finally secured for Parliament by Lord Grey of Groby, the active Puritan heir of the old Earl of Stamford.[18] This gain, however, was offset by the seizure of Belvoir Castle for the King, at the other end of the county, by the sheriff of Lincolnshire. Throughout Leicestershire conditions of near anarchy obtained, and for two years there were frequent raids on the countryside by the Royalist garrisons at Belvoir and Ashby de la Zouch. Indeed, the riotous Cavaliers of Ashby rapidly became infamous for their depredations. Needless to say, contemporary accounts of their pillage lost nothing in the telling. According to one Parliamentarian they were 'as debased wicked wretches there as if they had been raked out of hell . . .' They 'have three malignant priests there,' this writer continued, 'such as will drink and roar . . . and swear and domineer so as it would make one's heart ache to hear the country people to relate what they heard of them.'[19]

It was partly in an effort to provide more effective defence against these conditions that Parliament re-formed its County Committee in Leicestershire – that is its local governing body – in July 1644. A new Committee for the Militia was set up, with special powers to raise and pay local forces and suppress revolts. This arrangement, however, led to further local friction and even accentuated the indecision in the county, because it was complained that the best men were left out of the new Committee, and that Lord Grey had not been given adequate forces to restrain the Royalists.[20] Attempts were then made to reduce the garrisons at Ashby and Belvoir; but the temporary success of these efforts was reversed by Sir Marmaduke Langdale's victory, in March 1645, at Melton Mowbray in east Leicestershire. This victory was followed by the storming and capture of Leicester itself, in May 1645, by Prince Rupert.

The infamous and disastrous sack of the town that followed was the price that Leicester had to pay for its lack of decision in supporting either party during the previous three years. This is the essential lesson of all the rather confused events of 1642–5 in Leicestershire. If the town had unequivocally supported Parliament, its defences would have been more capable of withstanding Rupert's attack.[21] Indeed, he might never have ventured on making it. If, on the other hand, the town had firmly and consistently supported the King, it would have avoided a sack. Then, after Naseby, it would probably have been able to make advantageous terms of surrender with Fairfax, for as a rule Fairfax preferred to offer generous terms of surrender rather than engage in a wasteful and lengthy siege.

Quite different was the response of Northamptonshire to the similar decision with which it was faced in 1642. It is not necessary to enter into another detailed account of the local military events of the period. Suffice it to say that Northampton town, from the outset, was decisively on the side of Parliament. There was little of the shilly-shallying of Leicester about it, and within a few months of the beginning of the war, it had become the most powerful garrison in the south Midlands. Resolutely controlled by both corporation and county committee, it retained this position throughout the war. In the borough records of the time it is possible to trace how its proximity to attack only served to intensify its sense of somewhat grim and puritanical self-discipline. Not that by any means the majority of the inhabitants of town and county were in fact Puritans; but, after the manner of their kind, the more puritanical amongst them soon managed to secure leading positions on the corporation and the committee. In the corporation's right of presentation to the living of All Saints, moreover, a source of influence of unique importance was available to them. With its pulpit in their hands, the great church in the centre of the town virtually became the cathedral of Puritanism in Northamptonshire, both for the borough and for the surrounding countryside. Almost twice as large as its present successor, it provided the party with a splendid propaganda-hall.

## Local Leadership in Leicestershire and Northamptonshire

Such were the differences between these two provincial towns and counties in their response to the Great Rebellion. How do we account for their differing reactions? In the case of Northampton there can be no doubt that there was a certain economic basis for its allegiance to Parliament. That interesting mixture of holiness and hard-headedness which seems the peculiar prerogative of Puritanism was not altogether absent from this Midland entrepôt. The first major rendezvous of the Earl of Essex's armies was held just outside Northampton, and the town benefited greatly, both then and later, from the fact that orders for thousands of pairs of shoes for the army were from time to time placed with its cordwainers.[22] This was, indeed, the beginning of the great shoe-industry of Northampton. The town's prosperity as the chief horse-market of England was also stimulated by its ability to supply the armies of the Eastern Association under the Earl of Manchester.[23] Every subsequent war in English history, until Queen Victoria's reign, exerted precisely the same kind of stimulus upon the two basic trades of the borough. Northampton had a vested interest in other people's misfortunes.

These economic advantages were a contributory factor in the differing response of the two towns and counties; but they cannot have been the decisive one. Leicester, one might expect, would have been equally subject to commercial interests, and scarcely less addicted to Puritanism. The ultimate explanation is of a different kind, and seems, in fact, to have been a twofold one. Partly it lies in a difference in the quality of leadership in the two shires; and partly, at a deeper level, in the inherent dissimilarities in their social structure.

In Leicestershire leadership was implacably divided between two evenly-balanced rivals; on one hand Henry Hastings, later created Lord Loughborough, a younger son but the most forceful member of the ancient Leicestershire dynasty seated at Castle Donington and Ashby de la Zouch: and on the other hand Lord Grey of Groby, the Puritan heir of the old Earl of Stamford at Bradgate Park. This division was much more than a rivalry between Puritan and Cavalier, however. Traditionally, indeed almost until the outbreak of the Civil War, the Hastings family had been as notoriously Puritan as the Greys, though Loughborough himself, of course, was no adherent of that persuasion. But the division between the two families went back to personal feuds of far longer standing than the Civil War, in fact to their rivalry for the control of the county since the mid-sixteenth century. For these two families the Rebellion was, at one level, simply a further stage in the long-drawn out battle for local dominion.

Leicestershire had long been notorious for this family feud. According to Clarendon the whole county was violently divided between the Greys and the Hastingses, 'a notable animosity', he said, without the addition of any other quarrel. According to another contemporary the county was 'like a cockpit, one spurring against another'.[24] Further research shows the truth of these assertions. Behind the Grey family one finds aligned, during the Rebellion, such local families as the Ashbys of Quenby, the Babingtons of Rothley, the Caves of Stanford, the Faunts of Foston, the Hartopps of Buckminster, the Heselriges of Noseley, the Herricks of Beaumanor, and the Villierses of Brooksby. Ranged behind the Hastingses, on the other hand, were families like the Shirleys of Staunton Harold, the Turvilles of Aston Flamville, the Turpins of Knaptoft, the Poulteneys of Lubbenham, the Beaumonts of Gracedieu, and the Nevills of Nevill Holt. The division between the two parties in Leicestershire was in this manner remarkably evenly balanced.[25]

The even division of parties had several far-reaching consequences in the history of the county at this time. It explains, on the one hand, why the struggle for control was so indecisive. It also explains the long-drawn out contest for the control of Leicester town, and the almost morbid reluctance of the corporation to support either of the leading families so far as to antagonize the other. Finally it explains why Leicestershire people were so fully engaged with purely local issues that they seem to have had little interest in concerns of more far-reaching import. In marked contrast with the gentry of Suffolk, Northamptonshire, and Kent, few local families left the county to join the King at Oxford or the Parliamentarian armies under Fairfax. Events in Leicestershire were quite sufficiently exciting

and animosities quite sufficiently intense to confine their interests to the county itself. Most of the Parliamentarians were
fully preoccupied with their work for the County Committee,
though their frequent divisions seriously impaired the efficiency
of that body. Most of the Royalists were either engaged in
defending their estates from attack by the Parliamentarians, or
themselves became members of one of the predatory Cavalier
garrisons of the county.

The consequent insularity of the Leicestershire community,
though in the very heart of England, comes to light in the
reasons given for the sequestration of Royalist estates in the
county. These reasons are often mentioned in the records of
the Committee for Compounding, and from them we learn that
most Leicestershire 'delinquents' were sequestrated either because they were Papists or because they had joined one of the
local garrisons. Altogether there were about 150 'delinquents'
in the county, and the majority for whom relevant details survive confessed to some kind of connection with Belvoir Castle
or Ashby de la Zouch. Edward Farnham of Quorndon, for
example, was sequestrated because he had joined the garrison at
Ashby Castle. William Roberts of Sutton Cheney had also
joined the garrison there, partly in order to visit his kindred
and partly to secure himself from his creditors. Antony Allen
of Ilston had joined the Royalists at Ashby when still a mere
boy, no more than fifteen years of age. His case graphically
illustrates the tragic political and military pressures to which
even the most innocent Leicestershire people were subjected.[26]

Most of these Leicestershire Royalists came of quite minor
local families, and probably many of them were very moderate
in their adhesion to the King's cause. Local circumstances
forced them to take sides; but, in contrast with the Cavaliers of
Suffolk and Northamptonshire, few of them were sufficiently
dedicated to Charles I to join his forces at Oxford. Some had
spent only a few weeks in one of the local Royalist strongholds.
Not a few, like John Butler of Bilstone, confessed that they
had joined the King's garrison at Ashby merely because their
homes were under the power of the Cavaliers and they had no
alternative but to submit. Such pleas may sometimes have been
mere excuses; but they were accepted by the Parliamentarian
Committee, and they suggest that many delinquents, if

Royalists at all, were only so by force of circumstance.[27] In times of political pressure the moderate majority are always driven into positions they scarcely agree with by doctrinaire minorities and angry partisans. They are often the victims, of course, of their own lack of organization.

In Northamptonshire, in the early days of the war, leadership was for a short time divided very much as it was in Leicestershire and other counties. But here the Parliamentarian caucus had relatively little difficulty in securing the county-town and most of the shire for their party. Their success was principally due to the fact that the most powerful Royalist, the Earl of Northampton, together with many other local families, left the county in order to join the King. This migration of local Royalists was partly occasioned by the relative proximity of Oxford – barely forty miles from Northampton – and the consequent magnetism of the Court. It was also due, however, to the fact that Northamptonshire seems to have been a more politically-minded county than Leicestershire, and one where family divisions ran more naturally along lines of religious division, instead of cutting across them. As a consequence, out of a total of 103 Northamptonshire families who supported the King and whose activities can be traced, three-quarters were sequestrated, not for local rebellion, but for leaving the county to join the King's forces elsewhere. Of the rest, a number were recusants, and a mere 7 per cent were sequestrated for taking part in raids or revolts within the county.[28] In striking contrast with the Cavaliers of Leicestershire, Northamptonshire Royalists made remarkably little organized effort to challenge the dominance of the County Committee. There was a good deal of raiding and plundering in the shire, but relatively little of it was inspired by local Royalists. Much of it emanated from the garrison at Banbury, across the border in Oxfordshire. Most of the Northamptonshire Cavaliers were far away at the time, in other parts of England, many of them at Oxford or Newark.

*The Pattern of Society in Leicestershire and Northamptonshire*

Underlying these differences in the quality of leadership were deeper differences in the social structure of the two counties.

In some ways Leicestershire was still a curiously 'feudal' shire, dominated as it was by the age-old rivalry of its two great families. Between the Greys and the Hastingses, it was divided not only personally but geographically.[29] Altogether, it is possible to trace the allegiance of about 220 Leicestershire families, or probably about two-thirds of the gentry in the shire. About seventy-five of the gentry became at some date members of the County Committee under Lord Grey; and of these seventy-five the great majority were seated in the south and east of the county. About 140 became 'delinquents'; and of these more than two-thirds, or almost exactly 100, came from the north and west of the county, from the three hundreds of East Goscote, West Goscote, and Sparkenhoe. As these figures show, there were nearly twice as many nominal 'Royalists' as Parliamentarians in Leicestershire; but the two parties were evenly balanced because most of the former came of rather obscure minor families.

In Leicestershire, as in several other counties, there was also a marked tendency for the older, more deeply-rooted families to support the King, and the newer gentry to side with Parliament.

At least 57 per cent of the Royalist supporters came of families settled in Leicestershire for more than 150 years, and only 13 per cent of them had arrived in the county since 1603. The history of the Leicestershire Parliamentarians is less easy to trace, chiefly because many of them stemmed from mercantile or yeoman stock of rather uncertain origin. But it is safe to say that only about one-third of the committee men came of families with a lengthy local lineage of more than 150 years' standing. Of course we must be careful not to exaggerate these social distinctions between the two parties. Some of the oldest Leicestershire families, like the Greys themselves, were convinced Parliamentarians. Nevertheless, the contrast cannot be altogether ignored, and it is not, after all, very surprising. It was natural that the more deeply rooted and often smaller gentry should tend to support what seemed, in the 1640s, the more conservative side. It was equally natural for the brisker, newer, and more dynamic to support political innovations which might be expected to extend their power. Many of the former, of course, had themselves opposed the King in the

1620s and 1630s, when *he* had appeared to be the innovator, and Parliament – whether rightly or wrongly – the bulwark of traditional rights. Perhaps it would be more accurate to call these provincial gentry traditionalists rather than Royalists.[30]

It should perhaps be remarked at this point that, in endeavouring to trace the social origins of any county community, it is essential to cover every armigerous family in the shire concerned, or at least a very large representative sample. Estimates based on subjective impressions, or on selected examples for which documentary material happens to be abundant, are usually misleading and often quite valueless. The point is obvious, but it needs to be stressed, because so much nonsense has been written about the rise and decline of the gentry by historians who base their remarks on selected examples, instead of studying the local community *as a whole*. The tendency to notice the striking and dramatic instead of the typical is the besetting sin of most of us; but in elucidating the causes of historical development it is the typical and not the exceptional that we need to study.

Quite as significant as the social differences within the county of Leicester were the contrasts between it and its southern neighbour. Even today the most casual observer of the Midland countryside is struck by the fact that Northamptonshire is a county of superb country houses, usually dating from the sixteenth and seventeenth centuries: whereas Leicestershire, despite a few great mansions like Nevill Holt and Bradgate, is essentially a county of village manor-houses, sometimes little larger than farmhouses. In the seventeenth century the contrast between the two shires was at least equally striking. Kirby, Holdenby, Burghley, Drayton, Milton, Apethorpe, Althorp, Rushton, Deene, and Castle Ashby: Leicestershire had little to compare with these Northamptonshire palaces.

This is how Daniel Defoe described the contrast at the end of the seventeenth century. Northamptonshire, he said, is 'not so full of antiquities, large towns, and gentlemen's seats but this county of Leicester is as empty. The whole county seems to be taken up in country business ... particularly in breeding and feeding cattle; ... even most of the gentlemen are graziers, and

in some places the graziers are so rich that they grow gentlemen.' Two or three generations earlier William Camden had
made much the same observation, remarking that Northamptonshire was 'everywhere adorned with noblemen's and gentlemen['s] houses'.[31] And two or three generations later, largely
because of its lack of imposing and pretentious buildings,
Leicestershire was looked down upon as one of the most
'impolite' counties in England. The grandiose and somewhat
limited mind of the eighteenth century could not appreciate
the intimate, friendly charm of a house like the Palmers' at
Carlton Curlieu, lost among the lark-haunted pastures of East
Leicestershire. It was the same kind of mental limitation that
made sophisticated persons of an earlier generation, like John
Evelyn, speak disparagingly of the old manor-houses of the
Kentish Weald, set in their wooded, moated, romantic hollows.
Happily for us, a great many people in both counties kept to
the old ways, and were no doubt unaware how unfashionable
they were. Perhaps this is one reason why Leicestershire in the
eighteenth century was one of the earliest centres of the Gothic
Revival. The old Gothic, indeed, virtually never died out.

These differences in the architectural legacy of Leicestershire
and Northamptonshire express, of course, a profound difference
in their social structure. The basis of this difference is hinted
at in the comments of Defoe. The roots of the Leicestershire
gentry, like their manor-houses, were for the most part local
rather than alien. The interests were agrarian rather than
courtly. Many of them in fact were graziers. The phalanx of
Tudor and Stuart *nouveaux-riches* who dominated Northamptonshire had no real parallel in the adjoining county. Not
that by any means all the Leicestershire gentry stemmed from
medieval squires. In fact no more than about 41 per cent of
them came of really ancient armigerous stock in the county, a
figure which may be compared with nearly 75 per cent in
Kent. Nevertheless, many of them undoubtedly stemmed from
local roots of some kind. For the most part their ancestors
seem to have been small Leicestershire yeomen, who had
gradually pushed their way up into gentility, largely through
successful stock-farming. And, as Defoe implies, many of them
retained these grazing interests throughout the seventeenth
century. This interest in grazing was indeed equally apparent in

Leicester town. In striking contrast with Northampton, most of the townsmen still invested a good deal of their capital in stock-farming, and in the seventeenth century some of the wealthiest inhabitants were grazing butchers.[32] These facts certainly go some way to explain the introversion of the Leicestershire community during the seventeenth century. Where their treasure was, their heart was also.

In Northamptonshire the picture was very different.[33] More than almost any other English county, this shire had undergone a remarkable social transformation in the Tudor and early Stuart period, a transformation which seems to have been just about complete by the beginning of the Civil War. Out of a total of some 300 families whose history is traceable with fair certainty, only 27 per cent were genuinely indigenous to the county. As many as 40 per cent had settled in Northampton-shire under the Tudors, principally under Queen Elizabeth, and another 33 per cent since 1603. Moreover, most of the 80 or so indigenous families had only risen to the status of gentry quite late in the Tudor period. In other words, in 1640, at least three-quarters of the leading families of Northampton-shire, and perhaps more than four-fifths, were of very recent social origin. Through trade, or the law, or office under the crown, or simply by marrying a succession of heiresses, they had managed to purchase estates in the county and build or rebuild the splendid mansions we still marvel at today. If any county furnishes a classic example of the Rise of the Gentry, that county is Northamptonshire.

What is the explanation of this revolutionary change in the composition of society in Northamptonshire? Why was it possible for so many newcomers, often extremely wealthy newcomers like the Cecil's, Spencers, and Hattons to settle in the county? Partly it was because the open-field areas of the county offered adventurers admirable scope for enclosure and for large-scale investment in sheep- and corn-farming. Judging from the findings of the Enclosure Commissioners (though admittedly these are not very reliable evidence) the acreage of land enclosed in Northamptonshire seems to have been greater than in any other Midland county, possibly more than twice as much.[34] Partly, too, the change seems to have been facilitated by the fact that large tracts of royal forest were still available to be granted out to favourites of the Court, or disposed of to ambitious merchants by the impecunious crown. There were almost certainly other reasons, however, which at present we can only guess at until we know more about the basic economy of the county.

Whatever the reasons, by the year 1640 a more or less united phalanx of new and wealthy gentry had come into existence in Northamptonshire, with relatively few connections as yet with the indigenous gentry. Like families of similar origin elsewhere, they were often strongly Parliamentarian in sympathy, and more than able, as a group, to challenge the local power of the older, Royalist magnates like the Earl of Northampton. Within a few generations, it is true, the new families were destined to come to terms with the old, and during the eighteenth century, through frequent intermarriage, to become completely merged with them. But in 1640 they were still distinct. Cartwrights, Cleypooles, Crews, Danverses, Drydens, Harbys, Knightleys, Norwiches, Pickerings, Samwells, Thorntons, Yelvertons: all of these were relative newcomers to Northamptonshire, and it was they who formed the backbone of county society and provided the leadership in the County Committee. During the Civil War some of them went so far as to move house into the county town, partly of course for the sake of protection, but also specifically to reinforce the rule of the godly in the area. The consequent combination of urban Puritanism and landed authoritarianism was a phenomenon to which there was no real parallel in Leicestershire. It was, however, the overwhelming fact in both the economic fortunes and the political allegiance of Northamptonshire.

## The Texture of Provincial Life

Earlier in this paper it was remarked that the basic defect of the older local histories of the Civil War was their failure to relate the narrative of events to the development of local society. It was also stated that the lives of most provincial people were not simply polarized around the ideals of Cavalier and Roundhead, but rather around local rivalries and loyalties, and the common facts of daily life. In a world with poor communications and no country newspapers it was inevitable that most people should be chiefly concerned with the fortunes of their local community. It was not that they never heard any national news, but that they were not *continuously* preoccupied with it as we are today. There were other matters of more immediate concern, and most people lived too near the bone to spare much time for political speculation.

For these reasons few political actions in the seventeenth century could be determined by unfettered idealism, or by abstract principle alone. They had to work themselves out in a complex and intractable provincial world. Every decision, every loyalty was shaped, not so much by a fiat of government, as by the whole network of local society: by all the pressures of personal influence, family connection, ancient amity, local pride, religious sentiment, economic necessity, and a dozen other matters, now often very difficult to track down. In describing social conditions at this time, even in confining oneself to a couple of Midland counties, it is easy to invest one's story with a deceptive air of simplicity, and to forget the underlying diversity, the extraordinary density of this web of provincial life.

This density in the fabric of local life, this elaborate network of family loyalties and personal necessities that shaped the pattern of politics in the countryside, was, of course, neither a novel feature of the county community of the seventeenth century nor a merely ephemeral one. It had existed at least as early as Henry VIII's reign – no doubt a good deal earlier – and it continued to influence the pattern of the county society until the days of Queen Victoria. In the sixteenth century, for example, the evolution of the Reformation in the north was shaped, not only by religious developments affecting the whole of Europe, but by many confused influences peculiar to the society of the region itself. In elucidating the motives behind Sir Francis Bigod's Protestant revolt in Yorkshire, Professor Dickens has unravelled a whole tangle of personal and temperamental factors, problems of debts and land, and many other notions inextricably intertwined with them, 'not merely family affection and ancestral loyalty, but credit in the county and the very prestige of the Reformation movement upon the dubious soil of the north.'[35]

At the end of the nineteenth century, in a revealing passage, Richard Jefferies depicted strikingly similar conditions in Wiltshire, in his description of county society in *Hodge and his Masters*. 'Now the business of the county,' he said, 'was not very intricate; the details were innumerable, but the general drift was easy to acquire. Much more complicated to see through were all the little personal likings, dislikings, petty spites, foibles, hobbies, secret misunderstandings, family jars, and so forth, which *really decide a man's vote* or the scale into which he throws his influence. There were scores of squires dotted over the county, each of whom possessed local power more or less considerable ... Every family had its history and its archives containing records of negotiations with other families. People who met with all outward friendliness, and belonged to the same party, might have grudges half a century old but not forgotten. If you made friends with one you might mortally offend the other... Those who would attain to power must *study the inner social life*, and learn the secret motives that animate men. But to get at the secret behind the speech, the private thought behind the vote, *would occupy one for years* ...'[36] In these phrases Richard Jefferies might well have been describing the community of Leicestershire or Kent at the time of the Great Rebellion. The matrix of local society in which political opinion in the provinces was formed was essentially similar in both periods, though of course there were important differences as well.

Now and again the local historian lights upon some past event that momentarily illuminates these tracts of ordinary human life during the Civil War. The texture of provincial society and the pattern of politics woven into it suddenly begin to focus. The question forces itself upon one's attention: How much were ordinary people really affected by the events of the Great Rebellion? The present writer is gradually coming to the conclusion that we may have exaggerated the impact of the war itself upon daily life in the provinces. In the Midlands, of course, country people could not fail at times to be conscious of the fighting, and for some of them – the people of Leicester, for instance, on a May evening in 1645 – it brought horror and tragedy. Yet it would be misleading to suppose that daily life was *continuously* disrupted by fighting, even in the Midlands. The Great Rebellion was far from being a total war as we understand that term.[37]

When we read of the uproar occasioned in 1643 by Lord Northampton's seizure of a train of carriers' wagons at Daventry, drawn by fifty-seven horses on their journey from Cheshire to London, we need to remember, not only the outrage itself, but the fact that normally speaking these carriers' trains must have continued to reach their destination, otherwise there would have been no occasion for the outcry. When Sir Samuel Luke tells us how, after the King's astonishing victory at Leicester in 1645, the country people of Buckinghamshire and Bedfordshire suddenly refused to supply any further provisions for the local Parliamentary garrisons, we need to envisage, first the fact that farming life in the Midland counties had evidently continued, and secondly that for farming folk there were clearly more pressing matters than political allegiance. And when one finds the supposedly Puritan inhabitants of Hampden's county suddenly becoming 'so malignant, that neither the power of the army nor of the Committees could be sufficient to force in provisions' for the troops at Newport Pagnell, one need not suppose that all these country people were astute political cynics, but that, in a subsistence society, allegiance was unavoidably dictated chiefly by economic necessity.[38]

The suspicion that we may have exaggerated the impact of the Civil War upon provincial society is often confirmed if one isolates the experience of a single community in the seventeenth century, and studies its life-cycle as a whole. The town of Northampton need not be taken as a typical instance, and in fact the Great Rebellion probably played a larger part in its development than in most provincial boroughs. As we have seen, it not only stimulated the horse-trade and shoe-industry, but also encouraged the town's propensity towards Puritanism. Yet the impact of the Civil War also needs to be seen in perspective. Quite as decisive in the economic and religious development of Northampton were the effects of harvest-failure, disease, and fire. In 1605, for example, largely as a result of plague, one person in every six in Northampton died: a total of more than 600 people, or the equivalent, size for size, of more than 20,000 in the town of today. In 1638, barely a generation later, nearly 700 of the inhabitants perished, principally through a second visitation of the same disease.[39] Less than forty years later in 1675, four-fifths of the town was destroyed by fire, including its whole business centre. More than 700 families were rendered homeless, and the wealth that it had taken many tradesmen upwards of twenty years to accumulate disappeared in the space of three hours.[40] Important though the impact of the Civil War was, it was certainly not as catastrophic, for the people of Northampton, as these overwhelming local disasters. We may argue that such occurrences were merely local; but of course most towns and villages were from time to time smitten by very similar tragedies.

There is, of course, no need to minimize the impact of the Civil War upon seventeenth-century England. Its consequences for provincial society were obviously far-reaching. But we also need to see the Rebellion as one of a succession of problems to which society at the time was peculiarly vulnerable. The recurrent problems of harvest failure, and the malnutrition and disease that often followed in its wake, were, for most English people, more serious and more persistent than the tragic but temporary upheaval of the Civil War. As Professor Hoskins has remarked, the economy of Stuart England worked on a very fine margin between sufficiency and shortage. Probably at least a third of the population lived so close to the poverty-line that every poor harvest plunged them far beneath it. Even when vigorous action was taken locally to remedy the shortage, unrest and hardship remained acute. During the seventeenth century as a whole every fourth harvest, on the average, fell seriously short of basic requirements, and in some decades several successive years showed a marked deficiency. Those who lived through the Civil War and Commonwealth period, for example, suffered no fewer than ten harvest failures within the space of fifteen or sixteen years and in two years (1649-50 and 1661-2) the general price-level of food-stuffs was more than 50 per cent above normal.[41] This kind of situation affected every class in the country, and for hundreds of thousands of labourers, yeomen, craftsmen, and traders it might well mean ruin.

For us in the twentieth century it is hard to recapture how far provincial life under the Stuarts centred on the annual yield of the harvest. But in an agrarian society it was, of course, the basic fact of existence. It was the common talk of every market town, far more so than affairs of state. Perhaps we need to view the whole early modern period more frequently in this connotation. We need to study both the tragic consequences of harvest failure and disease, and the remarkable stimulus of abundance upon the life of the local community. The stubbornness and the resilience of country people, over the generations, in the face of this alternating harshness and generosity of nature were equally remarkable. Their experiences certainly go some way to explain that latent intransigence of the provincial world which, in the last resort, was one of the principal factors in the failure of both Charles I and Cromwell. For if you have been engaged for centuries in hand-to-hand warfare with the forces of nature, you naturally develop a certain dumb obstinacy towards the world at large – and not least towards the strange doings of princes and protectors.

## NOTES

1. D. H. Pennington and I. A. Roots, eds., *The Committee at Stafford, 1643–45* (1957); D. A. Johnson and D. G. Vaisey, *Staffordshire and the Great Rebellion* (1964); A. C. Wood, *Nottinghamshire in the Civil War* (1937); G. N. Godwin, *The Civil War in Hampshire (1642–45) and the Story of Basing House* (1904); E. Broxap, *The Great Civil War in Lancashire 1642–1651* (1910); A. R. Bayley, *The Great Civil War in Dorset, 1642–1660* (1910); C. H. Mayo, ed., *The Minute Books of the Dorset Standing Committee . . .* (1902); Alan Everitt, *Suffolk and the Great Rebellion 1640–1660*, Suffolk Records Society, iii (1960); Mary Coate, *Cornwall in the Great Civil War and Interregnum, 1642–60* (1933); Alan Everitt, *The Community of Kent and the Great Rebellion, 1640–1660* (1966).

2. 'Dalison Documents: Letters of Thomas Stanley of Hamptons', *Archaeologia Cantiana*, xvii (1887); 'The Expense Book of James Master, Esq.', *Archaeologia Cantiana*, xv-xviii (1883, 1886, 1887, 1889); Sir Roger Twysden, *Certaine Considerations upon the Government of England*, ed. J. M. Kemble, Camden Soc., 1st Ser., xlv (1849); *Proceedings, principally in the County of Kent, in connexion with the Parliaments called in 1640 . . .*, ed. L. B. Larking, Camden Soc., 1st Ser., lxxx (1862); 'Papers relating to Proceedings in the County of Kent, A.D. 1642–A.D. 1646', ed. R. Almack, *Camden Miscellany*, iii (1854).

3. Roger Howell, *Newcastle-upon-Tyne and the Puritan Revolution* (1967); Madeline Jones, *The Political History of the Parliamentary Boroughs of Kent, 1642–1662*, London Ph.D. thesis (1967).

4. Cf. Everitt, *Community of Kent*, p. 44.

5. Sabine Baring-Gould noted the same decline in Devon in *Old Country Life*, 1890, Chapter i, 'Old County Families'.

6. Quoted in Everitt, *Community of Kent*, p. 277.

7. The manuscript was originally in the Phillipps Collection and was sold at Messrs Sotheby's in 1967.

8. The phrase occurs in British Museum, Harleian MS 6918, f.34.

9. Cf. Everitt, *Community of Kent*, pp. 323–4.

10. Everitt, *Suffolk and the Great Rebellion*, pp. 28–34.

11. Ibid., p. 34.

12. For the military reorganization of this period generally see C. V. Wedgwood, *The King's War, 1641–1647*, Book 2, Chapter iv.

13. Everitt, *Community of Kent*, Chapter vii.

14. For Wales, see A. H. Dodd, *Studies in Stuart Wales* (1952); J. R. Phillips, *Memoirs of the Civil War in Wales and the Marches, 1642–1649* (1874).

15. There is a valuable narrative of political events in Leicestershire in these years by Prof. J. H. Plumb in V.C.H., *Leics.*, ii, pp. 109–18. The following pages are based on this account and on further research, chiefly in the Thomason Tracts, contemporary newspapers, records of the Committee for Compounding, Lords' and Commons' Journals, State Papers, and John Nichols, *The History and Antiquities of the County of Leicester*, iii, Pt. ii, App. iv. See also J. F. Hollings, *The History of Leicester during the Great Civil War*, 1840.

16. Edward Hyde, Earl of Clarendon, *The History of the Rebellion and Civil Wars in England*, ed. W. D. Macray, ii, p. 241.

17. Ibid., iv, p. 39.

18. Clarendon, however, described him as 'a young man of no eminent parts' (ibid., ii, p. 473). This view does not entirely square with his activities in Leicestershire.

19. Nichols, *Leics.*, iii, Pt. ii, App. iv., p. 39.

20. V.C.H., *Leics.*, ii, p. 114.

21. One of the best of the numerous accounts of the storming and sack is *A Perfect Relation of the Taking of Leicester...*, June 1645 (Thomason Tracts, E.288.4). This parliamentarian tract shows both the weakness of the defences and the fact that the carnage attributed to the Royalists was exaggerated at the time. There are other detailed accounts in *Perfect Passages of each Day's Proceedings in Parliament*, No. 32; *Perfect Occurrences of Parliament*, No. 23; *A Perfect Diurnal of some Passages in Parliament*, No. 97.

22. E.g., In 1642 thirteen Northampton shoemakers supplied the Treasurers at War with 4,000 pairs of shoes and 600 pairs of boots for troops in Ireland.—V.C.H., *Northants.*, ii, pp. 318–19.

23. Lt. Russell was paid £500 to buy horses at Northampton Fair for Manchester in April 1644, probably for about 80 horses. A further £1,256 was paid him to buy horses during the following seven weeks, probably at Northampton, though he also purchased at Cambridge.—Everitt, *Suffolk and the Great Rebellion*, pp. 90, 91.

24. Clarendon, op. cit., ii, p. 473; V.C.H., *Leics.*, ii, p. 109, quoting *Terrible News from Leicester* (Thomason Tracts, E.108.16).

25. Facts about Leicestershire and Northamptonshire family allegiance are based primarily on committee lists in C. H. Firth and R. S. Rait, *Acts and Ordinances of the Interregnum, 1642–1660* (1911); *Calendar of the Committee for Compounding*, Leics. and Northants. cases; and

miscellaneous references, chiefly in State Papers and numerous contemporary tracts in the British Museum. There seem to be few large local collections of family letters at present available for either county during this period.

26. *Calendar of the Committee for Compounding*, pp. 941, 962, 2290.

27. Cf. ibid., pp. 1121, 1133, 1166–7, 1987, 2615.

28. Ibid., *passim*.

29. This was first pointed out by Prof. J. H. Plumb in V.C.H., *Leics.*, ii, pp. 109–10.

30. For Leicestershire family history I have relied chiefly on John Nichols's *Leicestershire* (one of the most reliable of the great county histories), the usual printed genealogical sources, and in some cases the relevant sections of V.C.H., *Leics.*, topographical volumes.

31. Daniel Defoe, *A Tour through England and Wales*, Everyman edn, 1959, ii, pp. 89; William Camden, *Britannia, or a Chorographical Description of Great Britain and Ireland*, ed. Edmund Gibson (1753), i, col. 511.

32. V.C.H., *Leics.*, iv, pp. 99–104. By the mid-seventeenth century, few Northampton townsmen had any considerable agricultural wealth, to judge from their wills and probate inventories.

33. For the Northamptonshire gentry, see my article, 'Social Mobility in Early Modern England', *Past and Present*, xxxiii (1966), pp. 63–8.

34. Joan Thirsk, ed., *The Agrarian History of England*, iv, 1500–1640 (1967), pp. 241–2. With a total of 41,416 acres returned by the Commissioners of 1517–19 and 1607, the Northants. figure was more than twice that of any other county.

35. See A. G. Dickens, *Lollards and Protestants in the Diocese of York, 1509–1558* (1959), p. 69 and Chapter iii as a whole.

36. Richard Jefferies, *Hodge and his Masters*, 1946 edn. pp. 278–9. The italics are mine.

37. A superficial reading of contemporary tract literature sometimes gives the impression that it was a total war. But tracts, by their nature, do not usually record the *ordinary* facts of daily life, but its disruptions. It is the background of common existence that we need to visualize.

38. *Special Passages and Certain Informations*, No. 24; Hist. MSS Commission, *The Letter Books of Sir Samuel Luke, 1644–45*, ed. H. G. Tibbutt (1963), pp. 304, 306.

39. *The Records of the Borough of Northampton*, ii, 1898, ed. J. C. Cox, p. 238. The average annual mortality about 1605 was 139, and about 1638, 122. Deaths from plague alone were probably, therefore, about 500 in each of these two years, the total number of deaths being 625 in 1605 and 665 in 1638.

40. C. H. Hartshorne, *Historical Memorials of Northampton* (1848), p. 245; *A True and Faithful Relation of the late Dreadful Fire at Northampton . . .* (1675).

41. W. G. Hoskins, 'Harvest Fluctuations and English Economic History, 1620–1759', *The Agricultural History Review*, xvi, i (1968), pp. 15–21.

PART FOUR

Penruddock's Rising
1655

# PENRUDDOCK'S RISING
## 1655

*by*

*AUSTIN WOOLRYCH*

Three hundred years ago John Penruddock of Compton Chamberlayne and a dozen other brave men paid with their lives for their failure to raise the West Country in the name of King Charles II against the Protectorate of Oliver Cromwell. They had been in arms barely four days, and their little force, never more than 400 strong, had been sadly thinned by desertion before it succumbed to a single troop of regular cavalry. From all the teeming history of the 1650s such an episode might seem a small matter to commemorate; yet at the time it was a most serious business, alike to the government and to all Royalists at home and abroad, and it still claims an essential place in even the briefest account of the English Revolution.*

For one thing, the Wiltshire rebellion of 1655, like that in Cheshire four years later, was only the small visible appearance of a vastly greater mass of conspiracy which remained below the surface. It had been planned on a national scale, and it was the one general effort by the English Cavaliers between their defeat in war and the fall of the Protectorate to overthrow the revolution without recourse to Scottish or foreign arms. They were to plot again, of course, but not another party of them managed to appear in arms until Cromwell was in his grave and his son forced into retirement. Their attempt tells us much about their resources and morale, and more about the strength of the Protector's rule and the degree of support or tolerance it enjoyed in the country. But it is the consequence of their

* I am grateful to Colonel N. F. Penruddocke for permission to examine and quote from the unpubished Penruddock manuscripts in his possession. I also owe particular thanks to Professor S. T. Bindoff for placing transcripts of documents and other material of his own at my disposal.

failure which gives Penruddock and his comrades their niche
in history, for it provided the pretext for the most notorious
of Cromwellian experiments, the regime of the major-generals.
Why Cromwell took this step, which by setting a 'sword
government' over England drew upon him the bitterest wave of
unpopularity since the King's execution, can partly be understood through the events which prompted it – not merely the
tiny campaign in the west, but the gradual unfolding of the
whole sweep of the Royalist design.

Cromwell must have known when he took the title of Lord
Protector that he would not hold it long before he had to
reckon once more with the Cavaliers. They were unlikely to
accept Charles II's rout at Worcester as final, if only because
so few of them had then appeared for him; not for them a
restoration carried by an invading army of Covenanting Scots.
But since that disastrous campaign the young King had paid
more heed to his most responsible counsellors, Edward Hyde
and the Marquis of Ormonde, both of them tested in the long
years of war, and both opposed to any compromise with his
father's ideals in Church and State. They had striven to teach
him who his real friends were, and many of these (especially
the young) felt their strength had not yet been fairly tried.
Among the émigrés few had Hyde's patient faith that the King's
cause must one day be his people's too; plotting was the life's
blood of their hopes, and they itched for action. Those at home
who had been deeply committed to that cause would not forget for the sake of a grudging Act of Oblivion that they remained shut out for years to come from their natural place in
local and national affairs, denied by law the services of their
Church and the ministrations of the loyal clergy, their estates
sequestered or at best squeezed dry in the process of
composition.

Since they were last in arms, moreover, Cromwell had added
greatly to the number of his enemies; many who had fought for
a Parliament would not raise a finger for a Protector, and
might even help to overthrow him. Pride's Purge and the
King's execution had outraged the broad right wing which for
want of a better name was called Presbyterian. To the left, the
Levellers might be defunct as an organized party since the
suppression of the 1649 mutinies and the failure of John

Lilburne's last challenge, but the spirit of their teaching was to feed opposition to the Protectorate down to its end. More recently the expulsion of the Rump had raised the implacable opposition of the parliamentary Republicans, while later still the supersession of Barebone's Parliament by the Instrument of Government had roused the more fanatical brethren to even shriller heights of execration. To them Cromwell had not so much usurped as apostatized; he had taken the crown from the head of Christ and placed it on his own. Not much of this motley opposition could be expected to join hands with Charles Stuart, but in their mingled discontents might lie his opportunity.

*        *        *

The first serious exploration of the chances of a rising was carried out by Nicholas Armorer, a trusted agent who visited England in the autumn of 1653. He urged the need to commit authority and direction among the English Cavaliers to a very small number of picked men, and it was probably under his encouragement that towards the end of the year a secret council came into existence under the name of the Sealed Knot. Of its half dozen members Lord Belasyse was the natural leader of the northern Royalists, while the others, Lord Loughborough, Sir William Compton, Sir Richard Willys, Colonels Edward Villiers and John Russell, stood high in the midland counties. In the spring of 1654, with Armorer busy in London and else-where, their projects began to take shape, and in May Charles sent them a set of instructions urging the importance of simul-taneous action in all parts they planned to raise, and of a design upon London itself. In June and again in July he received from the Knot a general picture of its plan as it then stood, including the towns and garrisons to be attacked, the men responsible for the main enterprises and a rough idea of the forces they would furnish. Then, as later, the main centres of insurrection were intended to be in the north and west (especi-ally the vicinity of the Welsh border), though at this stage there were high expectations, too, of Kent, Surrey and Sussex. There was little as yet about Wiltshire and the adjacent counties which Penruddock was to call upon next year, for the death of Lord Beauchamp had caused a setback there, though it was hoped that his old father, the Marquis of Hertford, would not be idle, and that Grenvilles, Arundels and Courtenays would play their parts in Devon and Cornwall. Ireland was to be drawn in, and great hopes were placed on Scotland, where the Highland rising begun a year before under the Earl of Glencairn had swelled considerably since the King had sent Middleton over in February to take command. Already it had drawn off a number of veteran regiments from England, and Charles's advisers were deluded with reports that only 4,000 soldiers remained south of the Tweed.

To these offers of a general rising Charles responded eagerly. His actual letters belie Hyde's later picture, in his *History of the Rebellion*, of a patient and considerate king restraining his friends' rashness and warning them against a premature attempt which would only involve them in deeper ruin. He wrote in July that he would no longer hold them back until he could 'give them good encouragement from abroad'; in fact he would have them lose as little time as possible, and since they wished to act before Parliament assembled he suggested September as the best time. That proved impossible, for it was a slow business distributing commissions, collecting arms, concerting plans and sounding potential supporters. Fear of discovery made communication slow and imperfect; many of the more wary refused to treat with any but their own old friends, and there developed the confusion common to all unskilled conspiracies wherein confidence is denied to genuine agents only to be squandered amongst babblers and informers. To mutual suspicion must be added jealousy and personal pique, and even within the Knot itself Willys's old ill-feeling for Belasyse, which went back to 1645, flared up again to the point of a challenge. Meanwhile, as postponement followed postponement, Secretary Thurloe gradually pieced together a rough picture of the old enemy's new design. He had already tapped the brief reports of progress which Villiers wrote to Hyde, and among several other sources of intelligence none yielded such rich information as Colonel Bampfylde sent him from Paris.

That this spy could still pick up secrets of state and even continue to play a double game, long after Charles and Hyde had warned their friends of him, is a measure of the divisions which confounded the politics of the exiled Royalists. It was almost enough that Hyde should distrust a man for him to be taken up by Lord Jermyn, Sir John Berkeley, Sir Edward Herbert, Lord Balcarres and the rest of the clique which centred on the Queen Mother, and whose venom towards Hyde did more damage to Charles's cause than ever their plots did to Cromwell's. These precious spirits had pursued their own design against the Protectorate in 1654, and when the assassination plot which Gerard, Henshaw and others carried on under their auspices was discovered in May the projected rising received a serious setback through the large numbers of Cavaliers arrested on suspicion. But Henrietta Maria's courtiers thought little of Hyde's ideal of a restoration brought about as far as possible by the old Cavaliers; in their own interest they would rather the King owed it to Papists, Presbyterians and French soldiers. During the autumn Balcarres pressed Charles as hard as he could to go to Scotland and head the doomed Highland revolt, which was never to recover from Middleton's defeat at Dalnaspidal in July, rather than wait till his friends in England were ready. But Charles had left Paris in July, since the apparent imminence of an Anglo-French treaty threatened him with the humiliation of being expelled from French territory. Once he settled in Cologne at the end of September the ascendancy of Hyde and Ormonde in his counsels became firmer, and it was no small advantage to his cause that the courtiers who stayed behind were now able to do less mischief. Even so, the Queen did harm enough by her unscrupulous attempt late in the year to make a Catholic of the young Duke of Gloucester.

In spite of setbacks, however, the prospects for a rising seemed far less bleak in November and December than they became in the new year. Cromwell was already on bad terms with his first elected parliament, and even after he had got rid of the diehard Republicans by imposing on all the members a 'recognition of the government' as the Instrument had settled it in a single person and a parliament, the rest who subscribed persisted in regarding themselves as a constituent assembly rather than a mere legislature, and proceeded to redraft the constitution in a bill of their own. At a very different level, the agitation of that lunatic fringe of revolutionary Puritanism, the Fifth Monarchy men, was passing through one of its more violent phases. To them Cromwell had usurped not the rights of the people but the literal and imminent kingship of Christ, and Whitehall stank 'of the brimstone of Sodom, and the smoke of the bottomless pit'. During the winter he was forced into unwilling measures against their more incendiary preachers and their converts who could make trouble in the army, such as Colonel Rich, Adjutant-General Allen and (more dangerous) ex-Major-General Harrison, who was twice arrested and twice released before he was committed in February to a longer confinement.

But there was discontent of a more serious kind in the army, and it had reached the stage of active conspiracy. Behind it were those tireless plotters John Wildman and Edward Sexby, arch-Levellers since the first ferment of political consciousness in the New Model, organizers and spokesmen of the agitators elected by the regiments in 1647, and bitter enemies of Cromwell ever since he had wrecked their plans for a popular democracy based on an Agreement of the People. But busy as these were in fomenting and managing the movement, they were less prominent in it, and ultimately less important, than a group of officers who would have called themselves commonwealthsmen rather than Levellers. These had learnt much from Lilburne; they believed in government by a radically reformed sovereign parliament, elected on a wide franchise and renewed at fixed and frequent intervals, which would abolish tithes, preserve an unlimited freedom of conscience, fit the common law to the needs of the common man, and generally pursue the cause of social justice without regard to privilege or prescription. But for the most part they were less doctrinaire than the original Levellers, for they had supported the proceedings against the King and the establishment of the Commonwealth when Lilburne had denounced them, and though deeply suspicious of Cromwell's assumption of power, their hostility towards him was less violent and less personal than that of the Leveller leaders. They were after all soldiers who had fought his battles and shared his victories, and for that very reason the sympathy they could command and the pressure they could exert within the army were more dangerous than any incitement to mutiny from outside it.

The first manifestation was a petition, addressed to Cromwell and signed by Colonels Okey, Alured and Saunders,

which was to have been widely circulated for signatures within
the army and still more widely distributed as anti-protectoral
propaganda. Drafted by Wildman, it strongly challenged Cromwell's personal authority, military, legislative and financial, and
called for 'a full and free parliament' to 'freely consider of those
fundamental rights and freedoms of the Commonwealth' which
the Council of the Army had once adopted in the *Agreement
of the People*. It was seized in October before it could do much
harm, but at the same time another petition issued from the
fleet at Portsmouth which, though largely concerned with such
practical complaints of the seamen as impressment and lack of
pay, hinted also at political grievances in the unmistakable
language of the commonwealthsmen. The troubling thing here
was that Rear-Admiral Lawson was the probable author of the
petition, and that a council of war over which he presided approved the greater part of it. Lawson, a Baptist of Fifth
Monarchy tendencies, was anti-Cromwellian by religious as
well as political conviction, and if Thurloe was not mistaken
he and Wildman and the three petitioning colonels had all
met together early in September.

There was nothing here as yet that Cromwell could not deal
with. A court-martial cleared Okey of treason by a bare two
votes; he and Alured lost their commissions, while Saunders
only retained his after a full submission. A large meeting of
officers at the end of November unanimously declared its
devotion to the Protector and his government, and before that
the seamen had been so easily satisfied by the payment of
their arrears that there was no need to rake up charges against
Lawson. But the Levellers still had some cards to play, for they
had been conspiring with such leaders of the parliamentary Republicans as Haslerig, Bradshaw and Scot. Lord Grey of Groby
had promised to raise a large force for them, and they were
busy distributing thousands of printed copies of the three colonels' petition. One batch was carried to Scotland by Lieutenant Brayman, one of several of the old agitators of 1647 who
were active in the business, and it was in the Scottish forces that
the main action was planned to begin. General Monck was to be
seized in January and Major-General Overton placed at the
head of 3,000 foot and body of horse, who were to march
south and join forces with the commonwealthsmen of the

English army, gathered into rendezvous on Marston Moor, Salisbury Plain and elsewhere. By Christmas, however, Monck had his hands on a subversive letter which was circulating among his regiments, and he promptly clapped up the ringleaders and shipped Overton off as a prisoner to England. Overton was to suffer harsh measure in the form of over four years' imprisonment without trial, though according to Thurloe's information he had met Wildman when last in London, had subsequently written thither that there was in Scotland 'a party that would stand right for a commonwealth', had allowed disaffected officers to meet at his quarters, and had countenanced the dissemination within the Scottish army of propaganda against the government.* All the same the Levellers had cast him for a role which even Thurloe did not believe he would play, and the same is probably true of many of the men they relied on in England. Their design was in most respects chimerical, but it drew on a fund of real disaffection; one must not forget that it was a conjunction of army commonwealthsmen, parliamentary Republicans and extreme sectaries which eventually overthrew the Protectorate in 1659.

The question which most concerns us here is whether the Leveller design was directly linked with that of the Royalists. Cromwell believed it was, and said so when he dissolved Parliament on 22 January. He repeated the charge at length in a declaration published in the following autumn to justify the major-generals, though he was less positive when he returned to it in his opening speech to his next Parliament. The possibility of a treaty between King and Levellers had been discussed among the exiles as early as 1649; there had been some suspicious traffic between Lilburne and the Duke of Buckingham during 1652 and 1653; and only a few weeks after Penruddock's defeat Sexby launched his grandiose project for a restoration based on a Leveller rising and a Spanish army of invasion. Royalist leaders, when enlisting support for the rising, confidently promised that the Levelling party in the army would join with them, and we know they believed it because Hyde wrote to Ormonde that they expected the army to begin the

---

* The chief author of this propaganda, Samuel Oates, chaplain of Pride's old regiment, had a five-year-old son named Titus who was to outdo him in the art of plotting.

business, and that it might 'even do the work for us'. The rallying points planned by the Levellers on Marston Moor and Salisbury Plain were close enough to intended Royalist rendez-vous to excite suspicion, and Wildman was finally arrested very close to a town which the Cavaliers then meant to attack three days later.

Nevertheless, the evidence of collusion between the two interests is tenuous. That the King wrote letters to Overton and Lawson (both commonwealthsmen rather than Levellers) may prove no more than that he was misinformed of their in-tentions, and some subsequent allegations by Cromwellian spies in Cologne merely reflect his misplaced optimism. The large surviving body of correspondence between the exiled Court and its agents in England, though full of false hopes that the Levellers would bring out a large part of the army against the Protector, tells us almost nothing of actual contacts between the managers of the two enterprises or of any co-ordination of their plans. Thurloe on his part made a pretty full discovery of Wildman's and Sexby's activities, and his notes give us the names of most of the men they drew or sought to draw into their net. The only name common to both series, Royalist and Leveller, is that of Sir George Booth, who was engaged by the Cavaliers for the county of Cheshire which he was actually to raise in 1659. He himself was not a Cavalier, but a Presbyterian who had been turned out of the Long Parliament in Pride's Purge, and even if he did show some interest in the movement for a 'full and free parliament', it would go only a negligible way towards establishing an active connection between the two designs. That Levellers and Royalists each knew some-thing of the others' general intentions is beyond doubt, but the most that can be said with certainty is that each party hoped the activities of the other would play into its own hands. For the Cavaliers it was enough that Cromwell's left-wing opponents promised to hamstring his army; there was no sug-gestion as yet that the King should offer terms which would make his restoration acceptable to such as them, nor was it the Royalist policy in 1654–5, as it was to be in 1659, to declare merely for a free Parliament so as not to deter any disillusioned Parliamentarians from joining them by a premature proclama-tion of King Charles II. Some of the Levellers may possibly have been as ready now to treat with Charles as they proved to be soon afterwards, but they would never have carried with them the commonwealthsmen whose high standing in the army alone gave life to the movement against the Protector. Overton, Okey, Alured, Saunders and Lawson were chief of the band of Republican martyrs who suffered for the 'good old cause' under the Protectorate and were triumphantly re-instated by the Rump in 1659; their subsequent careers make it inconceivable that they would have considered exchanging Oliver's whips for Charles's scorpions. Lawson was the only one of them who finally came to terms with the Restoration, but when the rising broke in March there was no mistaking his readiness to help in defeating it. All in all, Cromwell's domestic troubles were a good deal less threatening than the Royalists imagined, and he had mastered them thoroughly before there was any chance of exploiting them.[1]

\*       \*       \*

We must now turn to the Royalist plan itself as it stood at the end of the year, when it first began to go seriously wrong. Yorkshire was to see the main effort in the north, with secondary movements in Cheshire, Lincolnshire and the north Midlands, and with York, Hull and Newcastle as particular objectives. In the west, active enlistment in northern and mid-Wales promised some link between an attack on Liverpool and the major enterprise aimed against Shrewsbury, while further south it was hoped to raise all the associated counties from Wiltshire and Hampshire westward to Cornwall, with Plymouth, Taunton and Portsmouth among the principal targets. The Western Association formed in these parts in 1650 had been revived, and within it John Penruddock, who had fought for the King with his father and lost a brother in the Civil War, had for some months been responsible for Wiltshire. His cousin, Edward Penruddock, returned from exile to help further his master's plans, and he was assisted too by Richard Pyle, an old agent of the King in the west. It was essential to seize at the outset some port at which the King himself could land at the first opportunity. Kent was too full of redcoats to do much at the start, but once the army had been drawn off to deal with trouble far away in the north and west, she and her neighbour counties were to make common cause with their friends in London.

In their general outline the plans for 1655 resembled those of 1657–8 and 1659, but in one respect they were weaker; the King could offer his supporters no military assistance from abroad. There was no hope from France; Mazarin was far too anxious for Cromwell's alliance, and family sentiment counted little against the claims of war and the French ambassador's reports from London concerning the stability of the English government and the present hopelessness of the royal cause. Spain from her dwindling resources was bidding scarcely less strongly than France for those veteran New Model regiments which might decide the issue of the twenty years' struggle in the Low Countries. Not till more than another year had passed, bringing with it the news of the capture of Jamaica and open war with England, could Charles wring a grudging treaty from the Spanish ministers in Brussels and not till then could he begin to raise the first few regiments he could call his own since Worcester. No help was to be had elsewhere, for the Dutch were all too anxious to keep the terms of their hard-won peace with Cromwell, and Denmark and Sweden were glad enough to keep his friendship. From Germany there may have been a chance of a few levies under the Count of Waldeck, but most of the reports reaching England of assistance from the princes probably arose from Charles's efforts to obtain payment of the grant which the Imperial Diet had voted for his subsistence a year before.

In England much had already been done in allocating commands, delivering commissions and gathering arms. From Penruddock's own papers we get a rare glimpse of what the prospect looked like to the men engaged in the undertaking, for in November he drew up a full statement of his debts, dues and disbursements (including a composition fine of £1,300 and a total of £1,500 incurred in the war and during six years of sequestration), and he closed it with these words:

'I have written this partly for my own satisfaction, and withal (in case it should please God to call me away) to satisfy my friends which I shall leave behind me, that the debts which I have contracted may not be laid to my charge. I hope God will

so bless me that I shall be able to go through this great trouble;
if I happen to die before it be done, I doubt not but my wife
and children will be so just as to see that no man shall suffer
a penny by me.'[2]

The gentlemen of the Knot, however, were far from satisfied
either with their own preparedness or with the auspiciousness
of the political situation. After sending encouraging messages
to the King in October, they wrote him such a gloomy letter
on 3 December that in replying he threatened rather wildly to
take service with the Dutch in the East Indies or with the
Venetians against the Turks, if they could not offer him better
hopes of an early return to his kingdom. There now developed
a fatal division among the English Cavaliers which played a
part second only to Cromwell's discoveries and counter-
measures in reducing the dangerous movement of the autumn
to the fiasco of the early spring. The Sealed Knot was later to
become a byword for caution and inaction – Booth was to
owe its members a bitter grudge in 1659 – but although on this
occasion they may have despaired a little early, events were
soon to justify them to the hilt. Since the summer of 1654,
however, a rival organization or 'Action party' had been com-
peting for the King's confidence and feeding him with much
more sanguine hopes. The plans for a rising, as they stood early
in 1655, were largely theirs. But their credit with the Royalist
gentry was on the whole inferior to that of the Knot, who, not
content with silence, spread increasing discouragement among
their friends and neighbours. The Action party nevertheless
decided that the time had come to fix a date, and they chose
at first 6 February, when the five months' span allotted to the
Parliament by the Instrument would have run out, and the
frustrated members would be spreading their discontent far and
wide.[3] It was not a bad idea in itself, though the assertion of
one responsible agent that 'half the Parliament were for the
King' was either insincere or just another delusive product of
the émigré mentality.

But before the dissolution came the Royalists' task was to
become far harder. During the latter part of December the
government, whether prompted by discoveries of the Army plot
or of the Cavaliers' preparations, took some ominous measures

for its security. Three thousand troops were sent for from Ireland, arms and ammunition were issued from peace-time stores, several regiments of horse and foot were brought into Westminster, the Tower garrison raised from 400 men to 900 and again to 1,200, and artillery planted around Whitehall and St James's. Then the last days of the year saw the exposure of the main Royalist organization for buying and distributing arms, and the arrest of Major Norwood, who managed it, with most of his accomplices. The tracking down of some crates and hampers of his purchases to their destinations in the country brought in a rich haul of prisoners, including the high sheriff of Worcestershire, Sir Henry Littleton, with his brother Charles and Sir John Packington, and among others Walter Vernon of Stockley Park in Staffordshire, his nephew Colonel Edward Vernon and the latter's brother-in-law, Edward Browne of Hungry Bentley in Derbyshire. This was only the beginning of a whole series of discoveries and arrests during January and February which should have convinced both the King and his agents, as it did Ormonde, that their enterprise had become hopeless.

The reaction of the more sanguine of them was to postpone the date by a mere week, and to send over Thomas Ross to get the King's consent to a general rising throughout England on 13 February. Since Cromwell had learnt so much, they argued, the only way to save the rest was to take to arms with the least possible delay. But hard on Ross's heels followed James Halsall with a letter wherein all six members of the Knot strongly condemned the fixing of a date, and warned Charles that any attempt at this stage would merely destroy his friends and close his enemies' ranks. Halsall, however, was delayed on the English coast for six days by contrary winds, and when he reached Antwerp on 1 February he found that the King had already approved Ross's proposals. From there he wrote warning Charles that such was the authority of the Knot that 'if they sit still and keep their chambers, I very much fear that by their ill examples our sword will be cut very short', though he judged that if the King sent them positive commands they would do their duty. Ormonde, who was himself at Antwerp and so acquainted with these messages before they reached Charles, sent a covering letter expressing the hope that he had either forbidden the enterprise firmly or else ordered the Knot to give it their full support. But Charles proceeded to take the one fatal course. He replied that it would not be reasonable for him either to restrain his friends who believed themselves ready, or to command the members of the Knot to act against their judgement; and he trusted that Daniel O'Neill, whom he sent over with this letter, would succeed in ironing out their differences and bring them to general agreement.

O'Neill, however, did not reach Dover until 14 February, and he spent eight precious days in detention before he managed to escape from the castle and get to London. The fact that the 13th came and went without word from the King was enough for the more cautious to give up hope, and it forced the activists into yet another postponement, though this was not sufficiently made known to prevent some abortive gatherings in the west. Even before these were reported Cromwell had had warning of the day. His arrests during the previous three weeks had included two gentlemen commissioned to raise regiments of horse and foot in North Wales; coupled with the landing of the regiments from Ireland, this ended all chance of action in that quarter. He had also secured Sir Humphrey Bennett, who had undertaken the attack on Portsmouth, Colonel Grey, brother of Lord Grey of Wark and pledged to secure Tynemouth Castle, a Lieutenant Read, who was caught with the letter the King had sent over last July – a splendid windfall – and a number of others, such as Colonels Thornhill and Gardiner, who would be sadly missed. To these was soon added the leader of the Devon gentry, Sir John Grenville. The breaking of the Leveller conspiracy was completed when Wildman was seized near Marlborough on 10 February, with the ink still wet on a declaration 'against the Tyrant Oliver Cromwell'. Two days later orders went out for the seizure of all horses in London and the suburbs, and for the delivery into the Tower of all private stores of powder which might fall into the wrong hands. All officers were sent to their commands, the guards were tripled, parties of cavalry scoured the city and four miles round, and a Royalist had to report that soldiers were posted at the end of every street. On the 13th itself Cromwell sent for the Lord Mayor and the city fathers,

read them Charles's letter and Wildman's manifesto, and persuaded them of the need to raise a strong militia under Major-
General Skippon. He was not disappointed. Only at Dover was
he ill-served, for with the mayor 'both weak and heady' and
some of the port officials engaged in the royal interest, messen-
gers still managed to pass.

O'Neill at first read in these signs, and in the general despair
of those he was sent to confer with, the sad truth that their
prospects had become hopeless, and Armorer when he joined
him thought the same. But O'Neill, alas, allowed himself to be
persuaded by Sir Thomas Armstrong that he could bring the
whole enterprise to life again by giving out that he carried full
authority from the King to call his friends to arms. He went to
work swiftly on these lines, and even got a pledge from
Compton on behalf of the Knot that though they believed little
good would come of it they would assist him in all they could.
8 March was now to be the day, and in spite of all Cromwell
had learnt and done, O'Neill was led to expect success at least
in the west and in Yorkshire, in Cheshire under Booth and in
Lincolnshire under Lord Willoughby of Parham, in the Isle of
Ely and at Shrewsbury. Willoughby deceived him into expecting hearty assistance from two other old Parliamentary generals,
Sir William Waller and Richard Browne, and (like other agents
before him) he accepted quite unfounded assurances that Lord
Fairfax would make a powerful appearance for the King in the
north.

All this false optimism is partly explained by the arrival of
another visitor from Cologne, two days after O'Neill. This was
Henry Wilmot, Earl of Rochester, who had persuaded Charles
months earlier to commission him as chief commander in
England in the event of a rising. Hard fighter, hard drinker,
fit father for the poet who inherited his title, Rochester had
learnt his trade in the Dutch service, been expelled from the
Long Parliament for his part in the 1641 Army Plot, advanced
in the wars to lieutenant-general of the horse only to be dis-
graced for intriguing with the Parliamentary commander-in-
chief, and finally confirmed himself in the young King's trust
and affection by his resourceful and selfless companionship
during their wanderings together after the battle of Worcester.
That Charles should send such a man half-way through

February to call the Cavaliers to arms shows how far he had prejudged the issue between the Action party and the Knot. Waiting to embark in Flanders, Rochester (so Clarendon tells us), 'in the hours of good fellowship, which was a great part of the day and night, communicated his purpose to anybody he did believe would keep him company and run the same hazard with him', and in this way he picked up Sir Joseph Wagstaff, who, like everyone else, had heard much talk of a rising and was waiting for a chance to slip across and try his fortune. Rochester spent five busy days in London, instilling his own sanguine spirit into all who would listen to him, then made his way to Yorkshire to take command in the north. He left O'Neill in London, while to the west he had already sent Wagstaff, who was a natural and acceptable choice as commander. He had been major-general of Charles I's western army and was known for a stout man and a good companion, though fit 'rather for execution than counsel'.

Charles on his side of the water was also preparing for adventure. It was not easy to leave Cologne without making a stir, but he sneaked out at daybreak on 14 February with only Ormonde and a groom for company, and after a slow, difficult and uncomfortable journey went to ground at Middleburg in the house of a wealthy citizen whose English wife had been brought up in the household of Elizabeth of Bohemia, the King's aunt. Hyde followed later to Breda, so as to be within a day's ride of his master. Extreme secrecy was essential, not only to conceal Charles's movements from the English government, but because the States of Holland made it offensively clear to his sister, the Princess of Orange, that his presence in their territory would not be tolerated, and he could expect no better in Zeeland if he were discovered. Cromwell, of course, knew what to make of his departure from Cologne and how to act on it, and he was soon much more accurately informed than the countless rumours which spread everywhere to the effect that the King was already in England. Charles was merely waiting to sail on the first news of success, and he had warned the Duke of York, who was still in France serving under Turenne, to be ready to follow at a call and to have if he could a frigate or two at his disposal.

The news, of course, never came, for what happened on the

night of Thursday, 8 March, was what any sober judge of the situation might have expected. None of the members of the Knot stirred, nor did the Presbyterians Willoughby, Waller and Browne. Portsmouth and Plymouth slept soundly, for the men who had undertaken them were Cromwell's prisoners. Hull was reinforced from Scotland, while Taunton lay quiet because the leaders of the Somerset Cavaliers, Sir Hugh and Colonel Francis Wyndham, had taken flight. At only half a dozen widely scattered points throughout England and Wales did the Royalists attempt to gather, and not a party of them was still in arms by the following morning.

All that materialized of the great rally on Marston Moor which Rochester had hoped to lead in an attack on York was a dispirited little company, probably little over a hundred strong, which dispersed so hurriedly that it left four cartloads of arms behind on the moor. The fugitives turned back a small body of fifty horse which Colonel Marmaduke Darcy was bringing to join them, and many prisoners fell to Colonel Lilburne's troops before they regained their homes, among them Sir Richard Mauleverer, Sir Henry Slingsby and Sir William Ingram. Rochester evaded capture and made his way south by quiet roads disguised as a grazier, and Mauleverer subsequently escaped and got away overseas. The poor appearance was not surprising, for successive postponements had caused confusion and discouragement. Rochester was personally none too well trusted, and many Yorkshiremen had hoped to have as a leader Sir Marmaduke Langdale, who as an old opponent both of Hyde and the favourite Rochester had not been called upon.

An ambitious plan to assault Newcastle from three sides fared no better, and three or four score men who met for the purpose at Duddoe, south of Morpeth, scattered before midnight. Chester, like Newcastle, was forewarned, and the mere discovery that sentries were pacing the castle precincts was enough to deter its attackers. Against Shrewsbury the design was more formidable, and that town might have gone the way of Salisbury had not Colonel Mackworth and his little garrison of seventy men received timely intelligence from the Protector. There was not time to get very far with raising the regiment of foot and troop of horse ordered on 5 March, but a regular troop from Hereford reached the city on the crucial evening,

and a warning about Sir Thomas Harris, the appointed leader
of the attack, made even that precaution superfluous. Harris
was taken at his house at Boreatton, eleven miles north-west of
Shrewsbury, with all the accoutrements of war only a few hours
before he was to head a rendezvous there. Another gathering
was frustrated near Llanymynech on the Shropshire-Mont-
gomeryshire boundary, and the general movement along the
Welsh border was finally rendered harmless when a hard-riding
messenger carried the alert to old Sir Thomas Myddelton at
Chirk Castle, which was also threatened.

    The largest party of Cavaliers to meet that night – some two
or three hundred – came together at Rufford Abbey in
Nottinghamshire. A number of old Royalist officers were on the
field, but the two chief men behind this venture, Lord Byron
and Sir George Savile (the future Marquis of Halifax), remained in London. Can they have despaired of success or received warning too late to call off their supporters? At any
rate the company gave way to panic, abandoned their arms and
made for home, though not in time to save some of them from
capture.

                    *        *        *

In Wiltshire the night of these alarms passed without a stir.
Wagstaff had meant to enter Winchester and seize the judges,
but the arrival there of a troop of horse made him postpone his
attempt by three days, when the assize would have moved on
to Salisbury. The odds were the more heavily against him because some of the western gentry had gathered prematurely
around Salisbury and Bristol on 12–13 February, and one of
them named Stradling had confessed all he knew of the design
up to that time. Nevertheless, when darkness had fallen on
Sunday, Wagstaff and Penruddock managed to collect about
sixty horsemen in Clarendon Park, three miles west of
Salisbury, and Thomas Mompesson brought them forty more
from the city. They marched out to the Blandford road to meet
another eighty of their friends from Dorset, then turned their
horses towards Salisbury again and entered it in the small hours
of Monday, 12 March. Posting a strong force in the market-
place and setting guards at the doors of the inns, they broke
open the gaol, enlisted many of the prisoners, and seized all the

horses which the usual concourse of visitors attending the assize placed unwittingly at their disposal. They dragged from their beds the two judges, Chief Justice Rolle and Baron Nicholas, and the high sheriff, Colonel John Dove, and Penruddock had difficulty in dissuading Wagstaff from hanging all three on the spot. Dove was spared most grudgingly, especially when he refused to proclaim Charles II, and he was roughly handled. He had trafficked largely in forfeited lands and had sat on the court which tried the late King; it was lucky for him at this moment that he had not put his hand to the death warrant. In the end the insurgents released the judges after burning their commissions, and carried off the sheriff, still in his night attire, as a hostage.

They had entered the city not far short of two hundred strong; they rode out of it at about eight o'clock with their numbers roughly doubled. But Salisbury's response had been cold, for most of their recruits were from the gaol, and the Marquis of Hertford, whom Penruddock had counted on for powerful support, had made no appearance. The little force was divided into troops, each intended to be the nucleus of a regiment, under Penruddock, Hugh Grove and Francis Jones. Blandford was their next halt, and there the unfortunate Dove was at last allowed to dress. There, too, Penruddock himself had to proclaim the King, for the town crier proved as obstinate in face of threats as the sheriff had been. From thence their route lay through Shaftesbury and Sherborne, though they may have split into several parties so as to cover more of the countryside in their search for recruits; at any rate they gathered on Babylon Hill east of Yeovil for a few hours' rest at one o'clock on Tuesday morning. There were still only three or four hundred of them, so Dove estimated when he was set free at daybreak, and they must have known that the thousands of supporters they had hoped to rally in Dorset would never appear. Their movements for the next twenty-four hours are obscure – they were seen at Crewkerne and Chard, and a party was reported to have entered Dorchester, broken open the prison and 'horsed the gaol-birds' – and we do not know where they spent Tuesday night.

By then the Protector's forces were well on their tracks. He had heard of the rising the day it broke out, and had promptly commissioned Desborough to go down as major-general of the west and take command of all the units in those parts. These included two troops of Berry's regiment at Bristol under Major Boteler and two more at Marlborough, while two troops of Colonel Twistleton's were ordered to join him from Chichester. But Boteler had set out from Bristol on his own initiative as soon as he got the alarm late on Monday, and collecting two more troops at Bath had reached Devizes the same night. Next day he was at Salisbury, but he stayed only for a night's rest and marched on to Shaftesbury, not knowing how much further the insurgents had travelled and intending to attack them at once if he got the chance. There, however, he got word of Desborough's approach and waited for his commander to join him.

Wednesday, as it turned out, was the last day of the rising. Wagstaff and Penruddock had no better hope now than to make with all speed for Cornwall, where they could expect a kinder welcome and, at the worst, ships ready to carry them overseas. They did well to avoid Exeter, where the high sheriff of Devon had rapidly raised a regiment of militia, and Taunton, where two or three thousand countrymen had come in to help against the disturbers of the peace. Only a typical local dispute over precedence among the officers of this force prevented it from marching out to meet the enemy. But Exeter also held a single troop of regular cavalry under Captain Unton Croke. As early as Tuesday he had marched out to Honiton in the hope of intercepting the rebels, though hearing they were too strong for his less than sixty men to deal with on their own he had withdrawn again to Exeter before they came up. Next morning, however, he learnt that he would miss them where he was, for they were reported at Cullompton about two hundred strong, though tired and dispirited. Knowing how important it was to prevent them from reaching Cornwall, he set out again at once, and though he was too late at Cullompton he kept on their tracks through Tiverton north-westward to South Molton. There at last, thinned still further by desertion during the long day's ride, they had halted at seven o'clock for the night's rest which both men and horses desperately needed. But by ten Croke was upon them, and for the next three hours or so the little Devonshire town saw some sharp street fighting, with the

Cavaliers firing hotly from their windows and Croke's troopers forcing them from house after house. He had nine or ten casualties, fortunately none fatal, but in the end the Royalists all fled or surrendered upon quarter, and he brought back to Exeter more prisoners than he had men.

Penruddock, Grove and Jones were among them, but not Wagstaff; he and other gentlemen made their escape, how long before the fight ended we do not know. It is a remarkable fact that all the men who came from overseas to further the rising – Rochester, Wagstaff, O'Neill, the Halsall brothers, Armorer, Ross and others – succeeded in making their way abroad again, sometimes after many weeks in hiding or disguise. The widespread eagerness to assist the government against those who threatened renewal of civil war did not generally extend to the tracking down of fugitives once they had become harmless.

Croke's triumph was later soiled by the assertion of Penruddock, Grove and Jones that he had allowed commissioners of his to grant them articles of surrender which guaranteed their lives, liberties and estates. The exact truth is now beyond reach, but two facts stand out in Croke's favour. In the first place, when Penruddock wrote to his wife on 17 March, instructing her in detail how to enlist all the influence she could command in his favour, he said nothing whatever about articles. All he wrote on the subject was this:

'The best that I can make of this is that it was our fortune to fall into the hands of one Captain Unton Croke, a generous and valiant officer, one that I hope will show something the better, for that we did not basely desert our soldiers as others did.'[4]

Though he later claimed he could produce the original document, he seems never to have done so. Secondly, as some indication of the honesty of Croke's denials, he did admit to granting articles to five obscurer men, for whom he interceded no less than three times, and to good effect. We need not suppose that Penruddock and Grove lied in their last moments when they repeated the charge against Croke on the scaffold, for they may well have persuaded themselves in their extremity that the terms which Croke admitted granting were general, and not particular to five of their followers.

Many more prisoners were brought in after Croke delivered his original haul to Exeter gaol, and a fortnight later Desborough sent up a list of 139. He explained that he had not brought in more of the meaner sort than he knew what to do with – most of them as it was had to be lodged in inns – but though if need be he could take up as many more as Cromwell pleased, he hoped these would be enough to proceed against 'to make a pattern for all the rest'. The list thus offers only the roughest of cross-sections, especially as the forty-three names of gentlemen and officers may include some who were not taken in arms but arrested on general suspicion. Among the rest may be counted eight yeomen, nineteen husbandmen, ten servants and two innkeepers, while most of the remaining fifty-seven were small craftsmen or traders, drawn largely from Salisbury and its neighbouring villages and from Blandford.

In dealing with these unfortunates Cromwell could afford to show moderation. His most remarkable decision was to allow them to be tried by juries of their countrymen, for special high courts of justice had been the rule for cases of treason since 1648. This was certainly a sign of confidence in his regime, though he probably remembered that when the last high court had sat, on the assassination plotters last summer, Mr Justice Atkins had refused to serve on the grounds that such cases must be tried by jury according to the due process of the common law. A special commission of oyer and terminer was issued, and assizes were held in turn at Salisbury, Exeter and Chard. By the standards of the time the trials were fair. Too much should not be made of the efforts of sheriffs and army officers to ensure that the jurors empanelled were 'well-affected', for in country where Royalism was rife it was an elementary precaution to select men who would accept the premise that rebellion against the Protector constituted treason and would judge the evidence on its merits. Although that evidence was in most cases quite clear, grand juries did not find true bills against all the prisoners indicted, nor did petty juries find guilty all who were tried. Rolle and Nicholas, though both on the commission, took no active part in the Salisbury trials lest the violence they had suffered there at the hands of some of the prisoners might be held to prejudice them. Penruddock was allowed to challenge twenty-two jurors before twelve were sworn, and his own full account of his trial permits no serious criticism of the justice he received. The contrast between these assizes and those which Jeffreys held in the same west country after another rebellion a generation later could hardly be more marked.

Less than a third of the prisoners in custody were brought to trial, and on the whole the commissioners and the government were satisfied with the results. Thirty-nine in all were sentenced to death for treason, but many were reprieved, and the rest were spared the barbarities of hanging, drawing and quartering. We cannot be certain how many actually suffered, for the newspapers differ in their accounts. There is no record of the fate of six men condemned at Chard, and some against whom treason could not be proved were condemned for horse-stealing. Certainly less than twenty were executed, and Thurloe's figure of fourteen or fifteen (given shortly before the sentences were carried out) is probably close to the mark. No mercy, beyond a comparatively honourable death by the headman's axe, could be expected for Penruddock; the rising bears his name rightly, for he had been the mainspring of the Wiltshire design since long before Wagstaff appeared on the scene. The persistent and heroic efforts of his wife won him no reprieve – her letter to him when she finally bowed to failure is among the most moving of all its kind[5] – and he died bravely. Grove faced the same death with the same courage, but Jones was reprieved, possibly because he could claim kinship with the Protector. Many of the reprieved prisoners and some who were not brought to trial were subsequently transported to Barbados, to suffer the hard lot of indentured servants.

A similar commission was issued for the trial of the prisoners in the north and midlands, but it was never executed. The three chief commissioners, Baron Thorpe, Justice Nicholas and Serjeant Hutton, at first took refuge in legal technicalities, but eventually they confessed to serious doubts whether the offences of the prisoners, even if proven, would constitute treason. To dispute the validity of Cromwell's Treason Ordinance was to question the legality of his government itself, and the two judges lost their posts. If the Northern Cavaliers had achieved nothing else, they had provoked the first of a series of disquieting conflicts between the Protector and his highest officers of the law. For themselves, they got off in the current year with nothing worse than a few fines for riot or misdemeanour, though later the hands of the major-generals were to fall more heavily on them.

\*    \*    \*

There is no need to dwell on the causes of the failure for which Penruddock and his friends paid the price; they have been sufficiently exposed already. The military strength of the Protectorate would have been proof against a far better mounted and more determined assault. The later projects of 1657–8 and 1659 were merely to confirm that the Cavaliers were incapable of the strength, organization and solidarity needed to shake any government which could still count on Cromwell's army and Thurloe's intelligencers, and they also saw the rift widen between the cautious ones who took their cue from the Sealed Knot and the bolder spirits who later fell under the leadership of John Mordaunt. Defeat in 1655 cast its shadow across all subsequent enterprises of the same kind – by its lowering of morale, its breeding of mutual distrust and recrimination, and above all by the further discoveries which prisoners and professional agents soon furnished. In May and June, for example, a whole crop of arrests and imprisonments, based largely on information from the spy Henry Manning at Charles's court, removed from the scene for long or short periods many leading Royalists who had been concerned in preparing the rising but had not actually taken up arms. Henceforth, whenever Royalist conspiracy became troublesome, the government knew pretty well whom to watch.

There would always be gentlemen like those of Wiltshire, ready to risk their lives and what was left of their estates at a call from the King, but without wider and more popular support no insurrection could hope to succeed. In this respect again the Sedgemoor campaign offers a telling contrast with the utter failure of Penruddock's company to raise the western countryside. The many recorded examinations of humbler prisoners, taken with the small numbers and the proneness to panic at the various abortive gatherings on 8 March, confirm that enthusiasm for the King's cause, though widely present, burned with but a low flame. It was not until the general breakdown of government in the latter part of 1659 that Charles II began to command a depth and breadth of popular devotion that would prove irresistible, and until the forces of the revolution began to disintegrate the master instinct of most people was on the side of preserving established authority against the threat of renewed civil war. For Cromwell had more to congratulate himself on than the absolute firmness of his regular forces under the mild shocks of rebellion. To the examples of Taunton and Exeter already mentioned must be added the prompt raising of 400 volunteers in Gloucestershire, the ready response of Bristol, the ease and speed with which London mobilized its large militia of 5,000 foot alone, and the rapid embodiment of volunteer forces in many other places from Kent to Wrexham and from Nottingham to the Forest of Dean.

But as was said at the beginning, history remembers Penruddock's rising chiefly for its direct consequence: the division of England into eleven districts under as many major-generals, the raising of a standing militia to reinforce the army's hold over the country, and to pay for all this the exaction, from all Royalists of broad acres, of the notorious 'decimation' which wrung a further ten per cent from their diminished incomes. It was not so much the four days' adventure in the west which prompted these extreme measures as the total picture of conspiracy and subversion which Cromwell gradually received, and which this narrative has tried to convey. It need not be thought that he believed every word of the greatly inflated accounts of the common enemy's machinations which he set forth from time to time in his speeches and declarations; we should bear in mind that he had to deal with the false accusation, revived in recent times,[6] that he had fabricated or engineered the whole plot in order to fasten a closer military domination over the country. We should remember, too, that much of the intelligence he himself received was alarmist and exaggerated, for spies like Manning were only worth their pieces of silver while danger continued to breed, and they certainly did their best to prove that conspiracy had not been scotched by the suppression of one insurrection. Information of assassination plots abounded, and there soon followed the first reports of Sexby's relations with the Spaniards and the exiled court, with all their suggestion of constant intrigue between Cavaliers, Papists and radical commonwealthsmen.

That the regime of the Major-Generals was a serious error of policy on Cromwell's part would be hard to deny. Apart from its injustice to the many Royalists who had lived peaceably since their original defeat, it was not necessary for its first purpose, since later events proved that Thurloe's intelligence system sufficed in itself, with the regular forces, to secure the Protectorate. There was certainly a strong case for a more effective police than the parish Dogberries provided, but in so blatantly military a guise, and with so little regard for existing local authority, the experiment could only be hated. It made much more immediate and irksome that 'sword government' which was the most unpopular and easily criticized aspect of Cromwell's rule. More than anything else he did after 1653, it hindered the reconciliation of the great numbers of the gentry who were neither Royalist nor Cromwellian, but indefinitely 'Presbyterian'. They did not only resent the exorbitant powers conferred on officers of low birth, or the enforcement of Puritan repressive legislation by a sort of moral police in accordance with Cromwell's own ideal of a 'reformation of manners'. What probably rankled most of all was the overriding of their own easy-going management of local affairs, as Justices of the Peace whose authority was a natural adjunct of their social standing, by a quasi-dictatorial discipline administered by a military satrap and his picked band of coadjutors, the 'commissioners for securing the peace of the country'. The Major-General and his commissioners mirrored at the provincial level the Protector and his Council, and extended into local life the authoritarian rule of a minority.

But the system grew with perfect naturalness from the challenge thrown down to this minority in March 1655. The final shape it took between August and October was merely an extension to the whole country of the sort of command committed to Major-General Desborough over the six western counties in 28 May, and that commission itself was an extension of the emergency powers conferred on him as 'Major-General of the west' on the very day Penruddock entered

Salisbury. The original and essential task of the Major-Generals was the prevention of conspiracy through their unified command over both regular units and the new permanently embodied militia; their other duties, which made them police-men, tax collectors, administrators and vice-squad chiefs as well as soldiers and in the end took most of their time, were all afterthoughts. As for making the Cavaliers foot the bill for the expense they caused, the idea was much in the minds of the officers who had to deal with them. 'I hope the great estates these blades leave behind them will pay for all the charge, if you forgive them not again'; ''tis the desire of all the good people that those who cause our troubles and charges might bear the burden now'; 'it would be an excellent course to raise about 2,000 horse equally out of all the counties on the north side of Trent, and to impose the charge of maintaining and finding them only upon such as are convicted or suspected notoriously for malignancy' – all these are from letters to Whitehall written by busy colonels in the middle of March.[7] Cromwell and his Council hardly needed so much prompting, for in the emergency commissions for the raising of a militia which went out on 14 March to twenty-one counties and cities they specially directed that the burden should be charged upon the malignant and disaffected. What followed in the summer and autumn was only an elaboration of these ideas, and the erection into a system of the immediate counter-measures prompted by Penruddock's rising.

## NOTES

1. Since the above was written, David Underdown in *Royalist Conspiracy in England, 1649–1660* (1960), pp. 123–4, has established that the Royalist Colonel Henry Bishop boasted of having a commission from the King to treat with the Levellers, and with two or three associates made contact with Wildman and others. But the negotiations broke down, and Professor Underdown concludes that although Royalists and Leveller conspirators knew enough to hope to profit from each other's activities, 'there was, clearly, no plan of combined action.'
2. 'A Note of such debts as are owinge by mee or that are dew to me Jo Penruddock', 4 November 1654. Hologr. Penruddock MSS.
3. The dissolution would be expected on 3 February, for it was not until 5 and 6 January that the newspapers began to hint that Cromwell would reckon the Parliament's term in lunar instead of calendar months, so as to put an end to it on 22 January. The date 6 February is derived

from two letters of 19 January, both informing the King that the rising was postponed by a week, and from the fact that James Halsall gave the date as 13 February (which is widely confirmed from other sources) *after* he knew of this postponement, which I am convinced was from the 6th to the 13th and not from the 13th to a later date. Firth in *E.H.R.*, III (1888), p. 333, assumed the latter, reading 'week' as a codeword for 'month'; but so confusing a substitution seems improbable in itself, and too vague to describe the final postponement from 13 February to 8 March. Most of the evidence is printed in *E.H.R.*, III, pp. 333–5; see also *Clarendon State Papers*, III, p. 266. Underdown's *Royalist Conspiracy*, ch. 6–7, throws a great deal of new light on the Action party and its role in the 1655 design.

4. *Wiltshire Archaeological and Natural History Magazine*, XIII (1872), p. 132.

5. It is printed from the Penruddock MSS in *Wilts. Arch. Mag.*, XV (1875), p. 1. There also may be found (pp. 3–5) two letters, entirely different from each other, but both purporting to be the last which Penruddock wrote to his wife. Neither is known to survive in MS, and both are of doubtful authenticity. The first appeared in the pamphlet describing Penruddock's trial and execution, published shortly after his death and probably prepared by Seymour Bowman, his friend and lawyer (for Bowman see Caroline Robbins in *Notes and Queries*, 196 (1951), 56–9). It is, however, in a style so much more high-flown and rhetorical than that of Penruddock's few undoubted writings that one cannot help suspecting it may be a pious fabrication by Bowman, who undoubtedly interpolated several passages into Penruddock's own account of his trial in order to heighten its effect. The pamphlet (B.M., E845 (7)) was privately reprinted (from a copy in his possession) by Colonel N. F. Penruddocke to mark the tercentenary of his ancestor's death. The second and shorter letter was first printed by Sir Richard Steele in *The Lover* for 13 March, 1714, with no mention of its provenance.

6. By R. F. D. Palgrave in *Quarterly Review*, CLXII (1886), pp. 414–42 and *English Historical Review*, III (1888), pp. 521–39, 722–51 and IV (1889), pp. 110–31. Palgrave's arguments were effectively demolished by C. H. Firth; see bibliographical note below.

7. *Thurloe State Papers*, III, 216, 227, 294.


BIBLIOGRAPHICAL NOTE

Information concerning the whole of the Royalist design as it reached the Secretary of State is to be found in the *Thurloe State Papers* (7 vols., 1742); they are somewhat meagerly supplemented by the *Calendar of State Papers Domestic*, 1655. For the correspondence between the English Royalists and the exiled Court, see the *Calendar of the Clarendon State Papers*, Vols. II–III (1869–76; a few items are printed in full in the *Clarendon State Papers*, Vol. III, 1786), and the *Nicholas Papers*, edited by G. F. Warner, Vol. II (Camd. Soc., 1892). Clarendon's *History of the Rebellion* adds some details, but is not to be relied upon. The *Clarke Papers*, edited by C. H. Firth, Vol. III (Camd. Soc., 1899), contain some useful news-letters, and Thurloe's dispatches to Pell in Switzerland are printed by R. Vaughan in *The Protectorate of Oliver Cromwell*, Vol.

I, 1839. Cromwell's long declaration, exposing the Royalist conspiracy in order to justify the Major-Generals, is printed in *The Parliamentary or Constitutional History of England*, Vol. XX (1763). Much matter concerning the rising, not always reliable, is to be gleaned from *Mercurius Politicus* and other contemporary newspapers.

David Underdown's excellent book *Royalist Conspiracy in England 1649–1660* (1960) has greatly illuminated the whole subject since this essay was written. There is also a mass of information in three linked articles which Sir Charles Firth published in the *English Historical Review* (1888–9) in reply to a misguided attempt by Sir Reginald Palgrave to prove that Cromwell deliberately engineered the rising in order to consolidate his own power. W. W. Ravenhill minutely investigated the rising in the west and the fate of its participants, quoting largely from the Penruddock and other manuscripts, in *The Wiltshire Archaeological and Natural History Magazine*, XIII–XV (1872–5). A. C. Wood covers the Nottingham episode in *Nottingham in the Civil War* (1937), and Maurice Ashley throws light on the Leveller conspiracy in *John Wildman: Plotter and Postmaster* (1947). On the Major-Generals, see C. H. Firth, *The Last Years of the Protectorate* (1910, reprinted 1963, 2 vols); D. W. Rannie, 'Cromell's Major-Generals', in *E.H.R.*, X (1895); and Ivan Roots, 'Swordsmen and Decimators', in *The English Civil War and After, 1642–1658*, ed. R. H. Parry (1970).

PART FIVE

# Charles II

# CHARLES II

*by*

## K. H. D. HALEY

The conclusions of historians change over the years, not only as a result of the discovery of new evidence, but as a result of the changing times in which historians themselves live and work. We have become familiar with the notion that each generation of historians may have its own questions to ask, its own standards and conscious or unconscious preconceptions by which to judge. The historical reputation of Charles II is a fascinating example of this. Broadly speaking, opinions about him may be divided into two sharply contrasting groups.

On the one hand there is what might fairly be termed the traditional Whig view – that of Macaulay,[1] and his grandnephew Trevelyan. Chapters XI and XII of Trevelyan's famous text-book, *England under the Stuarts*, first published in 1904, set out this highly critical view of the King and his reign in a way which must have influenced countless students; and Airy's biography of Charles, published in 1901, belongs basically to the same tradition. On the other hand there is the view which gained ground steadily in the next thirty years, and particularly between the two world wars, depicting Charles as a great and much-maligned monarch. This latter view owed a great deal, as will be seen, to Dr W. A. Shaw's introductions to the *Calendars of Treasury Books*, which began to appear in 1904. Two popular biographies which were relatively favourable to Charles were those of Imbert-Terry (1917) and John Drinkwater (1926); but by far the best-known expression of this view is that to be found in Sir Arthur Bryant's very skilfully written biography (first published in 1931),[2] and the same author's volumes on Samuel Pepys (1933–8) go still further in praise of the King and condemnation of his opponents. The old picture was never superseded: the three greatest authorities who wrote in the same period, David Ogg in his *England in the reign of Charles II* (1934), Sir Keith Feiling in *British Foreign Policy, 1660-72* (1930), and Sir George Clark in *The Later Stuarts* (1934) all continued to give unflattering portraits, and post-1945 works such as those of Andrew Browning and J. P. Kenyon have been no more favourable.[3] Yet anyone who lectures to extra-mural audiences knows how popular the Bryant view is.

The two pictures furnish as great a contrast as could be imagined. In its most extreme form, the traditional view represents Charles as a cynical, disillusioned rake, coming back from exile in 1660 resolved to enjoy himself and, in the words of that most famous of all historical clichés, 'never to go on his travels again'. Having no ideals himself, he set a notoriously bad example in a particularly dissipated Court in the pursuit of personal pleasures; his immorality and extravagance continued against a background of imprisoned Puritan preachers and unpaid starving seamen thronging the London streets in the second Dutch War. His laziness and inattentiveness to public affairs were illustrated from the pages of Clarendon or from Pepys's pictures of 'the silliness of the King, playing with his dog all the while, and not minding the business' in Council or (though this story is not first-hand) having supper with Lady Castlemaine and hunting a moth round the room while the Dutch fleet sailed up the River Medway. He was accused of calling Parliament as little as he could, ignoring its advice and bribing its members. He accepted French money in secret to pursue a highly dishonourable foreign policy in support of Louis XIV; and the Secret Treaty of Dover of 1670 included promises of French assistance in men and money for schemes to promote royal absolutism and Roman Catholicism in England. Sometimes, it may be added, condemnations of the Treaty of Dover were not altogether consistent with the accompanying charges of laziness and cynicism.

In this view of Charles's character the most that he could be credited with was a genuine love of the sea and an interest in the fortunes of the English navy, together with a certain low cunning which in the end allowed him to get the better of the Whigs and to end his reign in full authority over a loyal and subservient people. But, this apart, the fortunes of England

under this self-indulgent ruler were at a low ebb: Britannia on
the coins had the features of one of the ladies at Court, Frances
Stuart, while the Medway episode represented the greatest
naval disgrace in British history. Louis XIV was allowed to
pursue his way unchallenged on the Continent, while at home
there was chronic maladministration, embezzlement, friction
and disharmony between the King and the elected representatives of his people.

The rival view of 'Good King Charles's golden days' challenged this picture in several ways. Firstly, new facts came to
light, especially the discovery by Dr W. A. Shaw that Charles's
financial position would have been impossible quite apart from
his own personal extravagance or his lavish grants to his
mistresses. The House of Commons failed to provide sufficient
money for the government's genuine needs. In 1660 the
Convention Parliament had agreed that an annual peace-time
revenue of £1,200,000 was necessary; but in the early years
of the reign the average yield of the taxes actually voted for
this purpose was less than £900,000. Moreover inadequate
provision was made to enable Charles to pay off the debts
which he brought with him to the throne or which he took over
from the Commonwealth. It was calculated that these, together
with the expected deficit for the remainder of 1660, would
amount to some £4,000,000.[4] The financial situation was made
even worse by the depression caused by war and the natural
disasters of the Plague and Fire of London, and Dr Shaw's
conclusion was that it would have been hopeless even with the
best possible management of the resources available. It could
be argued that it was the chronic shortage of money which was
basically responsible for the great disasters of the reign, such
as those of the Second Dutch War. Dr Shaw went further, and
contended that it was the niggardliness of the House of Commons, and its failure to answer the King's legitimate demands,
that drove Charles to negotiate for subsidies from Louis XIV
and thus came to dominate his foreign policy. All this may be
taken as an illustration of the way in which the increased study
of official records, made possible by easier access to state
archives, had led generally to a greater sense of the difficulties
and the responsibilities of government. Whereas at one time
opposition criticisms (and particularly those recorded by

memoir-writers) were accepted at their face value, it had become possible to detect in them much ignorance, irresponsibility, prejudice, and sometimes interested motives. A case on these lines could be built up without difficulty against the opponents of Charles II, especially in their conduct of the Popish Plot crisis in the years 1678–81.

Another change of attitude also influenced the view which was taken of Charles. The mood of disillusionment with great political and religious issues, and the mood of moral self-indulgence which were so prevalent in the 1660s fitted in well enough with the post-1918 period. Charles's lack of idealism, his mistresses and fourteen officially recognized illegitimate children[5] no longer excited the same disapprobation. Like Pepys he was now regarded with some affection as an amusing old rascal, very 'human' in his failings, and it was even possible for Sir Arthur Bryant to argue that anyway Charles's 'affectionate generosity to his bastard sons . . . was no more costly to the country than the normal brood of younger princes denied them by a childless queen'.[6] This is not an argument which one would have expected to find used by a Victorian historian. Nor did parliamentary government itself, with its party fights, enjoy the same respect as in former days. Writers and thinkers from George Bernard Shaw down to less reputable authorities argued that parliamentary institutions often provided a happy hunting-ground for self-seeking, ambitious politicians and for vested interests, and a case was made for an enlightened, national monarch existing in some mysterious fashion 'above party' and ruling personally in the interests of the community as a whole. It was argued that there was positive evidence showing that Charles II was just such a clever and patriotic King. While the worst features of the reign were put down directly or indirectly to the influence of an intolerant and short-sighted House of Commons, stress could be laid on the King's genuine interest in the English navy. In one way it is curious that the biographer of Pepys should be at the same time a favourable biographer of Charles II, for many of the most scandalous stories about the King have their origins in gossip reported by Pepys; but King and Clerk of the Acts shared a devotion to the Fleet, and some contemporaries even thought that Charles took his technical knowledge further than was

fitting in a monarch.[7] At a time when the long national enmity
between England and France had been replaced by the *entente
cordiale* of the twentieth century, the idea was also put forward,
notably by Mr C. H. Hartmann,[8] that the French alliance of
1670 was not really as disastrous as older historians had made
out, but was a master-stroke of diplomacy against England's
commercial and naval rivals, the Dutch, who, it was alleged,
were the real national enemy in 1670. On these grounds the
Secret Treaty of Dover, ignominious failure though it was, was
described as a 'brilliant foreign policy'; and Charles was por-
trayed as a great King, who, far from tamely submitting to be
Louis XIV's pensioner, by sheer diplomatic skill managed to
make use of Louis XIV for English interests. And finally, in
the opinion of this school of writers, Charles, though harassed
by a gang of selfish, rich and unscrupulous opponents in the
'Country Party', managed in masterly fashion to outwit them
in the Popish Plot period, and deservedly ended his reign in
triumph.

It may be remarked that this highly exalted opinion of
Charles II would have been as much of a surprise to his contemporaries as it would to Macaulay and Trevelyan. Neither
friend nor enemy, neither brother nor minister, neither Louis
XIV nor William of Orange rated him very highly. They
recognized that he was full of tricks, completely untrustworthy,
skilful in manœuvre and an able politician in that sense, but in
that sense alone. It is indeed striking how many contemporary
writers, both Whig and Tory, when discussing the King's
character, took the line that he was plentifully endowed with
natural abilities, but that in fact he made too little use of them
except when his back was against the wall.[9] This of course is
not necessarily conclusive. Many of these authors wrote under
the uncomfortable and bitter knowledge that Charles, after a
lifetime protesting his undying devotion to the Church of
England, had on his death bed been received into the Church
of Rome, that a dangerous amount of power had been be-
queathed to his brother, and that revolution had followed. No
one, whatever his political standpoint, could look back upon
Charles II's policies with unqualified approval. And in any case
it is always possible that Charles had hidden merits which
escaped the observation of others who were unable to appre-

ciate the difficulties under which he laboured. At the same time
it would be folly altogether to leave out of account the opinions
of those who actually knew him.

\*     \*     \*

In attempting to discover which of the two conflicting schools
of thought comes nearer to the truth, it may be best to begin
by commenting on certain undoubted features of his personality. Those who are interested in the workings of heredity will
observe the contrast in all these respects between Charles and
his father.

In part this was the result of different environment in youth.
Whereas Charles I's early manhood had been sheltered and
comfortable, with an unquestioned succession to look forward
to, his son before his eleventh birthday appeared in the House
of Lords to plead for the life of Strafford – and pleaded in
vain; at twelve the boy saw his father having to fight for his
prerogative; at eighteen he heard the news that his father had
lost both his crown and his life on a public scaffold. Between
1649 and 1660 he had led a life of some risk and hardship. He
had been involved in unwilling Presbyterianism in Scotland; in
fleeing for his life after the battle of Worcester in 1651 – an
experience which he never forgot and was ready to recount in
detail at the slightest encouragement in after life – and finally
in an exile, among bickering courtiers, in which he was used
and dropped by foreign powers to suit their own convenience.
The result of this had been to give him a very hard-bitten
attitude alike to ideas and to people. He was already prepared
either to accept the Solemn League and Covenant (however
reluctantly) or to appeal for help to the Pope[10] as occasion might
offer. And in handling his courtiers he gave complete confidence
and friendship to none, not even to Hyde, but prided himself
on his 'skill in physiognomy' and his ability to make use of them
all, if necessary by playing off one against another. There was
no parallel to his father's relationship with Buckingham.

In contrast to his father, then, Charles was untouched by any
kind of religious or idealistic fervour. When he landed at Dover
in 1660 the Mayor (evidently a Puritan) presented him with a
bible and Charles declared that he loved it above all things in
the world. In later life he must have built up a collection of

such presentation copies, and he was even able to quote appropriate texts, as when he released the Puritan Lord Wharton from the Tower in 1677, telling him 'Go, and sin no more'. But he was very far from being a pious reader of the Scriptures. His stay on the Continent, almost always in Catholic countries, and his treatment by the Scottish Presbyterians in 1650 had destroyed any Protestant keenness that he might have had. He retained only the belief that 'Presbyterianism was no religion for gentlemen' and a conviction (bolstered by a little reading of Davila on the French religious wars) that religious disputes were only a cloak for political ambitions. It is likely enough that had he had a completely free and unfettered choice he would have declared himself a Catholic before he did: he had lived amongst Catholics, his mother, wife and two favourite mistresses were Catholics; Catholicism was frequently regarded as the religion most conducive to monarchical authority; his desire to relieve his Catholic friends from persecution was well-known; and on his deathbed in 1685 he was received into the Roman Catholic Church by the priest, Father Huddleston, who had been one of a number of Catholics who helped him to escape after the battle of Worcester. But the very fact that he was not received into the Catholic Church until he was on his deathbed shows the place of religion in his scale of values in his lifetime. If he had a vague preference for Catholicism, it was never strong enough to override political considerations, and even the explanation for the 'Catholic clauses' in the Secret Treaty of Dover must be sought elsewhere than in religious zeal.

Charles was therefore no crusader for any sort of ideological principle and his reign was marked by a series of reversals of policy on religion. In some ways this attitude, though to some people it might seem Laodicean and inglorious, stood England in better stead than his father's devotion to his conception of kingship and to the Church of England. He was not personally cruel or vindictive, and after the Restoration he countenanced no 'White Terror' involving serious loss of life amongst the defeated Puritans. It is true that this was partly the result of the political circumstances of the Restoration, and the way in which it was achieved by Monck's forces and ratified by a Convention which contained many Puritans; a policy of revenge would have been dangerous. But it is fair to give some credit to Charles for accepting this. Others, such as the Duke of York, might not have been as lenient in a similar position; and with only a little encouragement the Cavalier Parliament of 1661 might have repealed the Convention's Act of Indemnity and Oblivion. As for the 'Clarendon Code' which that Parliament went on to pass, this was certainly more severe than Charles personally would have wished. If at times he sanctioned persecution, it was not for religious reasons but because it seemed expedient in a temporary political situation. Though this may have been little consolation to the Puritans and Covenanters who suffered, there was a clear difference in motive from the persecution of Charles I and Laud; and at times the fact that the King was known to be lukewarm may have mitigated the severity of the enforcement of the acts. On the other hand, there is no evidence that Charles II believed in toleration as an abstract principle or that he appreciated the spirituality of the Puritans and the Quakers who supplied him with food for mirth; if he made concessions to Dissenters in his Declarations of Indulgence it was partly because he had thought them harmless and partly because indulgence to them would cover a relaxation of the penal laws against his Catholic friends, and it should not be forgotten that in the years of his greatest power, at the end of the reign, it was Catholics and not Protestant Dissenters who benefited from his increased authority.

If Charles's religious indifference contrasts with his father's piety, his immorality makes an equally obvious contrast with his father's devotion to his Queen. There is perhaps little point in making moral judgements about this; still less in enquiring into the validity of Charles's belief that 'God would not make a man miserable only for taking a little pleasure out of the way', or Reresby's plea that 'he was thus far excusable, besides that his complexion led to it, the women seemed to be the aggressors'. But it must be stressed that Charles's addiction to women was not merely a harmless personal weakness: it had serious political consequences. Though, as we have seen, his grants to his mistresses, their children and friends were not the root cause of his insolvency, and although not even Lady Castlemaine or the Duchess of Portsmouth had a fundamental influence on his

policy, this was not as obvious to his contemporaries as it may
be to historians dispassionately reviewing the evidence in the
twentieth century. Indeed his grants to his mistresses were undoubtedly far larger than those of a truly economical King, resolved to cut his coat according to his cloth,[11] and this was as
much a source of exasperation to his ministers – to Clarendon,
to Sir William Coventry, to Danby, to Ormonde and to Halifax
– as it was a cause of opposition to supply bills in the Commons.
A dissolute King with a dissipated Court is not in a good
position to ask Parliament for increased taxation. When, in the
course of casting about for new sources of money, someone in
the Commons suggested a tax on playgoing, and the courtiers
objected that this would be taxing the King's pleasure, one
member, Sir John Coventry, actually dared to enquire 'whether
did the King's pleasure lie among the men or the women that
acted' – a reference to Nell Gwyn and others. Fifty years
earlier no member would have dared to make such a remark; a
generation later no courtier would have dared to slit the nose
of the member who made it, as happened to Coventry on his
way home from the tavern one dark night; here we have in
miniature the transitional stage through which the constitution
was passing. Another famous story tells how two members of
the King's Court, Sir Allen Apsley and Sir Alan Broderick,
'did come drunk the other day into the House, and did both
speak for half an hour together, and could not be either laughed,
or pulled, or bid to sit down and hold their peace, to the great
contempt of the King's servants and cause'. One has to imagine
the effect of such incidents on country gentlemen called upon
to vote increased taxes and to explain them to their neighbours.

Charles's great enemy Shaftesbury once remarked that
reputation was the secret of all government. Whatever one
thinks of Shaftesbury's reputation, Charles's was poor. He was
a good companion, witty (though his sense of humour was
rather coarse); he made no bitter personal enemies; he was on
the whole well enough liked; but he was respected by few,
trusted by scarcely anyone, and held in awe by none.

On the other hand, in spite of his immorality, Charles shared
with all the Stuarts a readiness to be influenced by family ties.
During the Exclusion crisis he could have disarmed much of the
opposition by consenting either to the divorce of Queen

Catherine of Braganza, followed by his own remarriage, or to
the exclusion of his brother from the succession, but he would
not buy a quiet life by accepting either solution, though he was
repeatedly unfaithful to Catherine and held no high opinion of
James. His favourite sister Henrietta's part in the negotiations leading up to the Treaty of Dover is well-known; so also
is his over-indulgence of his son Monmouth. His attitude to
his nephew William of Orange fell into the same pattern and
was disastrously misconceived. Charles thought of himself as
the head of the family and expected William to follow the path
that Charles considered best for the general family interests;
and it came as a shock when in 1672 William refused to accept the inferior position that his uncle had planned for him,
and brought about the ruin of his uncle's foreign policy.

If we make one final point of comparison between Charles
and his father, there can be no doubt that Charles had a much
better mind, a much better judgement of men and situations, a
more accurate sense of what was possible, a keener intelligence
in general. Though he was not particularly widely read[12] nor
the possessor of artistic tastes equal to Charles I's, everyone
who reads and compares the speeches and reported conversations of the two Kings must agree that Charles II's mind had
an edge to it which his father's had not. Only Charles II could
have made the detached, sardonic observation, amidst the
general rejoicing of the Restoration, 'that it could be nobody's
fault but his own that he had stayed so long abroad when all
mankind wished him so heartily at home'. Contemporaries who
had no great admiration for him in other respects agreed about
his natural intelligence; but as we have seen, they frequently
thought too that he did not use his mind enough, that he was
lazy, and that he neglected public business for his personal
pleasures.

It is not easy to judge whether Clarendon, Pepys, Burnet and
others were right in this. What standards are we to apply for
laziness in kings? Many kings have not unnaturally taken the
view that their ministers were selected precisely to do as much
of the work as possible for them, while they themselves took the
responsibility for the final decisions. A general impression
might be that Charles was less consistently attentive to public
business than Louis XIV, the Great Elector, William of Orange

or James II, but rather more so than Louis XIII, Philip IV, or his own father and grandfather. But variations are discernible at different periods in the reign. In the early years the complaints of contemporaries about his lack of interest in business are far too numerous to be ignored. We have to remember that his past had given him virtually no administrative experience and no knowledge of the traditional procedures by which government was carried on; and naturally he fell back on those like Clarendon who had that knowledge. Later in the reign, when his own experience (especially in foreign affairs) came to equal or even exceed that of his ministers, the charge is less true; but one can easily observe that his interest depended on the urgency of the situation facing him. About financial details he cared little; no one could have been less likely to emulate Henry VII's personal supervision of the accounts, and as we have seen his ministers complained of his refusal to economize sufficiently rigorously. No one, however, could accuse Charles II of physical laziness; he took exercise of every kind, and left London for Newmarket at five o'clock in the morning when in his fifties; and usually he enjoyed such robust good health, that his unexpected illness in 1679 caused a first-rate political crisis. There are, however, some signs that after surviving the Exclusion crisis his mental grip relaxed in his last years.

But in this connection we must note also that the old charge of laziness resulted partly from Charles's predilection for informal methods of doing business. Whereas Louis XIV's ambassadors claimed to know what their master would be doing at any given time of the day, Charles had no such fixed and formal routine, and little penchant for ceremonial. To the Privy Council he preferred small committees like the committee of foreign affairs, or, still better, private chats with ministers or ambassadors, one at a time, often in the rooms of the Queen, or those of Lady Castlemaine or the Duchess of Portsmouth. There the real decisions could be taken or modified with the minimum of fuss. In this way it was possible to entrust different ministers with different secrets, and to play off one against another, while keeping the final control in his own hands. In spite of his formal Council meetings, his official audiences to ambassadors, and even his revival of the practice of attending debates in the Lords fairly regularly – he can scarcely have believed that it was 'better than the play', though he said it was – these were not his natural background. To that extent at least there is substance in the idea that Charles liked to mix business with pleasure.

This way of doing business, whether it be deemed lazy or not, also suited Charles's desire, partly temperamental and partly deliberate, to avoid committing himself to definite lines of action for as long as he could. Decisions were postponed wherever possible; different diplomatic policies were left open; he was disinclined to give all his favour to one minister, a fact on which the enemies of Clarendon, Danby and Ormonde were ready to play. He was not, in the present writer's view, a man with consistent and far-reaching plans. His reign was one of a long series of hand-to-mouth expedients, rather than one of deep and prolonged schemes. He was essentially an opportunist, seeking for measures to meet some present situation or to stop some immediate gap, and relying with great self-confidence on his power to manipulate other people for his own advantage. He prided himself on his knowledge of 'physiognomy' and his ability to read character. He used to the full his remarkable powers of dissimulation, so much so that it is as difficult for historians as it was for contemporaries to tell when (if ever) Charles meant what he said. The safest rule is certainly to judge him by what he did and not by the promises or professions of goodwill which he made in profusion.

It is, however, a mistake to over-rate Charles's cleverness, as is often done. Sometimes he was 'too clever by half', and many of his difficulties were brought on himself by his own excessive subtlety. But he had a shrewd sense of the weaknesses of his position, notably his lack both of financial independence and of armed forces and his consequent dependence on at least the acquiescence of the powerful classes in the country. When he was beaten, as he frequently was, he knew it, and unlike his father he knew how to give way. He abandoned his Declaration of Indulgence in 1673 and made no attempt to repeat it, even in the period when his authority was apparently unquestioned after 1681. Nor would he risk too much in support of an unpopular minister. In 1667 he was prepared not only to dismiss Clarendon (a step for which there was good reason) but even to encourage the Commons to impeach him and drive him out to die in exile (which is much harder to justify). The contrast between Charles's abandonment of a minister with Clarendon's long record of faithful service and his father's obstinate support of Buckingham against attack is marked. Yet it must not be forgotten that this greater flexibility, or opportunism, had accompanying disadvantages. His ministers always remembered how Charles had abandoned Clarendon to his enemies. They knew that they could not rely on him, and many of them took their measures accordingly.

There is however one apparent exception to this general opportunism of Charles. This was in the three years preparation for the Dutch War of 1672, including the Secret Treaty of Dover with Louis XIV in 1670. In more senses than one this is the central problem of the reign. More than any other act of policy in the reign the Treaty of Dover can be clearly distinguished as the result of Charles's own initiative; and whether Charles is to be considered a wise and patriotic monarch or something much less than that must consequently depend on one's view of his aims and motives at that point. Furthermore, the history of the second half of the reign takes its colour from the suspicions which the French alliance generated.

The controversies over the Secret Treaty have concentrated on two main points. Were Charles's motives in negotiating it selfish, personal ones or were they patriotic? and was the policy of a French alliance against the Dutch a disastrous underestimation of the danger from Louis XIV, or was it in England's true interests?

In relation to the first question, we may dismiss at the outset any idea that Charles was 'driven into the arms of Louis XIV' by the niggardliness of his House of Commons. The project of a further war with the Dutch made a bad financial situation not better, but even worse. The subsidy of 3,000,000 livres a year promised by the Treaty sounds impressive until it is calculated that this amounted to only some £225,000 in English money, and the further lump sum of 2,000,000 livres provided for in the 'Catholic clauses' brought in only a further £150,000. For the previous Dutch war Parliament had voted some £5,000,000, and considerably more than that had actually been spent. Useful as the French subsidy would be, the plan for war with the Dutch without a previous appeal to Parliament could only accelerate the bankruptcy which had long been threatening, and the Stop of the Exchequer in fact took place two months before war broke out, when the bankers failed to make the advances necessary to complete the naval preparations. Financial considerations, in spite of the time spent haggling over them, were only secondary, and the treaty's central aim must be sought elsewhere, either in the provisions for aggression against the Dutch or in the 'Catholic clauses'. In considering these it is safest to keep in mind that the bulk of the actual preparations made after the treaty was signed (as distinct from the talk which went on before it) were for the war with the Dutch, and so it is reasonable to conclude that the ruin of the Dutch was the main objective. Charles certainly had a keen personal interest in British supremacy at sea, and felt deeply the humiliation of the Medway incident in 1667, when the Dutch sailed unopposed into British waters, broke the chain across the river, burnt several of the capital ships and towed away the flagship, the *Royal Charles*.

If naval supremacy, with the attendant prospect of making inroads into the commercial position of the Dutch, was the main objective, what then was the purpose of the 'Catholic clauses'? For the French alliance was first made, not by ordinary diplomatic negotiation (as might have been possible, in view of Louis XIV's fixed resolve to destroy the Dutch for their 'ingratitude' in making the Triple Alliance against him in 1668), but by a private intrigue, known to only two of Charles's principal ministers, Arlington and Clifford, and involving a promise by Charles to declare himself a Roman Catholic[13] at some unspecified date in the future, in return for French assistance in money and even troops to crush any opposition. This was Charles's own idea, not that of Louis XIV, who was afraid that it might hold up the attack on the United Provinces and was pessimistic about Charles's prospects if he tried to carry it out. It is difficult, however, to take Charles's promise very seriously. His interest in Catholicism was lukewarm at best; and if the dangers of such a policy were obvious to Louis XIV across the Channel, they were far more so to Charles in London. He made no detailed preparations for keeping his promise, and was fertile in excuses for postponing it. The purpose of these clauses seems to have been the simpler one of enabling him to reach a closer and more personal relationship with Louis. Since the beginning of his reign Charles had striven without success to reach an alliance with Louis, the most powerful monarch in Europe, who had men and money at his disposal for his allies. Louis had sent plenty of expressions of good-will in return, but that was all. Instead of making concrete proposals he had preferred in 1662 to renew the traditional Franco-Dutch alliance; and in 1666 he had caused England considerable embarrassment by keeping his obligations to the Dutch and joining them in the Anglo-Dutch war, even though he kept his intervention to a minimum. If Charles was disappointed in this way, Louis on his side was disappointed by Charles's action in making the Triple Alliance with the Dutch in 1668 to restrict his conquests from Spain in Flanders. By 1669, therefore, a situation had been reached in which each monarch wished for his own purposes to gain the alliance of the other in order to attack the Dutch, but each feared from past experience that he could not trust the other's professions of friendship; and it so happened that neither trusted the other's ministers. The French did not like Arlington, and Charles did not get on well with the French ambassador in London, Colbert de Croissy, but could not easily ask for the replacement of the great Colbert's brother. It was the function of the 'Catholic design' to overcome this deadlock, with Charles's sister and Louis's sister-in-law, Henrietta, Duchess of Orleans, to act as an informal channel for communicating it. Entrusted with the secret of Charles's 'conversion', Louis was both convinced of Charles's sincerity and, as a pious son of the Church, unable to refuse to co-operate, whatever his misgivings about the practicability of the plan. By this means not only was agreement for joint action against the Dutch reached (including an additional subsidy of £150,000 which would at least keep the fleet at sea for a month) but Charles might hope to extract further advantages from the more confidential relationship which had been reached. The long-term disadvantages of incorporating such clauses into a treaty were not apparent until later.

If it is conceded that the main purpose of the Treaty of Dover may have been the attack on the Dutch in England's naval and commercial interests, and that the 'Catholic clauses' may have been rather a means to achieve the French alliance than part of a clear and deliberate design to 'restore absolutism and Roman Catholicism' in England as the older tradition would have us believe, it still does not follow that Charles's view of British interests was the correct one. Mr C. H. Hartmann and others argue that the historian should not allow himself to be influenced by hindsight – by his knowledge today that France became Britain's great overseas rival in the eighteenth century; they would say that *in 1670* Charles was justified in thinking that the Dutch were still the real danger – and in plotting to ruin them by a treacherous and cold-blooded attack. But this argument can be answered in two different ways.

On the one hand, the Anglo-French rivalry of the future was already discernible to some eyes in 1670: Colbert's policies were already beginning to bear fruit. Louis had always refused to yield that salute to the English flag which Englishmen prized as an acknowledgement of their supremacy in the Channel; his fleet had been strong enough to affect the English strategy in 1666 and was to be strong enough to defeat the great De Ruyter in the Mediterranean in 1676; there were colonial disputes in the West Indies, notably over St Kitts; and commercial interests in the city were already concerned about Colbert's protectionist policy.[14] Charles's own ministers had thought it worth while to keep a spy in the new dockyard at Brest, and Charles had asked the Duchess of Orleans to warn Louis of the danger that aggressive French commercial policies might spoil the good political relations for which he hoped. The East India Company and the City of London were markedly less enthusiastic about the war against the Dutch than they had been in 1664, and it seems that Charles was pursuing a line of thought which was already losing ground amongst those most directly concerned, for whom the French rather than the Dutch were becoming the enemy.

At the same time it was also true that in any case victory over the Dutch by means of a French alliance would have implied conceding to Louis XIV domination over the Low Countries. Under the terms of the Treaty of Dover the gains which Louis was to make were left unspecified; and the conditions which he actually offered to the Dutch would have had the effect of turning the United Provinces into a French protectorate. With the Dutch left helpless, or even in orbit round the *Roi Soleil*, Louis would have been free to deal with the Spanish Netherlands as he chose, or even settle the Spanish succession problem in his own way if Carlos II of Spain should die. His promise to maintain his peace settlement of 1668 with Spain would not have been worth the paper that it was written on. If this line of reasoning is justified, then Charles II's foreign policy can only be defended on the basis that Louis's advances in Europe, and particularly in the Low Countries, were of no concern to England. This runs counter to one of the main principles of English foreign policy from the sixteenth century to the twentieth.

Charles's alliance with France is sometimes defended on the negative basis that if he had not made it Louis XIV would have turned back to the Dutch and left England once more in the isolation from which she had suffered in 1666. This may well have been a genuine fear on Charles's part, but if so he did not appreciate the extent either of Louis's hostility to the Dutch after the Triple Alliance or of the anxiety of the Dutch about Louis's expansionist policies.

The claim that Charles's was a 'brilliant foreign policy' must fail on these grounds; but in any case such a claim could not plausibly be made for a policy which proved to be such a miserable failure. Charles miscalculated alike the stubbornness of Dutch resistance, the personality of his nephew William (who refused to accept the part of protégé assigned to him) and finally the reaction of his own subjects. Eventually in the Treaty of Westminster in 1674 he admitted defeat: under pressure from his Parliament he made the separate peace which he had previously promised not to make, and he had nothing at all to show for his efforts.

But the matter did not end there. Charles could not continue as though the Treaty of Dover had never been. It made it very difficult for him ever to pursue a truly independent policy in the future should he wish to do so; if he did, it would be in Louis's power to remind him about his promise to declare himself a Roman Catholic. Only once, in the summer of 1680, did Louis actually authorize his ambassador in London to drop hints about a certain secret which his master possessed, and which, if revealed, could ruin Charles; but the knowledge must have exercised a restraining influence upon Charles at other times as well, and it was a matter on which he dared not confide in his principal minister, Danby. At the same time, within England the French alliance bred distrust and suspicion of Charles's motives and led to mounting criticism, which was fostered by Dutch propaganda. The reversal of the policy of the Triple Alliance of 1668 against France could never be satisfactorily explained to the public; and in the minds of many the alliance with the authoritarian and Catholic monarch was given a sinister interpretation, which was connected with the Catholicism of the heir to the throne, the Duke of York. Time after time in the debates of the last sessions of the Cavalier Parliament opposition speakers used the argument that those responsible for such a foreign policy could not be trusted to control English affairs. Danby would have liked to counter this by declaring war against France, but this Charles dared not do, and his wrigglings only succeeded in losing him the French subsidies without conciliating English public opinion.

So far from the Dover Treaty being a masterstroke of policy, therefore, it led directly to the straits to which he was reduced in 1678, and from which he was only extricated in the end because his opponents overplayed their hand in the Popish Plot agitation. Unquestionably Charles showed considerable skill in outwitting the Whigs, and defeating their attempts to use the fears generated by Titus Oates's story to pass an Exclusion Bill; but even here his astuteness has probably been overestimated. His success was not the result of a consistent plan pursued from the very outbreak of the Plot, but rather a matter of clinging to certain assets which he possessed, and after several tactical defeats seizing his chances when they came. Through all the temporary excitements which the Whigs fostered he retained some very solid advantages. One of these was a House of Lords, which, containing many of his ministers, peers created by him and the 'dead weight' (in Shaftesbury's phrase) of a bench of bishops appointed by him, had a majority large enough to block the Exclusion Bill in 1680. An even greater advantage was the possession of the power to summon, prorogue or dissolve Parliaments as the King thought fit; from this, unlike his father, Charles never departed, and without a House of Commons in which to focus their discontent the

Whigs were helpless. Moreover, no external circumstances came to the rescue of the Whigs. This time Scotland and Ireland were firmly under the King's control; and an improvement in the yield of the customs duties and other taxation, fostered by Danby's administration to an extent which Shaftesbury probably never realized, meant that he was never so dependent on parliamentary assistance that he had to keep Parliament permanently in session. Eventually, in March 1681, Louis XIV rallied to his side and provided a subsidy which was sufficiently large to remove anxiety; and this left no reason why Charles should summon Parliament for the rest of his reign. Debarred from constitutional means of protest, the Whigs as a whole were not desperate enough to have recourse to unconstitutional ones; there was a general reluctance on the part of the aristocracy and gentry of all sides to run the risk of another upheaval such as had followed the events of 1642, and Charles's propagandists made effective use of the idea that ' '41 was come again', stressing and exaggerating the extent to which Whig support came from 'the rabble', the less respectable people, and Dissenters.

Charles's success, then, was less the result of a plan clearly thought out in advance than of keeping his nerve, and making use of his opportunities when Louis XIV (fearing that the situation might develop to William of Orange's advantage) came to the rescue at the same time as the spell of the Popish Plot tales was beginning to lose its power. Nevertheless his victory was a considerable one when it came. For the last four years of his life he ruled without Parliament; by the *quo warranto* process, whether used or merely threatened, he gained control over the City of London and other corporations; the Lords Lieutenant were nominated by him, and the commissions of the peace were remodelled to his advantage; to the bench he promoted lawyers like Jeffreys. From the pulpit doctrines of passive obedience to the King by divine right were proclaimed without opposition; his opponents were silenced by censorship or fear after the execution of Russell and Sidney for alleged participation in the Rye House Plot. Charles lived his last years in peace, without challenge to his authority. Yet if Charles had this considerable measure of personal success, it is improbable that the years 1681–5 can be called successful from the national point of view. If there was rest from political excitement, it was at best the rest of stagnation. In concrete terms Charles achieved nothing memorable; abroad Louis XIV made himself master of Luxemburg, and at home there was censorship and persecution which promised ill for the development of English polititical and religious liberties.

Even Charles's personal success was of a brittle kind. The French subsidy came to an end in 1684, leaving the financial situation just manageable, but vulnerable to any accidental circumstance; and if Parliament had to be called, even the remodelling of the corporations could not guarantee a completely acquiescent House of Commons, as was shown in James II's 1685 Parliament. Wisely he broke no law save the Triennial Act; unlike his successor he issued no Declaration of Indulgence and did not flout the Test Act. His shrewd sense of the limitations of his position, possibly strengthened by increasing indolence, did not desert him. And in the time of his death he was fortunate. Had he died five years earlier he would have been written off as a failure; had he died five years later his failure to make a positive use of his personal success might have been revealed. As it was, he died in 1685 and was succeeded by a brother whose rapid downfall contrasted sharply with his own peaceful end. But his brother's folly is not a satisfactory reason for exalting Charles. Perhaps the safest conclusion might be that although the graver charges of the Whig historians against him were exaggerated, he cannot convincingly be built up into anything like a great monarch.

## NOTES

1. *Essay on Milton*, in *Works* (1903), v. 35–6; and *History of England* (1913 edn.), i. 146–51.

2. It should be said that in the preface to his second edition (1955) Sir Arthur Bryant writes that 'If I were to rewrite it now . . . I might try to balance my understanding of the King and the men of the loyal party who stood by the Throne with a greater understanding and sympathy for those who opposed them' and that 'Charles cannot be called a great King or a great man'. But the book is substantially unaltered.

3. A. Browning, *Thomas Osborne, Earl of Danby* (1951); J. P. Kenyon, *Robert Spencer, Earl of Sunderland* (1958) and *The Stuarts* (1958), ch. iv.

4. *English Historical Documents, 1660–1714*, ed. A. Browning (1953), pp. 279–88.

5. The list is in G.E.C., *Complete Peerage*, vol. vi, Appendix F.

6. Op. cit. p. 240.

7. Burnet, *History of My Own Time*, ed. O. Airy (1897), i. 167.

8. *The King My Brother* (1954) combines the essential points from Mr Hartmann's earlier works.

9. See the examples printed by A. Browning, *English Historical Documents, 1660–1714*, pp. 899–902; also Halifax's 'Character of Charles II', printed in H. C. Foxcroft, *Life of Halifax* (1898), ii. 343–60; Burnet, i. 166–8 and ii. 466–74.

10. F. J. Routledge, 'Charles II and the Cardinal de Retz', in *Transactions of the Royal Historical Society*, 5th Ser. VI., pp. 49–68.

11. In the British Museum, Add. MSS 28094, fo. 54, there is an itemized list of payments to the Duchess of Portsmouth and to 'Nelly', between 27 March 1676 and 14 March 1679 The former received £55,198.7s.11d. and the latter £16,041.15s.6d., and the total for these three years for these two women alone was not far short of the equivalent of one month of the King's revenue.

12. Cf. Dr E. S. de Beer's article on Charles II in *The Royal Society, its Origins and Founders*, ed. Sir Harold Hartley (1960), pp. 39–45. Charles shared the fashionable taste for scientific experiments and had a private laboratory, but this was mere dilettantism and the Royal Society owed him little besides his name.

13. It is a fallacy to suppose that Charles promised to restore England to the Catholic faith; all that he undertook was to declare *himself* a Catholic (see the terms of the treaty, published in translation by A. Browning, *English Historical Documents 1660–1714*, pp. 863–7). But in a century in which the principle of *cujus regio ejus religio* normally operated, few people believed that a situation in which the ruler and ruled belonged to different faiths could be permanent – hence the anxieties aroused after 1673 by the knowledge that Charles's heir was a Catholic.

14. Cf. Margaret E. Priestley, 'Anglo-French Trade and the "Unfavourable Balance" Controversy, 1660–85', *Economic History Review* (1951), pp. 37–52.

## BIBLIOGRAPHICAL NOTE

In addition to the works mentioned in the text and the Notes, there is now a further biography by Maurice Ashley (*Charles II: the Man and the Statesman*, 1971), which reaches a general conclusion not greatly different from my own. The reader in search of more detailed information about the reign may now refer to Mary F. Keeler's second edition of Godfrey Davies's extensive *Bibliography of the Stuart Period* (1970), which includes works published down to about 1965; W. L. Sachse's *Restoration England, 1660–89* (1971) is less exhaustive, but includes works published down to 1970.

We still await Professor D. Chandaman's book on the financial problems of the reign, which, it is understood, will cast serious doubt on Dr W. A. Shaw's figures and interpretation referred to above on p. 136.

# PART SIX

# Mercantilism

# MERCANTILISM

*by*

## CHARLES WILSON

### The Changing Meaning of a Word

The word 'Mercantilism', Professor E. A. Johnson has written, 'has become a positive nuisance. It is confused with autarky, with nationalism, with protection... Journalists have taken up the word and use it carelessly, as they use many others. At their hands "mercantilism" may be an antonym for *laissez-faire* or a synonym for stupidity.'[1] Yet it would be difficult to abolish a word around which so much history and controversy has grown. Better, perhaps, to see whether a look at the historical origins of the word can disperse some of the confusion. The words 'mercantilist' and 'mercantilism' were unknown in the seventeenth and for most of the eighteenth century, and the phrase 'the mercantile system' only acquired meaning at the hands of Adam Smith. Smith borrowed it, in all probability, from the writings of the Physiocrats, where it appeared sporadically. From *The Wealth of Nations* the phrase passed into popular usage. Its first use by Adam Smith was not, seemingly, controversial: he merely used it to contrast a trading economy with an agricultural economy: thus the chapter 'Of the Principles of the Commercial or Mercantile System' begins:

'The different progress of opulence in different ages and nations has given occasion to two different systems of political economy, with regard to enriching the people. The one may be called the system of commerce, the other that of agriculture. I shall endeavour to explain both as fully and distinctly as I can, and shall begin with the system of commerce. It is the modern system and is best understood in our own country and in our own times.'

He passes on to discuss what is, to him, the economic crime of the system – its confusion of wealth with money which had led its supporters to regard the accumulation of gold and silver as the principal object of economic policy. Such erroneous ideas, he thought, had led governments in many countries to prohibit the export of gold and silver. Others, like Thomas Mun, claiming to see a trifle further, had argued that the flow of money was controlled by the balance of trade and had persuaded policy makers to adopt as their prime object the attainment of a favourable balance of trade. Such were the arguments 'addressed by merchants to Parliaments and the Councils of Princes, to nobles and country gentlemen . . .'; but between tradesmen who did not understand the principles of national policy and gentlemen who failed to grasp the principles of trade, policy fell into an erroneous obsession with trade balances. Thus 'from one fruitless care' (the prohibition of the export of bullion) men turned to another, 'much more intricate, much more embarrassing, and equally fruitless'. The erroneous maxims of Thomas Mun had spread outwards from England until they had been adopted by all other commercial countries. Disregarding the importance of home trade, governments had set themselves the totally unnecessary and mischievous task of preventing that 'scarcity of money' which they feared as the prime source of the recurrent trade depressions. Yet (Adam Smith thought) they had no more occasion to be anxious over the supply of money than over the supply of any other commodity. Like them, it would be regulated by the laws of supply and demand and it was about as sensible to try and keep unnecessary quantities of treasure in a country as it would be 'to attempt to increase the good cheer of private families by obliging them to keep an unnecessary number of kitchen utensils'. To those who tried to argue that precious metals represented a store of purchasing power with which the emergencies of war might be financed, he replied that this could be equally well done by the export of commodities and by the use of credit and paper money.

The 'two great engines' by which the mercantile system proposed to enrich every country with 'an advantageous balance of trade' were a set of measures designed to encourage exports and another set to discourage imports: or, more strictly, to encourage the export of manufactures and the provision of imported raw materials, and to discourage the import of manufactures and the loss of domestically produced raw materials. Yet in practice this government interference did not benefit the nation as a whole: it only benefited a section of it at the expense of other sections. The linen export bounty enriched the exporters but damaged the consumers and the spinners. Powerful industries had the ear of the government and got what they wanted: the occupations of the poor and indigent received scant attention. And this contravened the principles of nature; for

'to hurt in any degree the interest of any one order of citizens, for no other purpose but to promote that of some other, is evidently contrary to that justice and equality of treatment which the sovereign owes to all the different orders of his subjects.'

The gravamen of the charges brought by the author of *The Wealth of Nations* against the mercantile system is, then, that it is a conspiracy contrived by a minority for their own interests; '... our merchants and manufacturers have been by far the principal architects'. It professes so to regulate trade as to secure a favourable balance in the national interest but its real object is to secure our manufacturers a monopoly of the home market. The kernel of the argument is this:

Consumption is the sole end and purpose of all production and the interest of the producer ought to be attended to only so far as it may be necessary for promoting that of the consumer ... But in the mercantile system, the interest of the consumer is almost constantly sacrificed to that of the producer; and it seems to consider production and not consumption as the ultimate end and object of all industry and commerce.

Whether we regard Adam Smith's charges against the mercantile system as valid or not, there can be no doubt that he chose an apt title for his target: for him it was, without any shadow of doubt, a system of policy contrived *by merchants* for *mercantile ends*. The attack was brilliantly successful: for more than a century the sound of the blows reverberated through the

academic and political corridors. In one country, however – if
Germany may be so described at this time – Smith's views were
never popular. During the first half of the nineteenth century,
Germans found the views of Friedrich List more to their taste,
and List was violently opposed to most of what Adam Smith
stood for. Later in the century, as the work of unification in
Germany went on, List's disbelief in *laissez-faire* found a new
and more historical expression in the writings of the so-called
'historical school' of economists, and notably in the works of
Gustav Schmoller. Schmoller's studies of the economic policy
of Frederick the Great contained a long section on *The Mercantile System and its Historical Significance* which gave an
entirely new interpretation and was to have great influence, not
only in Germany but elsewhere. Schmoller's main theme is that
economic institutions are dependent on *political* bodies; the
notion that economic life was a process dependent on individual
action was fallacious. While all other States had made rapid
economic progress, Germany had failed to do so 'for lack of
politico-economic organization', viz. a state policy. For:

'. . . mercantilism . . . in its innermost kernel is nothing but
state-making – not state-making in a narrow sense but state-
making and national-economy-making at the same time.'

The central economic mechanism was to Schmoller much
the same as to Smith: the export of manufactured goods was
encouraged by export bounties, by the ban on manufactured
imports and on raw material exports. Trade was promoted by
commercial treaties, shipping and fishing were encouraged by
bounties and legislative aids, the colonial trades were reserved
to the mother countries in Europe. The balance of trade he
regarded as a secondary consequence of a conception of economic processes which grouped them according to states. The
wars which filled the seventeenth and eighteenth centuries 'had
economic objects as their main aim':

'In all ages [wrote Schmoller] history has been wont to treat
national power and national wealth as sisters: perhaps they
were never so closely associated as then.'

Later writers have sometimes regarded Schmoller as the prophet of 'power': yet this and other passages show clearly that, Prussian though he was, Schmoller did not regard power as an end in itself. Power is usually the servant, or at most the partner, in a dual system. States which followed mercantilist principles 'give the economic life of their people its necessary basis of power and a corresponding impulse to its economic movement . . .' He retained, too, sufficient objectivity to praise those governments which had thus wrested the lead in the struggle for supremacy from poorer, weaker, less organized states:

'. . . it was precisely those Governments which understood how to put the might of their fleets and admiralties, the apparatus of customs laws and navigation laws, with rapidity, boldness and clear purpose, at the service of the economic interests of the nation and state, which obtained thereby the lead in the struggle and in riches and industrial prosperity.'

Though the inspiration of Schmoller's ideas was undoubtedly parochial, they had a wide influence, partly because they were informed by a strong historic sense, partly because events were leading to a revival of nationalist economic policies in other countries besides Germany. In England, for example, William Cunningham shared the German scholars' conviction that political institutions had a profound influence on economic development: this idea is basic to his great work, *The Growth of English Industry and Commerce*, which owed much to Schmoller and his predecessors. Indeed, Cunningham appears at times to go further than Schmoller in defining power as the object of mercantilist policy – thus:

'Politicians of the sixteenth, seventeenth and the greater part of the eighteenth century, were agreed in trying to regulate all commerce and industry so that the *power* of England relative to other nations might be promoted, and in carrying out this aim had no scruples in trampling on private interests.'

The wheel had, indeed, come full circle in the century since Adam Smith had condemned the mercantile system as being a private conspiracy of merchants for their own ends. It was now seen as a policy of state-building in which private mercantile interests were, if necessary, crushed; and, as such, the system was seen by some as praiseworthy. (One may remark in passing that one school of historians, led by George Unwin, disagreed profoundly with this view, and said so.) The tradition thus established, that mercantilist policy was strongly orientated to the pursuit of power, reached its climax in the large-scale synthesis of material and views contained in Professor Eli Heckscher's *Mercantilism*, which had appeared in Sweden in 1931 and was published in an English translation in 1934. As a synthesis of ideas Heckscher's work was novel in important respects: for while he followed and extended the methods of those like Schmoller and Cunningham who had emphasized the element of power in mercantilism, he did so not to praise it but to condemn. A firm believer in orthodox classical economy theory, he found it (one suspects) difficult to keep patience with those who saw any economic virtue in this system of wholesale interference with the economic process called mercantilism (the German *Merkantilismus* now came to replace the older English label in common speech). Beginning with the modest presentation of mercantilism as 'an instrumental concept' to help towards understanding a particular historical period more clearly, Heckscher built up the idea of a uniform body of doctrine and practice throughout the states of Europe which he grouped under five headings: (1) Unification, (2) The Pursuit of Power, (3) Protection, (4) Monetary Policy – the accumulation of treasure, (5) A Conception of Society. Of these objects the Pursuit of Power was clearly the most important, and though in subsequent controversy Heckscher seemed to concede that mercantilists sometimes had other, e.g. commercial, ends in view, he did not ever stray far from the main thesis enunciated in the following passage:

'The most vital aspect of the problem is whether power is conceived as an end in itself, or only as a means for gaining something else, such as the well-being of the nation in this world or its everlasting salvation in the next.'

The *laissez-faire* school of thought, he believed, aimed at power only as a means to wealth, while medieval economic thought had been a branch of theology. Mercantilists alone had given power itself pride of place until *laissez-faire* thinkers and statesmen had changed the order of priority. 'All countries', he wrote, 'in the nineteenth century made the creation of wealth their lodestar, with small regard to its effect upon the power of the State, while the opposite had been the case previously'. The rights and wrongs of this may for the moment be disregarded. Two unsatisfactory points about Heckscher's interpretation may be noted at this point. First, that it did not make for clarity to use the term 'mercantilism' to describe a system of *Staatsbildung* which aimed not at 'mercantile' objectives but at 'power'. Second, Heckscher did not explain how it came about that the principal authors of mercantilist literature – Mun, Misselden, Molynes, Child, Gee, Decker and many others – who were, almost without exception, *merchants*, should have shown such a tenacious interest in power politics. It seems improbable, to say the least of it, that they would have done so if they had not thought the system served some useful 'mercantile' purpose.

Finally, no survey of changing attitudes towards mercantilist ideas should neglect the contribution of Lord Keynes, in the Appendix to his *General Theory of Employment, Interest and Money* (1936). Keynes was an economist, not an historian, but his views on mercantilism are significant for historians, for it is unlikely that they can go on treating as merely antique ignorance economic policies which resemble remarkably closely policies followed today by scores of Governments disposing of the help and advice of an army of statisticians and economic advisers. Keynes's thesis, briefly, was that the postulates of classical theory could not be held to apply universally. For 200 years theorists and statesmen alike had been agreed on the 'peculiar advantage' of a favourable balance of trade if it resulted in an efflux of precious metals, and much practical policy had remained based on this belief, even when the theorists had become converted to the view that the mechanism of foreign trade was self-adjusting. Keynes was not therefore disposed to accept without question the view that the mercantilist argument represented merely intellectual confusion. On the contrary, he thought that it contained a certain logic that was

related to the economic condition of the times. The volume of
economic activity depended on the volume of investment. This,
in turn, would be stimulated by the low rates of interest which
a favourable balance would tend to create by increasing the
quantity of precious metals inside the economy. 'We, the
faculty of economists,' he wrote, 'prove to have been guilty of
presumptuous error in treating as a puerile obsession what for
centuries has been a prime object of practical statecraft.'

Keynes's attempt to rehabilitate the mercantilists brought
down on his head the wrath of the orthodox, including a
spirited rejoinder by Heckscher, for whom all this was un-
historical and heretical, an ephemeral by-product of the depression and unemployment problem of the early thirties. Others
found it difficult to resist the conclusion that the mercantilist
essay in the economics of intervention deserved more serious
sympathetic study than it had received, especially as the suspicion grew that the age of *laissez-faire* had perhaps been an
interlude between the mercantile age and what threatened to
be another extended period of regulation according to principles not unlike those of the earlier period. Thus the
Chancellor of the Exchequer speaking in November 1946
could lay it down that 'the first principle to be adopted in our
export policy was to export fully manufactured goods in preference to partly manufactured goods and goods in which the raw
material values were as low as possible compared to the value
of work done on that raw material. The more brains and
craftsmanship we can export, the better for our balance of payments position and thus the higher our standard of living.'
That economists and Cabinet Ministers had come back to
beliefs and policies so close to those of the mercantilists did not
mean that such views need necessarily be accepted as correct.
It did, nevertheless, suggest that it was hardly decent for a
generation which attached so much importance to the balance
of trade argument to acquiesce in condemning 'the puerile
obsession' in their ancestors without more careful enquiry.

## The System in England

This brief survey of the idea of mercantilism makes it clear
that interpretation has varied from age to age, from country to

country, and from writer to writer. Yet it is worth taking another look to see if there is any ground common to these interpretations. So far as the *literature* is concerned, mercantilism is a mirror large enough to reflect an infinite number of economic viewpoints. Yet most of the accounts of the mercantilist age, though they have differed as to the motives, the origins, the efficacy and the wisdom of mercantilism, have agreed that it was essentially bound up with the notion of the balance of trade. In England, at any rate, few things are more striking than the growing concordance between thought and policy from the mid-sixteenth to the mid-eighteenth century.

Before that time, many diverse strands of later thought are already present – men were forbidden to export the materials needed by the clothiers and other manufacturers, the export of coin and bullion was prohibited, numerous Acts for the encouragement of English shipping were already on the Statute Book: and so on. Yet they were not so far bound together by any clear or comprehensive set of expressed ideas. By the mid-eighteenth century, new, critical and challenging ideas of economic freedom were coming forward. The two intervening centuries form the Mercantilist Age, when thinkers and policy makers drew the scattered acts and notions of earlier ages together within a framework of national, often nationalistic, economic policy which can be briefly expressed in terms of the balance of trade doctrine. The idea of a 'balance' may have been drawn from experience of double-entry book-keeping which Englishmen borrowed from Italy in the sixteenth century. A growing consciousness of the corporate character of the nation-state combined perhaps with contemporary scientific notions of equilibrium to turn it into a popular criterion of economic welfare. Round about the middle years of the century a number of writers refer to the balance of trade directly or indirectly, none more clearly than the author of *The Discourse of the Common Weal of this Realm of England* (1st edn. 1549: 2nd edn. 1581). His injunction that '. . . we must alwaies take care that we bie no more of strangers than we sell them . . . for so wee sholde empoverishe owr selves and enriche them', was elaborated into a schedule of occupations that could be regarded as enriching or impoverishing the nation; and William

Lambarde, the Kentish antiquary, added an explanatory note in his copy of the *Discourse* which was to be echoed many times later: 'If we send out more comodities in valeu than we bringe home, the overpluis cometh in in coyne; but if we bringe in more, then the overpluis must nedes be paid for in moneye, and this is the measure of increasinge or diminishinge the Coyne, except of that little which is found within the realme.' Thus the main principle of mercantilist thought and policy was clearly enunciated: a favourable balance would lead to an influx of treasure. But what was the merit of treasure? Nothing could be more lucid, balanced or sensible than the passage in which the author of the *Discourse* deals with this question. Precious metals are light to carry in relation to their value, they do not perish, they go current everywhere, they are most easily divided into many pieces: for these reasons 'they are chosen by a common consent of all the world, that is known to be of anie Civilitie, to be instrumentes of exchange to mesure all thinges by, most apt to be ether caried far, or kept in store, or to receave [for] thinges whereof we have aboundance, and to purchase then by theim other thinges which we lacke, when and wheare we have most [neede].' In less sensible minds such ideas might degenerate into false doctrines of wealth, but little objection could be taken to the explanation as it stood.

Thus the central dogma of the mercantilists came into being. It was restated in its classical form, three-quarters of a century later, by Thomas Mun in his *Englands Treasure by Fforraign Trade*. This, the bible of later mercantilists, was composed of material assembled, in all probability, for the discussions of the Commission of 1622 which was set up to deal with the prevailing trade depression. On this occasion, as on so many others, we are listening to the economics of crisis. 'The ordinary means to encrease our wealth and treasure is by *Fforraign Trade*', wrote Mun, 'wherein we must ever observe this rule; to sell more to strangers yearly than wee consume of theirs in value.' And he illustrates his point by a case: if we export goods to the value of £2,200,000 and import goods valued at £2,000,000, we must win the difference in treasure: and vice versa. This central principle could naturally be interpreted in many different ways on any particular occasion, but that it remained the core of thought and policy there can be no doubt.

More than a century after Mun wrote his tract, another writer,
Sir Matthew Decker, whose *Essay on the Causes of the Decline
of the Foreign Trade* (1739) is thought by some authorities to
have influenced Adam Smith towards free trade, could also
write as though it were an unquestionable article of faith.

'Therefore if the Exports of Britain exceed its Imports,
Foreigners must pay the balance in Treasure and the Nation
grow rich.

But if the Imports of Britain exceeds its Exports we must
pay the Foreigners the Balance in Treasure and the Nation
grow Poor.'

The dangers – inflation and competitive difficulties in export
markets – which might be logically inherent in such policies
did not go by any means unperceived. But the alternative risks
of the unfavourable balance seem to have been regarded as
unquestionably graver for the national welfare. The 'favourable balance' survived as an object of high policy, therefore, and
not merely in the mercantilist age. 'The gilded image of clay
and mud stood for more than a century, an object of slavish
adoration, after its foundations had been rent in all directions.'
Thus McCulloch in 1856.

The doctrines of the mercantilist pamphleteers might nevertheless have been of little more than antiquarian interest if
these writers had merely been philosophers speculating on the
workings of the economic system. But there is more to it than
that: bit by bit the conception of the balance of trade was
built into the economic legislation of the seventeenth century.
In this respect the Commission of 1622 was decisive in linking
together thought and policy more closely than they had ever
been linked before. The depression was itself, in part at least,
the result of the ill-fated Cockayne Scheme by which a group
of merchants trading to the Baltic tried to break the Merchant
Adventurers. The Merchant Adventurers monopolized the
export of unfinished cloth which formed a high proportion of
total English exports. The projectors' scheme was to set up
great industries to dye and dress cloth and thereby deprive the
Dutch – who purchased, finished and sold a large proportion
of English cloth – of their apparently disproportionate share of

the profits in the cloth trade. For many reasons the plan, which itself claimed to promote the balance of trade, failed disastrously. In putting forward their proposals to alleviate the distress and unemployment left in its wake the Commissioners – Thomas Mun among them – adumbrated a considerable part of what was to prove mercantilist policy for the next century or more. Their six main principles were (1) To reserve English raw materials to the cloth industry by prohibiting the export of wool, fullers earth, pipe clay, etc., especially to Holland. (2) To injure Dutch competitors by stopping English ships and merchants from supplying them with Spanish or Turkish wool. (3) To reduce the need for imports and the drain of treasure by developing manufactures; linen would be made here and home-grown hemp and flax would make England independent of the Baltic. (4) The fisheries, now exploited by the Dutch, would be exploited in future by English companies and the Dutch ousted. (5) Foreign merchants and shipmasters who earned money in England by importing goods to England were to be compelled to spend the money they earned here on English manufactures. (6) Goods imported from abroad must come either in English ships or ships belonging to the country producing the goods. All but one of these principles – (5) – was to prove a root from which elaborate later policies were to stem. Jointly, they represent a strategy of attack, in the name of economic nationalism and the balance of trade, on the profitable but vulnerable positions held by the Dutch in the European economy – as middlemen, brokers, refiners, finishers. It is not difficult to see here the work of the same hand that sketched out the principle of 'natural' and 'artificial' wealth in *Englands Treasure by Fforraign Trade*.

'If we duly consider England's Largeness, Beauty, Fertility, Strength, both by sea and land, our multitude of warlike people, Horses, Ships, Ammunition, advantageous situation for Defence and Trade, number of seaports and harbours, which are of difficult access to enemies, and of easie outlet to the inhabitants, wealth by excellent fence woods, Iron, Lead, Tynn, Saffron, Corn, Victuals, Hides, Wax and other Natural Endowments; we shall find this Kingdome capable to sit as master of a Monarchy. For what greater glory and advantage can any

powerful nation have, than to be thus richly and naturally possessed of all things needful for food, Rayment, War and Peace,
not only for its own plentiful use, but also to supply the wants
of Other Nations, in such a measure, that much money may
be thereby gotten yearly, to make the happiness complete.'

Unfortunately, a second look showed that not all these natural
riches were made the most of. The Dutch, on the other hand,
occupying a small country with no natural resources, 'not fully
so big as two of our best shires', had shown what could be
done by *artifice*, by 'their continual industry in the trade of
Merchandize'. By this way they had made themselves the richest nation in the world, not least at the expense of the English.
For the foundation of their trade was shipping, and this in turn
was founded on their herring fisheries, and these lay along the
coasts of England. Here, within sight of the English, sailed the
Dutch fishing fleets for a large part of the year '. . . whereby
many thousands of Households, Families, Handicrafts, Trades
and Occupations are set on work, maintained and prosper,
especially the sailing and navigation', together with the public
revenues for the State.

Jealousy, ambition and common sense were then the principal springs of the policy later called mercantilism. The prohibitions on the export of raw materials used in cloth-making
were repeated and strengthened year by year through the
century to survive as a principal target for the attacks of Adam
Smith. For Stuarts, Parliament men and limited monarchy
alike, they were a common article of faith. The difficulty of
enforcing these measures and the fact that other lines of supply
were open to competitors kept alive the idea of blockading
alternative sources of wool. A scheme of 1651 planned to pre-
empt all the wools of Segovia and Castile through a private
Company which would make an agreement with the King of
Spain and thereby cut off four-fifths of the Dutch supply of
raw wool. The idea was revived again in 1662. Whether anything came of these schemes in practice is doubtful, but it was
a device always liable to be thought of in times of crisis, as
1622, 1657 and 1662 all were for the clothiers.

Plans for new industries like linen manufacture, and the
growing of crops such as hemp and flax, which provided

industrial raw materials, were all closely tied to ideas for reducing imports and boosting exports. Rich as England was
(said Mun) she might be much richer 'by laying out the waste
grounds (which are infinite)... hereby to supply ourselves and
prevent the importation of Hemp, Flax, Cordage and Tobacco
and divers other things which we now fetch from strangers to
our great impoverishing'. The theme that because we were
'weak in our knowledge' we were 'poor in our treasure' was
repeated constantly throughout the century: but it was not
until the end of it that persistent effort presented England with
a cloth industry that could rival the Dutch at Leiden in their
skill at all branches of technique and export a fully finished
article, or a linen industry that could rival that of Haarlem.

The schemes for 'the waste grounds' matured more quickly.
As early as 1589 an early projector conjured up visions of the
Fens round the Wash drained and converted into a land of
plenty, 'a storehouse for the whole Realm, with a super-
abundance to save for foreign lands'. Here 200,000 people
would live in laudable abundance, shipping would thrive on
the grain trade and so would the blacksmith, the shipwright,
the seaman, the sailmaker, etc. A million acres would support
300,000 cattle and 25,000 cavalry horses. Here was 'a regal
conquest, a new republic and a complete state'. In the 1620s
the draining of Hatfield Chase, an impassable morass of 70,000
acres between Humber, Trent and Ouse, raised the value of
land from 6d. to 10 shillings an acre. From there the great
Dutch engineer, Vermuyden, turned to the Fens proper – 'the
sink and drain of 13 counties', a land 'of great waters and a
few reeds thinly scattered...' By the mid-1650s, Samuel
Hartlib described the reclaimed land as 'growing the best
Hempe in England as well as Flax, oats, wheat, Cole seed for
oil, and wood.' Altogether the projectors must have reclaimed
the largest part of half a million acres.

The condition of the fisheries, touched on by the Commission of 1622, was an old occasion for lamentation. From June
to December the Dutch herring fleet followed the shoals down
from Shetland to the Thames Estuary. English critics of this
insult to national pride estimated in huge and no doubt exaggerated figures the value of the catch to their rivals. But they

scarcely outdid the Dutch themselves in assessing its importance and, indeed, it was difficult to overstate the value of an
industry which was as much the base of the Dutch economy as
agriculture was of the English. Here, then, was a persistent
source of friction in Anglo-Dutch relations and the origin of
fundamental disputes over the legal basis of maritime
sovereignty. For while the Dutch claim to freedom of fishing
found its classical statement in Grotius's *Mare Liberum*, the
English replied through John Selden's *Mare Clausum*. There
was besides a series of attempts, all ill-starred, to organize
English fishery companies. But just as the English appear to
have lacked the skilled techniques of dressing and dyeing cloth,
so they lacked the no less mysterious skill required for catching,
salting and barrelling herrings. The fishery question therefore
continued to act as a provocation to those wilder spirits who
thought England's best short cut to wealth and strength lay
through a Dutch War. Their theories were tested in 1652 and
1665 and found wanting.

The many motives and ambitions, private and public, which
churned together in men's minds in the seventeenth century
to produce the complex of thought and policy known as mercantilism produced their *chef d'œuvre* in the Navigation Laws.
To understand their purpose we must remember the growing
importance of the new colonial territories. The original economic motive of exploration had often been the search for
precious metals. This had given way in time to a popular hope
that the Colonies would form alternative, cheaper and safer
sources of supply for those necessary commodities which
England drew from foreign countries. Yet such hopes had been
repeatedly thwarted by the skill of the Dutch in inserting
themselves between colonial producer and English buyer.
Hence, it was thought, a drain of money to pay for cargoes and
freight; hence the nation was robbed of the chance to build up
a fleet and a body of seamen not only for economic profit but
for defence. The neat and ingenious formula of the Act of 1651
aimed at cutting out the Dutch merchants and shipmasters
from all the *import* trade into England. Before there was satisfactory evidence as to its exact results it was replaced by the
Acts of 1660, 1662 and 1663 which extended the scope of the
earlier Act; the aims were more limited, the administration

more efficient, and the most recent historian to examine their operation in detail has formed a high opinion of their efficacy.² Under the guidance of Sir George Downing, to whom the title of architect of the mercantile system in England should perhaps be awarded, the whole trade between England and the Colonies was henceforth enclosed and protected, and canalized in English shipping. The old attempts to prevent the drain of treasure by directly banning its efflux were now largely abandoned. The emphasis had moved towards building up the volume and value of exports, reducing the volume and value of imports, controlling the latter to an important extent by eliminating what were thought of as indiscriminate imports in Dutch and foreign shipping, and winning as much in the way of income from freights as possible. So after an interval of nearly forty years, the proposals of Mun and his colleagues came into full operative force.

The emphasis has thus far been placed on the conception of the balance of trade within the framework of mercantilist thought and policy, principally because so many accounts of the system have subordinated this, with all its potentialities of economic expansion, to the notion of the pursuit of treasure as an end in itself. It would be foolish to deny that mercantilists as a whole set great store by precious metals. Some even fell into a fallacy of virtually identifying wealth with treasure, but in general (as Professor Heckscher himself said) there was no conscious idolatry of money. Did they then put (as he added) 'a halo of significance round gold and silver not explained by functions consciously ascribed to them'? The answer must depend on what those functions really were in the contemporary economy; and one may doubt whether some of the critics of mercantilist policies in this respect have adequately appreciated the problems of conducting either domestic or foreign trade at the time. Much thought and policy was devoted to ensuring that a supply of precious metal was maintained adequate for a sound and plentiful currency. The anxiety lest 'a scarcity of coin' should slow down the volume of trade and bring about an economic depression affected writers repeatedly every time a crisis threatened. To Adam Smith such anxieties were absurd. Yet his sense of historical change was not strong and his own chapter on *Metallic and Paper*

*Money* contained implications which he does not fully consider. If the growth of new methods of payment had been of such significance in the century before 1776, how had Mun and his contemporaries fared without these later devices of paper money, bank credit, etc., whose effects Adam Smith found so beneficial? Mercantilists have been criticized for their 'fear of goods'; yet it is by no means certain that the dire recurrent crises of overproduction may not have been made worse by physical scarcity of currency. It may be wise to suspend judgement over mercantilist concern for a sound currency and the efficacy of their measures until we have more evidence. There can, however, be no doubt that some branches of foreign trade demanded the use of large supplies of precious metal. By the end of the seventeenth and in the early years of the eighteenth century, the East India Company alone was compelled to export large quantities of silver to pay for the spices which it imported from the East. It seems likely that purchases of Baltic corn in the first half of the seventeenth century similarly absorbed bullion supplies; so did the purchase of timber and stores for naval shipbuilding in the second half of the century. There was a chronic tendency for the value of goods leaving the Baltic to exceed the value of imports to that area. Evidence from English and Dutch sources suggests that merchants trading to the Baltic found it at least convenient to take coin and bullion with them for trading purposes. Unquestionably, bills of exchange and credit instruments were in common use on the well-worn paths of trade in Western Europe. But it seems as though the expansion of the European economy into the peripheral areas of Asia, India and America may have emphasized the traders' need for what one authority has called 'capital in a solid and ponderable form'.[3] It may be, therefore, that the monetary preoccupations of mercantilism – the obsession with 'treasure' – have their roots in the times – in the political uncertainty and violence, in the limited knowledge and efficacy of more sophisticated conceptions of money and credit which later more skilled and less troubled ages were to utilize.

It seems clear that no interpretation of the complex of ideas and policies called 'mercantilism' which attributes to it a single end or credits it to one type of creator can be satisfactory. In Britain, at any rate, the system stems from a dual authorship and has twin objectives – though contemporaries, not having analysed their purposes into economic and non-economic, saw those ends as a single end. Throughout the seventeenth century the pressure of the merchant interests on government grew, and in this respect the current form of polity – monarchy or republic – seems to have been of less importance than is sometimes assumed. It is the continuity of economic policy throughout the seventeenth century that is truly remarkable. Kings were as ready to lend an ear to the merchant's pleas as republican governors, and in some ways readier. It was typical that in the Commission of 1622, merchants like Thomas Mun and government servants like Cranfield sat side by side, both subscribing to the broad programme designed to achieve the ends of the merchant community and the nation at large. Merchants of the great Companies bombarded the Council of State with petitions, energetically pressing their private views, before the Act of 1651 took final shape. This Act, and its successors of the early Restoration years, did not represent the whole desires of any one group, but a compromise in which public servants like Downing attempted to reconcile the interests of the Companies and the State. On the boards of the Fishery Companies and the Royal Africa Company, merchants, nobles, and court hangers-on all sat together in amiable and (it was hoped) profitable conspiracy. Not the least hopeful were the King, who saw promise of larger revenues, and James, Duke of York, Lord High Admiral, who sought support for that larger Navy which would ensure booty for all and glory for himself and his officers. There was thus a partnership in mercantilism. Kings, governments and bureaucrats saw in the expansion of mercantile prosperity the chance of larger revenues for themselves, and of a more prosperous and tranquil people to govern. Merchants saw in the 'State' the helping hand necessary to aid and protect them. To trade to far countries required the aid of Royal embassies and the backing of government prestige. To sail through European and Asiatic waters, merchant ships might need convoy or armed protection against pirates or belligerents. At home, protection of a different kind was demanded – against excessive competition (as they regarded it) from foreign importers, for example. Infant industries needed bounties and subsidies, and incentives to skilled foreigners to settle here and teach denizens new techniques. In all such matters, the mercantile community sought the help of the State and saw in it the highest embodiment of that corporate form of organization to which the traditions of gild and company had accustomed them.

## The System Elsewhere

Talk of 'the uniformity of mercantilist doctrine' should not lead us to suppose that the programme or its authorship were everywhere the same. The origins and methods of the mercantile programme differed from State to State, reflecting differences of social structure, national resources and characteristics, and the stage of economic and social development attained by different societies. If, for convenience, we think of England with its fairly equally balanced partnership of merchant and State official as the norm, the mercantilism of other European States seems to diverge on either side of that norm. In the mercantile republics, first of Italy and later of the Netherlands, economic policy leans towards private initiative and profit. In France, on the other hand, there is a stronger flavour of *raison d'Etat* than in England, while in Prussia all the impulse of change seems to come from above, powerfully directed towards the attainment of strategic strength. Let us look at some of these other types of policy in more detail.

As with the Italian trading cities, the success and prosperity of the towns of the Dutch Republic was an excellent advertisement of the virtues of economic self-government. The merchant governors of Holland had not rid themselves of one dangerous and expensive dynasty to saddle themselves with another. Throughout the century of their most rapid expansion, therefore, they asserted their determination not to be ruled by a Prince. *Ab furore monarchorum libera nos Domine* was their cry. The society they helped to create rested on the enterprise and initiative of the merchants, shipmasters and industrialists who made Amsterdam and the other great cities the *entrepot* of the word. This precocious display of economic skill by the *entrepreneurs* of a score of ports and cities left little room or need for 'State' action – if, indeed, the loose federal machinery of government could be regarded as a 'State'. Decentralization was the most marked characteristic of the Republic. The great trading companies were divided into their municipal chambers; even the navy was organized in five admiralties. Such extreme emphasis on local authority could be a source of weakness where defence and strategy were concerned – as it undoubtedly was in the first war against the English in 1652 – but the powerful trading classes remained convinced that it was the form of government best suited to their needs and those of the Republic as a whole.

In spite, therefore, of a degree of control and regulation within some industries, the presence of gilds down to the time of the French Revolution, and the existence of scattered tariffs and prohibitions, there was no systematic protection of local industry such as characterized the economic policy of other more centralized States. As the warehouse of the world, Amsterdam and the other cities were committed, not by doctrine but by interest, to securing a free flow of trade through the *entrepot*. With local authority strong and central prestige weak, with so much revenue dependent on international freight, with so much capital at the mercy of other governments, the Dutch had generally to pursue a cautious policy of no embroilments. Economically ahead of their rivals, they did not need to rely on government action to the same extent, and the notion of a balance of trade was absent from their calculations. To a large extent, therefore, the conventional apparatus of 'mercantilism' was neither appropriate nor necessary. Yet in one respect, the Dutch conformed to contemporary modes of thought: the value to a trading community of precious metals, both for domestic and foreign trade, is repeatedly stressed. Normally, they relied on the unhampered working of trade to bring in enough bullion – especially from the Spanish trade – to serve their needs. But it is worth noting that in the closing years of the seventeenth century, the silver shortage gave rise to a battle between the mintmasters (who were concerned for the currency and wished to stop the export of silver) and the traders to Northern Europe and the Far East (who insisted that such export was vital to their trades). The dispute offers some interesting glimpses of the reasons why seventeenth-century thinkers held precious metals in such high esteem. Perhaps in general the Dutch merchants were right to feel that a conscious policy of striving after 'power' could do little for their economy. It was vulnerable by nature. Certainly, in practice, little was done to strengthen it, and the Republic had to rely on policy rather than force to protect itself against the inherent violence of the seventeenth-century world.

In France, mercantilist ideas showed many points of resemblance to those of English writers. At the close of the Middle Ages, the famous *Débat des Hérauts* sounded a note of combative satisfaction that was to characterize French mercantilist thinking for a long time to come, and reminds an English reader of Thomas Mun's mood of self-congratulation on the 'natural riches' of England. The reflection that France, too, was a land of vast natural resources constantly comforts French writers: yet even they are conscious of certain deficiencies. In the *Cahiers* and royal edicts of the sixteenth century, successive rulers urged a programme very like that of English kings. France must aim at importing raw materials, not manufactures, said a *cahier* of 1560. An edict of 1572 bans manufactured imports so that the people of France 'can better devote themselves to the manufacture and working up of wool, flax, hemp and tow . . . and get the profit that foreigners now make'. Skilled foreigners and *entrepreneurs* were enticed in to set up new industries, especially those which would increase France's stock of gold and silver. It became a matter of increasing anxiety to governments and writers like Bodin, de Laffemas and Monchrétien that 'the nerves and support of Kingdoms and monarchies' should be lost through ignorance and the idle purchase of luxurious goods and entertainments. Just as the English blamed the Dutch for draining away their treasure, so Frenchmen blamed Italians for the same offence. A *Commission de Commerce* inspired by de Laffemas held 150 meetings between 1601 and 1604, promoting the fortunes of new industries and especially those like the silk industry, which would reduce dependence on Italy. As in England, there was a strong emphasis on drainage and reclamation of land, on river navigation, and on the improvement of the textile industries. To them Monchrétien added a thrust towards the exploitation of colonies, of local fisheries and the development of shipping, and these were taken up in practical form by Richelieu. In many respects Richelieu anticipated Colbert, and two of his trading companies – dealing with Canada and the West Indies – managed to survive the fate that overtook most of the projects of these years.

Under Colbert the naive aspirations of earlier writers and the largely ineffective regulations of earlier administrators were clarified and given unprecedented force. While in England Downing and others were laying the foundations of a commercial empire, Colbert was launching his own schemes to rescue France from the poverty and chaos of the Mazarin era. The regulation of trade stood high in his scheme of things and to his predecessors' attempts to oust Italian enterprise from French trade, Colbert added a direct attack on the Dutch. Yet the centre of Colbert's beliefs was the conviction that manufactures were the true source of wealth and social contentment. He therefore set himself to develop them by means of tariffs, privileges, the enticement to France of ingenious *entrepreneurs* and skilled artisans. Production was to be left to the individual but supervised in minute detail to ensure quality, through gilds, and through local and general règlements. Thus could industry, with trade, play its part in winning and keeping a supply of bullion whose principal purpose was to keep trade moving by its free circulation.

Nothing, however, could be further from the truth than the view which depicts Colbert as a pacific economic planner thwarted in his purposes by a rash and aggressive royal master. Colbert shared the common mercantilist view (for which there was in fact some rational basis) that the amount of international trade was fairly static. 'Commerce,' he said, 'is a perpetual and peaceable war of wit and energy among all the nations': yet as Pooh-Bah to Louis he shared fully in the schemes to down the Dutch, and had all the major bureaucrat's contempt for the business man – 'merchants, who nearly always understand merely their own little commerce and not the great forces which make commerce go'. Like his predecessors in France, Colbert saw himself first and foremost as the servant of King and State, and herein lies a major difference between the French mercantilist writers and the English, most of whom were merchants. In France, economic regulation came from above: it was 'royal Colbertism'. Companies were formed at the instance of the King and Colbert. Colbert would consult merchants, but it is doubtful whether their advice did much to affect either the economic doctrines he held or the economic organization he imposed. It is a curious feature of his system that though it was nearer *étatisme* than its English counter-part, it was slower to focus attention overtly on the balance of trade, though of course the conception underlay all that was done in the name of Colbertism. While England had an Inspector General of Customs by 1696, it was not till more than half a century later that France followed suit: possibly Colbert's failure to break down local autonomy had something to do with it.

The effects of the Colbert system remain a matter of controversy. It has been suggested that it probably promoted technological progress in some textiles and in metallurgy but that the gild organization may have tended towards ossification by hindering the coming of machines and by making it difficult to follow changes of design and fashion. Be that as it may, down to 1763 or probably later, France led the world in its volume of industrial production, foreign commerce and domestic trade. The resources of France made this possible: but mercantilist aspirations, if not mercantilist policy, may well have encouraged a basically rural economy to turn to the methodical development of its resources by trade and industry.

The whole structure of mercantilism in the lands along the Atlantic seaboard was under attack from philosophers, and even merchants were growing doubtful of its advantages, by the time the peripheral States began to turn their attentions to the possible advantages of an induced economic birth. Undoubtedly, to the so-called Enlightened Despots who ruled beyond the Elbe, north of the Baltic, or south of the Pyrenees – places never mentioned in those guide-books devised for gentlemen on the Grand Tour – the framework of mercantilist ideas promised to offer a short cut from feudal poverty to a developed economy. The familiar doctrines seemed to fit the case of Prussia as well as they had those of England or France: 'The basic rule to follow in connection with all trade and manufacture,' wrote Frederick the Great,

'is to prevent money from flowing permanently out of the coun-

try; an attempt should always be made to bring it back into
Prussia. The exodus of money can best be prevented by producing in Prussia all kinds of goods which were formerly
imported . . . The second way to prevent an undue exodus of
money . . . is to purchase necessary foreign commodities at
their original source, thus taking the trade in one's own hands
instead of leaving it to foreign agents . . . Manufacture results
in large quantities of money within the country . . . All these
reasons must cause the ruler of Prussia to encourage manufacture and trade, whether through direct subsidies or through
tax exemptions, so that they may be in a position for large
scale production and trade.'

In Prussia, even more clearly than in France, the stimulus
came necessarily from the top. Land was reclaimed, canals
built, forests cleared, companies and banks founded, industries
promoted, immigrants encouraged on land and in factory.
Under devoted administrators like von Heinitz and von Hagen,
a business community was coaxed into being, and a large
variety of trade and industry achieved. Much of it disappeared after Jena, but not all depended on Frederick's
personal energy. Almost all industrial beginnings can be said to
look artificial. The seeds sown by Frederick were to germinate
much later.

If the idea of a body of mercantilist economic thought and
practice in Western Europe has any validity, Spain must be
excluded from our definition before the eighteenth century.
There all traces of a rational economic policy had disappeared
beneath a mountain of taxation, and the protests of thinkers
and traders had been silenced by the exigencies of the tax
gatherer. Even more clearly than France, the example of Spain
shows how fiscal necessity and private privilege could frustrate
mercantilist principles just as they could later frustrate those of
*laissez-faire*.

The Spain of *Don Quixote* was no place for business. Not
until the 1720s are voices raised again against the absurdities
of the Spanish economy. First Geronimo de Uztariz, then
Bernardo Ulloa held up the mercantilist doctrines of England
and France and the business acumen of the Dutch as a model

for Spain to follow. As in Prussia, there was little to hope for from the dwindled band of business men whom social prejudice had turned into a caste of untouchables. The appeal was therefore to authority; the instrument was the balance of trade and the end the revival of military glory as well as national prosperity. Under the enlightened despotism of Charles III (1759–88) a programme of mercantilist endeavour, mixed with physiocratic zeal, went forward. Campomanes, the Asturian statesman, promoted industry and commerce, technical education and transport. The results were not negligible but they did not compare with the progress which had been seen earlier in more northerly countries. Spain remained obstinately traditional.

By this time, in any case, mercantilism was becoming unfashionable in the places of its origin. The attack on it is a story in itself: all that can be said here is that the attack came, broadly speaking, from two quarters: (1) From a growing school of philosophers who held that it was an offence against the natural order to interfere with economic affairs. The idea of 'natural harmony' goes to the roots of eighteenth-century thought: in the economic sphere it emerged in the identification of self-love and social welfare. (2) At the other extreme were those merchants who believed that the existing regulations harmed their own interests. In between were writers, like Boisguilbert in France and Matthew Decker in England, who combined an attack on monopolies and other forms of corruption and privilege, with a hint of philosophical detachment. 'Everything will work out all right provided nature is left alone . . . ,' wrote Boisguilbert. It was not philosophy but it was philosophical, though it was a long time before the conjunction of interest and philosophy dispersed the last remnants of the old system.

## Conclusion

The mercantile system was composed of all the devices, legislative, administrative and regulatory, by which societies still predominantly agrarian sought to transform themselves into trading and industrial societies, to equip themselves not only to be rich but to be strong, and to remain so. And these very measures made up the system which the *laissez-faire* school of thought was to condemn as corrupt, futile and disastrous. Almost everything about the system is open to theoretical objection, almost all the possible theoretical objections have been urged at one time or another and a considerable number gained wide currency. The motives, logic, morals, methods and behaviour of mercantilists have all been examined and (quite rightly) found wanting by later persons and ages thinking themselves more virtuous or more intelligent. We have been concerned in this essay not to 'defend' mercantilist policy but to analyse and understand it. It has been shown that to suppose that it sprang everywhere from the same motives and the same kind of social groups is to oversimplify. In some countries it came from the top – from rulers, governors and state officials – while in others it came from further down the social and political scale – from tradesmen, in fact. Likewise, the ends it sought varied; they ranged from the immediate profit of individuals and the pockets of princes to the power of the state and the welfare of great communities of people. The purposes of governments were not limited to strategic or military objectives, to 'power' (as some have claimed): they extended to the peaceable employment of more of their subjects and the enrichment of the merchants who were recognized as important contributors to the national welfare. Catherine the Great thought that the English were 'first and always traders' and many others agreed. Yet the wiser heads repeatedly observed that economic and political ends went together. 'Profit and Power,' observed Sir Josiah Child, 'ought jointly to be considered.' And to Hobbes is attributed the maxim: 'wealth is power and power is wealth'. Such views on the *dual* nature of policy and its twin objectives could be multiplied indefinitely. The fact was that the age was one of violence when the pursuit of economic ends constantly demanded the backing of force. It was too early for men to allow themselves the luxury of a separate science of wealth. To judge mercantilist thought by the criteria of later economic logic is to misconceive its character. Its inventors had not attained, and perhaps would not have been interested to attain, to the philosophic detachment of a later age. Their ends were at once more immediate, yet in some senses larger, than those of the 'economist', for they insisted on seeing economic institutions in their political setting.

Mercantilism, it is as well to confess, often looks less like the onset of economic virtue than like an attack of economic lust. Certainly its basis was national gain, not universal philanthropy. Its logic often led to plunder, violence and warfare, overt or disguised. Yet it had one virtue which, from a materialistic standpoint, can hardly be exaggerated. It was the embodiment of enthusiasm for economic gain, and its relentless, systematic pursuit of material ends constitutes, it may be, one of the factors which help to explain the more rapid material progress of the West as compared with the stagnation of, say, Asia. The great age of mercantilism in action – the century between 1660 and 1760 – was, in Western Europe, an age of economic expansion. By later standards progress was slow enough, but it was remarkable by comparison with what had gone before. Yet the purely economic phenomena often used to explain expansion in, say, the sixteenth century, are lacking. There is no inflation, no rising tide of silver. By Adam Smith's time much of the mercantilist apparatus was otiose or corrupt; even in its prime, many plans undertaken under its aegis had misfired and ended in disaster. It would be rash, nevertheless, to dismiss too hastily the possibility that the economic growth of this period owed something to the remarkable concentration of human energy and organized effort we call the mercantile system. Few governments at the present time fail to pay tribute in the interests of economic progress to one or another of those aspirations which, jointly, represented the economic programme of Leviathan.

## NOTES

1. E. A. Johnson, *Predecessors of Adam Smith* (1937), 4.
2. L. A. Harper, *The English Navigation Laws*, Ch. xxiii.
3. G. N. Clark, *The Seventeenth Century*, 27.

## NOTE ON LITERATURE

*The Wealth of Nations* (Book IV) and Schmoller's *The Mercantile System and its Historical Significance* (London, 1896) will repay further study as two classic sources of opinions on the subject. The fullest modern survey is Heckscher's *Mercantilism* (revised edn., London, 1955). Chapter III of Sir George Clark's *The Seventeenth Century* (Oxford, 1947) gives a very clear and valuable account of the way the different States developed their particular versions of the mercantile system. More detail on these may be obtained from Herbert Heaton's *Economic History of Europe* (New York, 1948). Although this is a general textbook covering a vast field, it is marked by consistently sound judgement and itself has valuable bibliographical notes. The most thorough studies in English of Continental mercantilism are Professor C. W. Cole's *Colbert and A Century of French Mercantilism* (New York, 1939) and *French Mercantilism 1683–1700* (New York, 1943). *Profit and Power* by Charles Wilson (London, 1957) examines English mercantilist policy in the seventeeth century in its context of strategy and diplomacy.

Heckscher's work has stimulated a number of articles, all in some degree critical of his interpretation. The following cover special as well as general aspects of the problem:

D. C. Coleman: 'Labour in the English Economy of the Seventeenth Century' (*Economic Hist. Review*, 1956).

H. Heaton: 'Heckscher on Mercantilism' (*Journal of Pol. Economy*, 1937).

S. Viner: 'Power versus Plenty as Objectives of Foreign Policy in the Seventeenth and Eighteenth Centuries' (*World Politics*, 1948).

C. Wilson: 'Treasure and Trade Balances: the Mercantilist Problem' (*Econ. Hist. Review*, 1949); 'Mercantilism: Some Vicissitudes of An Idea' (Ibid., 1957).

The Cambridge Economic History of Europe Vol. IV (1967) – the final chapter and generally for reference.

# PART SEVEN

# A Commercial Revolution

# A COMMERCIAL REVOLUTION

*by*

## RALPH DAVIS

The pattern of overseas trade is always in movement; new commodities are constantly appearing, old ones fading into unimportance, different trading partners coming to the forefront. But between the latter end of the sixteenth and the second half of the eighteenth century, change took specially far-reaching forms. In 1570 England was a country with one major export, woollen cloth, accounting for some four-fifths of the value of its trade, and that trade was nearly all with places on the North Sea or Atlantic coasts of Europe. By 1770 it had a wide range of manufactured exports (among which woollens were still the foremost) and a big re-export of colonial and Asiatic goods; and its trade not only extended to the farthest corners of Europe, but far beyond to America, Africa, India and China. The ultimate origin of this transformation lies in events of the sixteenth century, but its pace and scope were very limited until after the Civil War. Just as the most striking economic changes of the century after 1760 were associated with Industrial Revolution, so those of the century or so after 1660 were associated with trade. They did not have nearly such a great immediate impact on English economic and social life as a whole. But their consequences were so important, not only for the development of merchant organization and services ancillary to trade, but also in wider fields of capital accumulation and investment, in the changing opportunities they offered to industry, and in their influence on social habits, that we may well attach to the period running from the English Restoration to American Independence the title of 'The Commercial Revolution'.

In the period of preparation for this, 1570–1640, the collapse of old marketing arrangements through Antwerp had driven

Englishmen to extend their trading activities to all the ports of Europe and the Mediterranean coastline, to widen their range of production of woollen cloth, and to find room for new kinds of imported goods. But from the time of the Restoration (or perhaps a little earlier) changes were beginning to show a much wider character, first in the geographical spread of trading activity, and then in the diversification of exports. Two phases of very rapid expansion may be distinguished, with a slowing of growth between them. From 1660 until the outbreak of the long war with France in 1689, there was a continuing enlargement of trade with Europe. Nevertheless much the most striking feature of this period was a great extension of the area of trade as America and India began to send very large quantities of goods to England; and the counterpart was a huge re-export of colonial and Indian goods, which by the end of the period accounted for a third of all exports. Progress was checked when war came, and for a variety of reasons it was not resumed at the same rate after peace was restored in 1713. But in the early decades of the eighteenth century the rapid growth of colonial population and wealth were laying the foundation for a new period of advance in trade, which got under way in the thirties, was brought to a standstill by renewed war in 1739, and finally matured after the peace of 1748. In this new phase, the leading feature was an enormous American demand for English manufactures of every kind, and for the first time in history, woollens came to be rivalled in English export trade by other manufactures.

Throughout these two centuries the significance of foreign trade in the English economy was increasing. Its value was probably growing rapidly in proportion to total national income (with a brief pause in the first decades of the eighteenth century), and in terms of capital requirements its relative weight in the economy grew even faster than statistics of trade value would indicate, because of the extension of its geographical bounds, and the emergence of a big re-export trade. The attention that writers of the latter part of the seventeenth and the eighteenth centuries gave to problems connected with overseas trade is no accident, but a testimony to its importance in English economic life.

*　　*　　*

The principal purpose of this pamphlet is to summarize the developments of the period 1660–1776; from the Restoration of Charles II, which had real importance to commerce in bringing back stability to England, to the revolution which ended the political dependence of the American colonies and initiated changes in their economic relationship with England. But to understand how the commercial developments of this period came about it is essential to look briefly at the previous hundred years, when great cracks appeared in the old pattern, preparing the way for its complete reconstruction.

In the first half of the sixteenth century English trade had come to be intensely concentrated on a London-Antwerp axis, to the detriment of the English ports of the east and south coasts. In this trade, the London merchant class acquired wealth, self-confidence, and experience of European trading conditions. For Antwerp, where most English cloth was sold, was not the ultimate destination, but a market where cloth could be further processed, sold, and forwarded to buyers in nearly all parts of Europe. Antwerp, and English trade, were recent beneficiaries of the growth of prosperity in central Europe north of the Alps, after some hundreds of years in which the principal centres of commercial activity had been in Italy.

By the middle of the sixteenth century the position of Antwerp as entrepôt for much of the trade passing into and through central Europe was beginning to weaken, as more direct exchanges were established between different areas. Moreover, the religious wars in central Europe in 1545–55 disrupted the life of the main trading cities, from time to time bringing financial crises and ruin to continental merchant houses trading through Antwerp. By the time the restoration of more peaceful conditions in central Europe might have made possible a renewal of Antwerp's trading expansion, these political and religious quarrels had spread to the Netherlands, and Antwerp itself was involved in the vast upheaval of the revolt against Spain. This was the end of Antwerp's great period as a trading city; it was fought over, sacked by mutinous Spanish troops, finally cut off from the sea by the Dutch in 1585, and abandoned by the English, German, Spanish and Italian merchants who had for so long resorted there.

It was not easy for English exporting merchants to adjust themselves to this sharply changing situation in the 1570s and 1580s. The English cloth trade relied not merely on Antwerp's commercial facilities to sell its goods, but also on Antwerp craftsmen to put the finishing touches to the cloth. Consumers in central and eastern Europe wanted English broadcloths and kerseys which had been dyed and finished in the Netherlands, and persistent efforts by English governments to change this demand by limiting the export of cloth 'undyed and undressed' had had no success. When the obstacles to trade through Antwerp became serious it was possible to find alternative routes for carrying goods into Europe; but the problem of getting cloths finished to suit European customers' tastes presented difficulties for a great many years. The methods and skills for dyeing and finishing the better types of cloth were not firmly established in England itself until well into the seventeenth century.

The decline of Antwerp weakened the domination which London had over other English ports in carrying on overseas trade, and compelled the London merchants themselves to look for new channels for their operations. The process of adjustment to new kinds of trade was delayed by the long war with Spain, which lasted from 1587 to 1604; in the first decade of the seventeenth century well over half of English cloth exports still entered Europe through the handful of trading cities of the Netherlands and north-west Germany which had now taken over Antwerp's role. Nevertheless, in the decades round 1600 England was being forced along the first steps on a path of change which was to transform her overseas trade.

Most of the exports from London to Antwerp had been unfinished cloths, supplied by the west of England broadcloth and kersey producers. But many other types of cloth were made, dyed, and finished in England, and some of these already had markets overseas. Cheaper cloths from the southern counties had found useful markets in France, Spain, and Portugal, which were supplied through Bristol and south coast ports. East coast ports sent good-quality East Anglian broadcloths, and cheap Yorkshire kerseys and dozens, to the Baltic. The growing opportunities in these trades attracted the interest of London merchants when the Netherlands market entered on its troubles. From London, too, direct relations by sea were opened with Italy in 1570, and with Turkey in 1581 – markets previously served through Antwerp. The difficulties of Antwerp, in fact, forced English merchants – and especially the richest group of them, operating from London – to find new paths of entry into the markets of Europe, and the most natural places to go were those where English goods were known already. But trading directly with Danzig, Leghorn or Smyrna was a very different matter from dealing in well-settled grooves with Antwerp, less than two hundred miles away; it called for more capital, more complicated organization, more shipping. Thus the movement was a precursor of the much greater geographical widening of trade that came a hundred years later.

Several further developments presently aided this movement towards more direct trade with European and near-Eastern markets. Dyeing and finishing of woollen fabrics of every kind at last became firmly established in England before the Civil War, so that west country cloths as well as others increasingly went out in finished form, whether to central Europe through Hamburg, Middleburg, or Amsterdam, or by sea to Danzig or Istanbul. Moreover, long-continued fighting had made havoc not only of Antwerp's trade but also of the great Low Countries woollen industries making light, thin cloths. This helped York-shire cloths to expand their European market; and it enabled a new branch of English industry to grow up in East Anglia, producing, at first under the guidance of immigrants from the Netherlands, the so-called 'New Draperies', which were cloths of the worsted type. After the war with Spain ended in 1604 these began to find a big sale in southern Europe. Spanish industry had been declining in the latter part of the sixteenth century under the influence of price inflation, and in Italy the cloth industry was in similar difficulties from the early seventeenth century. The new English manufacturers found great export markets opened by the weakening competition of these native Mediterranean industries.

In the first half of the seventeenth century, therefore, English cloth exports were becoming much more diversified and were increasingly being carried from England by sea, beyond the narrow bounds of the London-Low Countries route. The two developments went hand in hand, for in the new or vastly expanded trades with Spain and Portugal, France and Italy, Poland and Sweden, the old-style broadcloths had little place. English ships were to be seen from Helsinki to Istanbul; and in seaports and centres of trade all over Europe English factors – sons, apprentices and employees of English merchants – settled and began to build up the experience and connections needed for the full development of trading relations.

This movement of traders' attention to new export markets involved some significant changes in imports; for selling in Spain or Turkey necessarily had its counterpart in buying the goods available in those places. The system of money transfers by bills of exchange, which made multilateral trade possible, was as yet little developed outside the main cities of western Europe. Antwerp, the universal entrepôt, could supply goods of nearly every kind, but a Mediterranean or Baltic port could offer only a limited range of products. The greater part of English imports in the sixteenth century had fallen within two categories; wine (mostly from France) and a great variety of central European manufactures brought from the Netherlands, especially linenwares and a great variety of metal goods. When English ships appeared in the ports of the Baltic and Mediterranean, they found few things of this kind could be obtained – a few coarse linens, Spanish wine. Instead they had to bring home various kinds of semi-luxury foodstuffs which had until then had little sale in England (though privateers' hauls in the later years of Elizabeth's reign had widened the English taste for them) and a range of new raw materials. From the Mediterranean came raisins and currants, sugar and drugs, cotton, silk and dyestuffs. The Baltic ports sent flax and hemp, timber and iron. At first much of the import from the Mediterranean could not be absorbed by English industry, and cotton, dyestuffs and above all raw silk were re-exported in some quantity; but by 1640 most of these imported materials were being used up in England. For the combination of the wartime troubles of continental industry, of artisan immigration, and of contact with these sources of raw materials, made possible the establishment of a new range of industries. Cloth dyeing, and linen, silk and cotton manufacture developed slowly from the end of the sixteenth century, and all became important during the next hundred years. As to Baltic goods, these were the very things which the English shipping industry, expanding rapidly to meet the new demands of trade, needed for its building and maintenance.

The attempt of the Netherlands to throw off Spanish rule, and the Anglo-Spanish war of 1587–1604, were aspects of the wider European – and especially European Protestant – revulsion against the threat of domination of Europe by the Spanish Habsburgs. The influence of this spread far beyond Europe; for defiance of Habsburg authority led the rulers of England, the Netherlands and France to encourage settlement and trading by their subjects in America and Asia, where priority of discovery, and Papal blessing, had secured a fairly general acceptance of Spanish or Portuguese monopoly throughout the sixteenth century. The development of shipping and navigational skills in distant trades and fishery in the later decades of the sixteenth century equipped Englishmen to attempt voyages across the Atlantic or round the Cape of Good Hope; and with the ripening of political conditions they took their first serious steps beyond Europe. The first English trading stations in Asia were established by the East India Company from 1601 onwards, and effective English colonization on the American mainland began in 1607, and in the West Indies in the 1620s.

The American and West Indian colonies were of little commercial importance before 1640, though by then they were sending a good deal of tobacco to England, some of which was re-exported. The trade of the East India Company, however, quite rapidly reached a significant level. The existing English requirements for goods from Asia were very limited, and the volume of trade which would have satisfied them could not maintain eastern establishments of the size needed to support English trade against Dutch and Portuguese power, and to convince local rulers of the desirability of giving countenance to English traders. Almost from the beginning, therefore, the quantity of pepper (the main commodity of the trade) brought to England was far in excess of English consumption, and most of it was re-exported, at first to northern Europe but soon to the Mediterranean, which had until then relied on supplies coming through the Red Sea.

Despite these developments, extra-European trade in 1640

was only a small fraction of the total English trade. Woollen cloth still supplied some 80 per cent of all exports, just as it had done a hundred and fifty years before. The character of cloth exports, and the relative importance of different markets, had been greatly modified in the early decades of the seventeenth century, but English trade continued to be founded, essentially, on the export of cloth to Europe.

\*    \*    \*

The second half of the century saw an astonishing change in the nature of the export trade, largely accomplished, indeed, between 1660 and 1689. By 1700 woollen cloth, so far from dominating export trade, had fallen to less than half the total of exports. This was not because exports of woollens declined – on the contrary, they continued to grow rapidly. Nor were new exports of other kinds of English products coming forward in significant quantities, though a number of minor branches of manufacture were in fact finding a new market in the colonies. The reason for the change was the great expansion of re-export trade from its small beginnings before 1640. Between 1640 and 1700 exports of English products increased from £2½–3 million at the earlier to some £4½ million at the later date; in the same period re-exports went up from a negligible figure – a few score thousands – to almost £2 million.

So a new phenomenon entered English commercial life, with far reaching consequences. Re-export of East India goods had begun because the trade opened by the East India Company was not founded on England's own needs. The growth in the re-export of colonial goods came about for a different reason; because the new English settlements across the Atlantic were presently able to produce quantities of tobacco and sugar far beyond English needs, and were prevented by the English Navigation Acts from sending them directly to any but English ports. Once the English settlers in the West Indies, and in Virginia and Maryland, had found the staple products most suitable to their lands and climates, they were able to produce and export them at prices far below those set by the existing producers in Spanish and Portuguese America. Consequently they extended their production very rapidly; competition among the planters brought prices down fast, and this in turn greatly widened the market, turning their products from semi-luxuries into near-necessities for English and many European consumers. Tobacco offers the most striking illustration of this process. Tobacco had been coming to Europe from Central America, expensively and in small quantities, since the late sixteenth century; in James I's reign it was sold in England at prices ranging from twenty to forty shillings a pound. But production was firmly established in Virginia before 1620, and in the next few years it became the main product of the new English settlements in the West Indies. An extraordinary expansion of supply followed, leading to a collapse of the price in the colonies to no more than a penny a pound in 1630, which drove West Indian producers out of the market before mid-century. Even at this price the mainland producers could still make money, and they continued to increase their crops. In 1619 Virginia and Maryland sent some 20,000 lb of tobacco to England; by the sixties the figure had risen to 9 million, in the late eighties to 15 million, and at the end of the century to 22 million pounds. The colonial price recovered a little from the bottom levels of the 1630s; but even with the addition of heavy duties on import to England, tobacco retailed in London at a shilling a pound in Charles II's reign – a small fraction of the price of sixty years before. It had ceased to be a luxury in England; now everyone had his pipe. Moreover, the smoking habit had spread through much of Europe. Some tobacco was already being sent abroad in the 1660s; and by 1700, despite strong competition from Dutch and German growths, two-thirds of the tobacco brought to England was re-exported.

The development of the sugar trade shows some similarity. This had once come from the eastern Mediterranean and the Canary Islands, in small quantities, but in the late sixteenth century the price was brought down, and European consumption expanded, by the development of Portuguese sugar plantations in Brazil. After the 1630s the English West Indian islands, still attracting settlers, found they could not compete with the mainland colonies in tobacco production, and sought new products to market to Europe. Not until sugar planting was established did they find one that gave adequate scope for expansion. It was introduced to them in the 1640s by Dutch settlers expelled from Brazil by the Portuguese; and first in

Barbados and more gradually in the other islands sugar became the main crop. The West Indian planters came into a European market which had already been widened by the advent of cheap Brazilian sugar; but they were able to produce great quantities much more cheaply still, and after the Restoration their production brought European sugar prices tumbling down, to touch bottom about 1685. Again, therefore, the cheapening of the product rapidly expanded the market; and for some decades English colonial production was the cheapest, and it was saleable throughout western Europe. Sugar imports to London (which handled nearly all the early trade) were negligible before the Civil War; they rose from 148,000 cwt in 1663–9 to 371,000 cwt in 1699–1701. Again, colonial production was far in excess of the capacity of the English market, and a third of the total was being re-exported at the end of the century.

These two commodities, tobacco and sugar, with minor re-exports of such colonial goods as ginger, logwood and pimento, accounted for some two-fifths of England's re-export trade at the end of the seventeenth century. A similar proportion was supplied by re-export of goods brought in by the East India Company; for the character of eastern trade, too, had been transformed. Although pepper was cheapened considerably, the European market offered little further opportunity for growth after about 1640, since the demand for a commodity so long known in Europe was rather inelastic. The East India Company, seeking to extend its activities, was firmly excluded from the spice trade by the Dutch, but it found an entirely fresh field, with immense possibilities, in the import of Indian cotton fabrics. Cotton was a textile material hardly known in Europe before – since European cotton industries were very small and specialized – and one that was light and far cheaper than linens or woollens. Before the Civil War the Company had imported small quantities of cotton goods; after 1660 it built up the trade very rapidly, and in the last quarter of the century it was rewarded by an outburst of a fashionable demand for Indian cottons for clothes and coverings, scarves and hangings. This demand extended from England into Europe, and a great deal of the East India Company's import was re-exported for sale on the continent. In every country the demand for Indian cottons alarmed local textile producers, and by 1700 many

European governments were putting restrictions on imports. Nevertheless, a big re-export trade from England continued through Amsterdam and Hamburg. By this time, too, the East India Company had established connections with China, and was importing Chinese silks, which were preferable, either for cheapness or for quality, to many European silk products. England's re-exports of Indian and Chinese textiles, which had been negligible in 1640, accounted for a third of all re-exports in 1700; and the total of eastern goods re-exported, including pepper and some minor items, was roughly equal to that of re-exports of American goods. A third branch of the developing re-export trade (of which more presently) was in European manufactures sent to the colonies.

The character of English export trade, therefore, changed markedly during the second part of the seventeenth century. Woollens now accounted for less than a half, instead of four-fifths; and a third of the goods sent out of England were re-exports, most of which had been brought to England from places far beyond Europe.

This widening of the range of trade had important consequences for the English economy as a whole. Because of the distances over which goods were now carried and the new kinds of uncertainty involved in very long-distance trades, the amount of capital needed for carrying on trade grew very much faster than the value of trade itself. Trade no longer employed merely a small fleet of small merchant ships upon short voyages; it was trans-oceanic and required the services of a greatly expanded merchant fleet, with far more ships of fairly large size, which were sent out on long voyages. Instead of traders' capital being laid out for quite short periods in goods dispatched to great markets only a hundred or two miles away, it had to be sufficient to cover the time involved in sending goods thousands of miles, to places where sale was often irregular and payment uncertain. Even if shipments could be geared to the timing of return crops of colonial products, the merchant's outlay of his own capital was still likely to be a long one.

*     *     *

On the other hand, because so much of the growth of trade was associated with the import and re-export of goods from abroad, trade expansion had a much more limited effect on the expansion of English manufacturing industry. It stimulated the investment of capital in trade itself and in its ancillaries such as shipping, but only to a much smaller extent in manufacturing enterprise. When, for example, rising cloth exports in the seventeenth century called forth growth in the cloth industry this required the cloth producers, or clothiers, to find more capital, so as to hold larger stocks and to allow for a larger total of debts from the purchasing merchants. By contrast, the growth of re-exports did not in any such direct way call for an expansion of industrial capital; nevertheless, the merchants still had to find capital to finance the holding of stocks of goods in transit, and the granting of credit to buyers. Moreover, instead of getting credit from their suppliers (as they did when they bought manufactured goods to export) English merchants commonly found themselves advancing money for their planter clients to buy English goods and pay English expenses; and the East India Company certainly had to settle large capital in its Indian agencies. Merchants, too, provided most of the funds for building and equipping the ships that carried the goods.

The import of produce of the colonies and Asia, whether for home consumption or re-export, was not as yet wholly paid for by a corresponding export of English manufactured goods. Asia had its own manufacturing industries and did not want European goods in any quantity, so much the greatest part of the import from Asia was paid for by sending out silver bullion. The American colonists used a great part of the funds they earned from sales to England in paying for shipping and insurance services, for English organization of the supply of slaves (in which, again, the cost of manufactured goods sent out to Africa was only a small element) and for meat, timber and horses, dispatched from Ireland. Their demand for manufactured goods was quite small and even that could not entirely be met by English industry, but had in part to be bought in Europe and re-exported to the colonies.

These transactions did, of course, have indirect influences on manufacturing industry, but it is hard to gauge their importance. More shipping meant a growth of the shipbuilding and ship repairing industries and all their ancillaries; earnings from selling pork or horses to Barbados put purchasing power

into Irish hands which was likely to emerge in the form of bills
of exchange on London merchants which could be used to pay
for English goods; the silver sent to India was largely earned
by the sale of English goods in Spain, and would have had
influence of some kind if put to other uses. When all this is
said, however, it almost certainly remains true that in these
decades after 1660 merchant capital had to be expanded much
faster than industrial capital. This accounts for some features
of this period that every student of it is familiar with; the
relative increase of the weight of the merchant in the community; the concentration of economic writings on merchant
affairs and on balance of payments problems; the identification
of national interest with high exports to a degree which is surprising in a country so nearly self-sufficient, exporting only
about a twentieth of its national output. If we look at the other
side – the earnings of enterprise – it seems probable that the
flow of profits into the hands of merchants was growing excep-
tionally rapidly in this period; most of the great new fortunes
which can be identified in the period, if not made by war
financiers and contractors, were merchant fortunes.

There may have been some tendency for credit terms to
shift part of the burden of financing trade back to the manu-
facturer. The length of credit granted by producer to merchant, and by merchant to his customers, is evidently a main
determinant of the capital requirement of the individual firm.
There is some evidence that credit terms given both by manufacturers and by traders were lengthening during the
seventeenth century – this was necessary for the expansion of
long-distance trade. On the other hand – again, possibly as a
counterpart of this – it seems that at least in the broadcloth
branch of the woollen industry, clothiers giving long credit to
merchants depended on being given corresponding credit by
their own factors, who were traders of a sort. Changes in
credit terms might modify the picture presented here of a
rapidly growing need for merchant, rather than industrial,
capital; but probably not very greatly.

Developments in long-distance trade had a further effect, in
attracting sustained government interest to the problems of
trade. In particular, the shipping industry, which was always
seen by governments as a bulwark of national defence, was the

object of a long series of measures to ensure that the English merchant fleet was built up to the greatest size that the new trading activities made possible, in order that it might be able to provide seamen and auxiliary ships for the navy in time of war. This policy has its roots in Orders-in-Council in the reign of James I, which were aimed specifically at securing for English ships the carriage of goods in the new English long-distance trades which were then being opened up. The Commonwealth Act of 1651, and the Navigation Act of 1660, which followed them and developed the policy much further, had the same purposes. But the precise terms of these measures emphasized the importance of extra-European connections, and above all of the American colonial trades, excluding foreigners and foreign ships from them. Though the Navigation Laws were brought into operation to assist the growth of English shipping, they had the result of giving to English merchants a near-monopoly of trade in products of the English colonies, not merely with England but also – so far as Europe was served with English colonial products – with Europe as well. In addition, by requiring foreign goods sent to the colonies to go through England, so adding to their cost, they gave English manufactures a real price advantage in the colonies. But for the provisions of the Navigation Acts, Amsterdam rather than London might well have been the European distributing centre for English colonial products in the seventeenth and even the eighteenth century.

At the end of the seventeenth century both the growth of trade and the pace of changes in its character were slowing down; and the outbreak of war in 1689 crystallized the new situation. In the first place, the developments which had pushed woollen cloth exports upward through most of the century were now losing their force. Broadcloths of the old type were meeting serious competition from continental woollen industries, which in some markets had government protection against English competition, so the value of these cloths exported from England were slowly falling away. Even more important, the new branch of the industry, producing serges, bays and other of the woollen cloths known as 'new draperies', also began to encounter new competitors in the cottons and cheap silks brought from the East. These threatened the markets of all the lighter textile industries – silk, cotton, linen and in England, light woollens. Their cheapness no doubt enabled more people to buy textile fabrics; that is, they did not simply drive out European textiles, but also widened the whole market. Nevertheless, contemporary comment makes it evident that they were thought to have had serious effects on the markets of such industries as the English 'new draperies'. Hence exports even in this section of the woollen industry, which was doing well in relation to its European competitors, began to falter at the end of the seventeenth century. The tumultuous growth of the woollen cloth exports, which had lasted for nearly a hundred years, was brought to a halt with the outbreak of war in 1689, and after that it made little further progress until late in the eighteenth century. Costs must have been declining, for the price of wool was low for a century after the Restoration; by the early eighteenth century Lancashire and Devon producers were using great quantities of very cheap Irish wool and woollen yarn; the destruction of most other branches of the industry by the advance of West Riding production must have been brought about by a growth in productive efficiency there which should have favoured export trade. But despite this, sales of English woollens in most European markets were falling in the eighteenth century; and when advance was resumed after mid-century, it was a minor aspect of a general growth of *American* demands for English goods. Since woollens were still, at this time, the largest single element in exports, stagnation in woollen exports meant a slowing down of all trade growth.

But the check to growth was not experienced by woollens alone. The major re-export trades which had been responsible for so much of the advance in trade since the Civil War also ran into difficulties at the end of the seventeenth century. Of course the explosive rate of their growth in the previous thirty years could not have been indefinitely maintained; but in fact each of the main re-export commodities met special trading difficulties around 1700. The French acquisition of the large island of Hispaniola from Spain in 1697 was followed by the rapid building up of sugar plantations there, and this presently faced the small, over-cropped British islands with competition at prices which they could not face outside the protected home market. Sugar re-exports to continental Europe fell away to negligible proportions quite soon after the Peace of Utrecht. Tobacco re-exports continued to grow fast, but after the Treaty of Union brought Scotland within the orbit of the Navigation Acts in 1707, much of the increase was channelled through Glasgow, to the benefit of Glasgow merchants, who had few links wth England. Until Glasgow had fully worked up its trading opportunities the English tobacco re-export could make little further progress. The popular demand for Indian cottons in Europe, which seemed to offer possibilities of almost limitless expansion of this branch of trade, was frustrated by the restrictions imposed by many European governments.

In the first quarter of the new century, therefore, the total of tobacco, sugar and cotton goods re-exported ceased to grow. There was still room for some expansion of the re-export trade through the introduction of new commodities. The trade in Chinese silks came to full development (though this, too, was hampered by prohibitions and restrictions); tea was launched towards a career that would in time make it the first beverage of Europe; rice and coffee added their quota to the total of re-exports. But none of these could quickly find such wide markets as to maintain the old momentum of growth of re-export trade.

*     *     *

The expansion of trade slowed down very markedly, because both the dynamic factors in it – first the woollen cloth trade and then re-export – were losing their vigour. Two waves of progress had nearly spent their force; there would be no revival until new waves gathered their strength. This revival, in fact, did not become effective until, towards mid-century, the markets and products of the colonial empire offered new opportunities for expansion. They took two forms; the first and most important, a sudden upsurge of new kinds of manufactured exports around mid-century; the second a fresh wave of growth of re-export trade, coming a little later, after the Seven Years War.

Seventeenth-century England had had only one very large, highly specialized industry with an international market – the woollen industry; alongside it a great variety of small industries served most English needs but had no advantages which could enable them to sell their products across international frontiers and tariff barriers. The major European countries showed similar characteristics; each had specialist industries – linens in parts of Germany, silks and high-grade linens in France – which could sell their products abroad, and each had a variety of minor industries which served only their home markets, in which they were protected (largely by distance) from foreign competitors. England imported some European manufactures – chiefly linens, but including silks and a variety of brass, copper and iron goods. The trading developments so far discussed had not yet made major alterations in this picture; but they had begun to prepare the way. Thus, as we have seen, minor English industries were growing during the seventeenth century; and some of them – notably linens and silks – received a sharp stimulus from the virtual banning of trade with France after 1678 and the immigration of large numbers of skilled Huguenot artisans. The raising of the English tariff wall after 1692 (to provide revenue for war) gave new protection to English industry, and in the early eighteenth century most of the minor imports of manufactures – metal goods, silks, paper – were dispensed with. A large import of linen goods continued, in spite of a gradual building up of government aids to the British linen industry, because the overall demand for linens was growing very fast.

So England was becoming much more self-sufficient industrially. At the beginning of the seventeenth century there was a wide range of manufactures which England obtained from abroad, if only in small quantities; a hundred years later there were few. English industries had squeezed most foreign competition out of the home market by the early decades of the eighteenth century; they were still far from strong enough to compete with other European producers in their own countries. But much more than the home market was open to them, for the overseas lands under British rule were now not merely extensive, but also prosperous and populous; yet they had no native industry beyond a handful of specialisms.

One of these overseas territories was Ireland, which had little industry except textiles. Ireland's export trade was nearly

all to Britain and the colonies (as English law prohibited the
selling of its main products elsewhere) and it was ready to
take manufactures of every kind, so far as its purchasing
power allowed. Ireland had been thrust far below even its normal levels of poverty by the civil wars of the seventeenth
century and the English reconquest of the 1690s, but it recovered very fast in the unaccustomed peace which lasted
throughout the next century. The once shattered Irish market
became one of the chief outlets for the products of English
industries.

The opportunities of expansion which opened in colonial
markets were even more important, and the outstanding feature
of English export trade in the middle decades of the eighteenth century was the great widening of the colonial market
for manufactures. The potentialities of this had long been
plain; before 1700 the export of English (and the re-export of
European) manufactures to the colonies, though small, had
been one of the fastest-growing elements in trade. The 300,000
inhabitants of the colonies in 1700 could only have a limited
demand for manufactures, despite the importance of their
staple products. But by 1776 the population was nearing three
million – a useful market to supplement England's seven
million. In these seventy years, colonial purchasing power
overseas, as measured by the goods they sent across the Atlantic to England, increased at least fivefold; their purchases of
English manufactures grew much faster.

There was little development of industry in the colonies
themselves. With unlimited land to tempt them, wage-earners
in mainland America expected high wages; this, rather than
occasional ineffective measures of the English government to
suppress particular American industries, gave the English their
advantage over most native manufacturers. In the West Indies,
the sharp social division which emerged between a small white
landowning, managing and professional class on the one hand,
and slave manual labour on the other, effectively kept away all
but the most essential of wage-earning artisans. The colonies
therefore imported most of their manufactured needs. They
imported them from England, in the first place, because the
Navigation Laws compelled them to send nearly all their exports to England, where they earned pounds sterling rather

than ducats or livres or rix-dollars. They imported British goods (except for some quantity of German linen) because these were the goods most cheaply available in England. Moreover, by the eighteenth century the strength of habit had been added to the pressures of legal requirement; the merchant connections were firmly established with England, and buyers did not seriously think of looking for their needs elsewhere.

These colonial imports of manufactures were naturally of immense variety, for they served nearly the whole of the requirements of the colonial population. Metal goods of all kinds, however, stood out ahead of everything else – and among these perhaps, the nails which were needed in tens of millions for putting together the wooden houses that in towns, in settled countryside or on the forest frontiers were to house civilized Americans; not the one-inch nails of suburban England, but six- and ten-inch spikes for holding treetrunks and thick wooden boards firm against the winter gales. Axes, pots, plough-shares, harness metal, anchors, watches, buttons and buckles, spoons and pewter mugs – presently vessels and dishes and candlesticks of silver – all swelled the total. English silks in moderate quantity, British (no doubt mainly Scottish) linens in mid-century, and beaver hats, can be distinguished as of some importance among a host of other items; but almost everything that could be made by craftsmen was sent across the Atlantic in some quantity. Even English woollen goods, which had not at first sold well in the colonies because there was some domestic manufacture of coarse woollens there, found a big colonial market after mid-century, so that the total English woollen export began to rise again after remaining stationary for over sixty years.

The expansion of the American market for iron- and brassware was on so great a scale that it must have contributed very significantly to the eighteenth-century development of those industries in England, and so to the process of rationalization, of division of labour, of search for new machines and new methods which helped so much towards the Industrial Revolution. Colonial demands may well have made similar contributions to the improvement of some other branches of industry. The division of labour, the specialization of workers in narrow processes or tasks, was the principal means of raising productive efficiency and lowering costs which operated before the coming of the rush of mechanical inventions; the division of labour, as Adam Smith said, is limited by the extent of the market, and the market freely open to English manufactures was immensely widened by colonial development. This wave of commercial expansion therefore carried with it expansion of industry as well.

Moreover, after mid-century there was a new advance in re-export trade, taking place all along the line, but with a powerful new supplement derived from coffee, grown in West Indian islands taken from the French in 1763. On the eve of the American Revolution, despite the greatly increased trade in manufactures, re-exports accounted for well over a third of the total of exports from England.

While trade with America and the West Indies was growing so fast during the two decades before the American War of Independence, European trade failed even to maintain its old level. Exports of English produce to European countries (outside the specially linked market of Ireland) actually dropped by a quarter between 1752–4 and 1772–4 – a decline attributable in equal proportions to a heavy fall in the export of woollen goods (which fell below the level reached at the beginning of the century) and the abrupt disappearance of the export surplus of corn which had brought a new factor briefly into English commerce towards the middle of the century. The important markets of Spain and Portugal, which had continued to grow in the first half of the century (partly because they supplied colonial needs) now declined as both countries initiated protective policies to build up their own industries. Only the rise in re-exports kept total trade with Europe close to its old level.

European countries earned English currency in a variety of ways. They sent goods to England – the dwindling legal supply of manufactures, the smuggled linens and haberdashery of France and Flanders, the food-stuffs, wines and raw materials of the Mediterranean and Baltic lands, wine and brandy smuggled from France. Spain and Portugal sent a great quantity of silver and gold, which built up the English gold currency and supplied the bullion needed for Indian trade. Dutch investors were entitled to draw large sums in interest on their holdings of the English national debt, and of Bank of England and similar stocks. Yet England had a great surplus on its publicly recorded balance of trade with Europe, and even on its real balance that allowed for smuggling. Despite interest payments and bullion movements it is probable that there was a surplus even on its overall current balance of payments during this period, and that in peacetime there was some net English investment on the continent. It seems that Europe had increasing difficulty in finding enough to sell to an industrializing England, to pay for the growing quantities of goods it wanted to buy there. And within the total of European purchases in England, the value of colonial and Asian goods was growing rapidly.

The colonies had no difficulties in selling to England, especially as they were prohibited from selling their principal products directly in the markets of continental Europe. The preferences they were given by the English tariff system assured a virtual monopoly of the British market (and the Irish market which England supplied) in nearly all their major staples. The British Isles, with their population growing after 1750, and perhaps some spread of modern prosperity in the middle ranks of society, were able to absorb colonial production at a quite rapidly increasing rate. The colonies were the main suppliers, through England, of coffee, tobacco and rice to northern Europe – and again, these products had an extending demand there. While England showed a deficit on the balance of trade with her colonies, her overall current payments position with them, taken as a whole, was probably very roughly in balance. There was still a large invisible export to the colonies in such things as shipping and insurance services and commissions. Net investments in the colonies had nearly ceased; the mainland colonies were now almost completely self-financing, and if West Indian colonists were still running heavily into debt with London agents, this was partly because of considerable repatriation of planter capital to England.

The whole colonial trade with England depended on the production of a few staples in the warm southern colonies – above all rice, tobacco, sugar and coffee. The northern mainland colonies, from Pennsylvania to Maine, acquired much of their purchasing power in England by supplying provisions and timber to the West Indian planters. Continual growth in the production of the colonial staples was made possible by the steady extension of the cultivated area in Jamaica, and on the mainland in Virginia, Maryland and Carolina; it was sharply increased by the acquisition of several French West Indian islands in 1763. Colonial supplies to England were therefore growing rapidly; we have seen that there was a balance between England and the colonies in trade and services; consequently the colonists were no less rapidly increasing their purchases in England. Nearly everything they bought in England was now English produce, and by the time the American War of Independence began the colonies had outstripped continental Europe in their purchases of English manufactures.

The part played by colonial trade in English economic development during this period was evidently a very great one. It helped to create national wealth and individual fortunes; it provided an important market for much of English industry, which helped towards the building of new forms of organization; it contributed heavily towards that general spiral of development, that expansion of demand, which was fast making England an industrialized nation. English trade, which had been turning rapidly towards the colonies and Asia from the mid-seventeenth century, therefore went through a new phase of expansion after the pause of the early eighteenth century. Moreover, in this new phase it was the colonial rather than the East India trade that made the running; and this had special significance because Asia still expected to be paid for its goods in silver rather than in goods, and made little use of the products of English industry. A still greater proportion of English trade was now carried on over long distances; shipping was tied up in colonial trading operations. On the other hand, colonial demand for English exports was now making necessary the growth of many branches of English industry; above all the metal industries, which were heavier users than most of fixed capital in relation to output. It has been suggested above that, for some decades before and after 1700, merchants as a group were adding to their weight in the English economy, merchant earnings rising as a proportion of national income and (more certainly) merchant capital rising as a proportion of all capital. We may suppose that around the middle of the century this relative rise was being brought to an end because trade expansion, in its new form, now carried industrial expansion with it. But there are so many imponderables here that this suggestion can be put forward only with great caution. Certainly economic literature continued to be very much pre-occupied with questions of foreign trade, even though, in-creasingly, it related these to industrial productivity, and so began the approach to a labour theory of value and a new system of economics built round it.

\*     \*     \*

We have seen that after a very long period of slow change English foreign trade erupted in this period of about a hundred years into a series of violent changes affecting its size, com-modity composition, geographical extent, methods, capitaliza-tion and general role in the English economy. What happened, in essence, was that an exchange with Europe, mainly of manufactures for manufactures, which constituted much the greatest part of English foreign trade in the early seventeenth century, was replaced by an exchange, on a world-wide scale, of manufactures for food and raw materials (with a large transit traffic associated with it). The beginnings of this movement of the sphere of trade away from the industrialized areas of northern Europe can be dated right back to the upheavals in the Spanish dominions in the late sixteenth century – the ruin of Antwerp, the ending of the inviolability of Spanish claims in America and Asia. English trade by sea spread to the Baltic and Mediterranean countries which had few manufactures to offer and then to the American colonies which had none. (Trade with Asia, of course, showed a rather different pattern.) The colonies were able to introduce a range of new or nearly new commodities into Europe so cheaply that demand for them grew all through our period, almost as fast as knowledge of and taste for them could be spread about Europe; and this eventually gave the colonists great purchasing power for English manufactures. As England expanded many branches of industry, and reduced its reliance on the woollen industry, whose raw material was a native product, imported raw materials accounted for a rapidly growing proportion of English trade. The relative weight of this extra-European trade was accentuated because as each European country (including England) built up new industries, it tended to create government protection for them; intra-European trade was, very slowly, being strangled.

Towards the end of the century, huge advances in productivity in certain industries brought about the transformation in the English economy and society which we label the 'Industrial Revolution'. The earlier, lesser but still important changes in industry and in the English economy as a whole, under the influence of developments in overseas trade which have been discussed here, were undoubtedly essential as a prelude to the greater movement. Much has still to be learned about the intimate connections between 'Commercial Revolution' and 'Industrial Revolution'.

### BIBLIOGRAPHICAL NOTE

This pamphlet is concerned with showing the progress, development and influence of English overseas trade, rather than details of its organization. Most books on trade, however, are about its organization in particular fields, and if these are excluded a bibliography is necessarily slim. An excellent general bibliography will be found in G. D. Ramsay, *English Overseas Trade* (1957), which is itself a good and useful survey covering the whole period. R. Davis, *The Rise of the English Shipping Industry* (1962), chaps. IX–XIII, surveys areas of trade in turn and the commodities they dealt in.

Modern views on the movement towards change in the sixteenth and early seventeenth century are largely based on F. J. Fisher, 'Commercial Trends and Policy in Sixteenth Century England' (*Economic History Review*, X, 1940) and B. E. Supple, *Commercial Crisis and Change in England, 1600–1642* (1959). Complete summaries of the trade statistics at intervals from 1663 to 1774, with a discussion of their implications, can be found in R. Davis's 'English Foreign Trade 1660-1700' (*Economic History Review*, VII, 1954) and 'English Foreign Trade 1700–1774' (ibid., XV, 1962). T. S. Ashton has useful brief discussions of eighteenth-century trade in *Economic Fluctuations in England, 1700–1800* (1959) chaps. III and VI; and in his introduction to E. B. Schumpeter, *English Overseas Trade Statistics 1697–1808* (1960). Mrs Schumpeter's selection of statistics is invaluable for trade in particular commodities; but it is a selection, and aggregates derived from it are misleading.

Stockton - Billingham
LIBRARY
Technical College

# INDEX